ETHELREDA, VISCOUNTESS TOWNSHEND

From a portrait by Zincke, formerly in the possession of Horace Walpole
at Strawberry Hill. Now the property of Lady Agnes Durham

Photograph by Nicholas Durham, Esq.

# THE
# LIVELY LADY TOWNSHEND
## AND HER FRIENDS

AN EFFORT TO SET FORTH THE DOINGS
AND THE SURROUNDINGS OF A TYPICAL LADY
OF QUALITY OF THE EIGHTEENTH CENTURY

BY

## ERROLL SHERSON

"So he looked silently at the days that were, as they
came dancing back again to him from where they had long
lain lost in chasms of Time." — *Chronicles of Rodriguez.*
                                    LORD DUNSANY.

19 26

LONDON: WILLIAM HEINEMANN LTD.

*First Published* 1926

*Printed in Great Britain by* R. & R. CLARK, LIMITED, *Edinburgh.*

# INTRODUCTORY DEDICATION

### TO THE HON. MRS. OTWAY CUFFE,
### ABIDING NEAR THE CARAGH LAKE.

MY DEAR LIL,

Most books are dedicated to somebody or other. When my first, dealing with the Past, was ready to face a doubtful reception from a very modern world, I had not to hesitate as to whom the dedication should be inscribed. My sister, who has never failed in her untiring goodness to me and all of us, had the first claim. So my memories of the Lost London Theatres were offered to her.

I did not then realise that I should so soon have more stories of the Past ready for the commendation or condemnation of readers of to-day: now that such a volume is let loose on a long-suffering public, I cannot but think that you are the proper person for the dedication.

You and I are in the same degree of descent from the "Lively Lady Townshend", for you, like myself, are one of her numerous great-great-great-grandchildren: you, like myself, are a reader of books (which certainly does not apply to others whom I know among her children with three preliminary

v

" greats ") : you have been so sympathetic about my literary efforts made so late in life : and to you I owe so many advantages accruing from opportunities to get at books of reference, that the dedication belongs to you as if by prescriptive right.

Ethelreda, more often called Audrey, Harrison, who became the wife of Charles, third Viscount Townshend, was, as you know, one of the most beautiful, witty, and audacious women of fashion in the eighteenth century. Audacious she certainly was, not caring in the least what other people said about her, and going her own way as best she pleased. Her beauty made her the envy of other women of the time : her wit caused effeminate creatures of the Horace Walpole type and others to write of her with the jealous spite of a jealous woman : and her independence of character prevented her from being a hanger-on of the subservient Courts of the Georges. In her own time she was set in the pillory by spiteful men and women, and pelted with mud by jealous termagants like our other grandmother (with four " greats "), Lady Mary Wortley Montagu : even in this twentieth century, nearly two hundred years afterwards, there are not wanting writers of her own sex who lose no opportunity of getting in a word of depreciation. But none have been able to shake her position as the outstanding Lady of Quality in the Age of Wig, Hoop and Powder, once she had ousted her rival, Lady Mary. She has been written of as celebrated for her Beauty, her Eccentricities, her Gallantries and her Wit. Her beauty none can deny who look on the various portraits still extant : her wit shines out and sparkles in many a letter of Walpole or Selwyn or their contemporaries, though the sharp edge of it has been somewhat blunted in the passing of over a hundred and fifty years : and what were dubbed her " Eccentricities and Gallantries " may be, to a large extent, excused by the unfortunate circumstances of her married life.

Her life story has never been written down. Material for a complete memoir is lacking. If her name be mentioned, some one will probably say, " Oh, yes, the original from whom Fielding drew his Lady Bellaston and Coventry his Lady Tempest ", thereby handing down a tradition for which there is but scant foundation and repeating malicious gibes of her rival, Lady Mary, whose position as " reigning toast " she had so successfully usurped.

In writing of this " lively lady " I have endeavoured also to compress into a small space, a picture of the doings and surroundings of a Lady of Quality of the eighteenth century, and though I am well aware that the social atmosphere of that time has been realised infinitely better by experts like Mr. Austin Dobson, Mr. Andrew Lang, Mr. Chancellor and others, yet I hope that you, for one, will find something to interest you in a modest book dealing with our witty and beautiful, if somewhat eccentric and wilful, ancestress.

Your affectionate cousin,

ERROLL SHERSON.

# CONTENTS

# CHAPTER VII

# CHAPTER VIII

# CHAPTER IX

# CHAPTER X

# CHAPTER XI

# CHAPTER XII

# APPENDIX

# LIST OF ILLUSTRATIONS

# CHAPTER I

CONCERNING THE FOREBEARS OF THE LIVELY LADY
TOWNSHEND AND HER EARLY MARRIED LIFE

Balls Park: Sir John Harrison: *Mariages de Convenance*:
Hertford in the eighteenth century: Marriage of Ethelreda
Harrison to Lord Lynn: the rival Courts at St. James's and
Leicester House: Eccentricities of the third Viscount Towns-
hend: Separation of the Lively Lady Townshend from her
husband: her bitterness against him and his family.

AMID THE SURROUNDINGS of grossness, immorality and corruption in which the fashionable world
of the Georgian era passed their lives, lived also
Ethelreda (or Audrey)[1] Townshend, wife of Charles,
third Viscount Townshend, one of the most beautiful,
fascinating and witty women of a fascinating and witty
age, who held her own, brilliantly and audaciously as
a lady of quality, from her marriage in 1723 almost
to the date of her death in 1788.

[1] Mr. Justin M'Carthy, Mr. Percy Fitzgerald, even Mr. Jesse, in speaking
of Lady Townshend, ridicule her for calling herself " Ethelreda " instead of
" Audrey ", though she always signed her letters " E. Townshend ". Indeed,
Mr. Justin M'Carthy, with characteristic inaccuracy, writes " Ethelfreda ".
Though her grandmother and her own daughter were both called " Audrey ",
Ethelreda is the real name and Audrey only a corruption, like Harry for
Henry and Dolly for Dorothy. At the great fair of Ely (in the cathedral
of which city was the shrine of St. Ethelreda) cheap and flashy goods were
largely sold, especially a particular sort of rosary called " St. Audrey's beads ".
Hence the word "tawdry", signifying cheap stuff bought at the fair of
St. Audrey or Ethelreda. The village of St. Awdries in Somerset is so called
because the parish church was dedicated originally to St. Ethelreda.

Born in the early years of eighteenth century, she passed her girlhood in the days of good Queen Anne, married when George I. was yet king, and gaily led the world of fashion, not only throughout the long reign of his successor, but for twenty-eight years of that of his grandson. She came into the world before the last echoes of the English Revolution had died away, leaving it only when the thunder of the French upheaval was beginning to stun the ears of Europe.

My Lady Townshend came of a good old stock— the Harrisons of Balls, near Hertford, descendants of a Sir John Harrison who had fought stoutly for King Charles against the rebel Roundheads.

When the Civil War broke out, Sir John had but lately purchased the Balls estate from one Sir Richard Willis, whose wife Jane was the heiress of the Henmarsh family, owners of Balls in the days of Elizabeth.

The place was originally so called from one Simon de Ball (or Bawle), a burgess in Parliament for the borough of Hertford as long ago as the twenty-sixth year of the reign of Edward I. The name, variously spelt, occurs again and again in the list of freeholders of the neighbourhood. A meadow in the parish of All Saints, Hertford, was known for two hundred years or more as Ball's (or Balle's) Hook, and there was a brass on the floor of the church of All Saints, asking for prayers for the soul of Thomas Barle (1456), who might well have been one of the same family.

The old hall on the estate, existing in Tudor times, had been pulled down in the reign of Charles I., and a new house was built by Sir John Harrison about the year 1642 or 1643. Evelyn, in his *Diary*, writing under date of April 16, 1643, says, " . . . and near the town of Hertford, I went to see Sir John Harrison's house

new built. . . ." It is described by Chauncey in his
old *History of Hertfordshire* as—

. . . a fair stately fabrick of brick in the middle of a warren,
consisting of a square pile with a court in the middle thereof,
every side equally fronted and exactly uniform, the ceilings
within the house wrought with several and distinct patterns of
fretwork: the steps in the great staircase wainscoted in panes:
the hall paved with black and white marble : the inward court
with fine stone. . . .

Sir John Harrison and his immediate family merit
more than a note in passing. He was born at Bemond
in the county of Lancaster, and was M.P. for the city
of Lancaster in three separate Parliaments of Charles I.,
by whom he was appointed a Farmer of Customs.
Throughout his life he employed his energies and his
fortune in promoting the interests of the King. When
Charles unfurled the Royal Standard at Nottingham,
he at once attached himself to the cause, and in 1643
joined his Sovereign at Oxford.

Dr. Salmon, in a *History of Hertfordshire*, says that
he was forced to leave his house "when the Parliament
drove, as the rest of the King's friends did their
habitations and estates", and that he made himself
obnoxious by his loyalty in the House of Commons,
where he sat for his native borough of Lancaster. The
old chronicler of the county continues quaintly to
note that—

. . . his malignant estate was sequestered, and he passed the
Purgatory of the Times in a private Retirement or Voluntary
Exile. Yet he lived to see the Tragic Past of his Fortunes blown
over, to enjoy Nine Years of the serenest Weather England ever
knew. . . .

His daughter Ann, wife of Sir Richard Fanshawe,
describes the distresses suffered by her family when

the rebels had expelled her father from the House of Commons, and deprived him of his estate.

. . . My father commanded my sister and myself to come to him at Oxford, where the Court then was, but we, who till that hour lived in great plenty and great order, found ourselves like fish out of water, and the scene so changed that we knew not at all how to act any part but obedience ; for, from as good houses as any gentleman in England had, we came to a baker's house in an obscure street : and from rooms well furnished, to lie in a very bad bed in a garret : to one dish of meat and that not of the best ordered : no money, for we were as poor as Job, nor cloaths more than a man or two brought in their cloak bags : we had the perpetual discourse of losing and gaining towns and men : at the windows the sad spectacle of war, sometimes plague, sometimes sickness of other kind, by reason of so many people packed together as I believe there never was before of that quality : always in want, yet I must needs say that most bore it with a martyr-like cheerfulness : for my own part, I began to think we should all, like Abraham, live in tents all the days of our lives. . . .—(*Memoirs of Ann, Lady Fanshawe,* 1600–1672.)

At the Restoration, Sir John Harrison's estates were restored to him.   He lived to a good old age, dying when past his eightieth year.  According to his daughter Ann, he was a handsome gentleman of great natural parts, a great accountant, of vast memory, an incomparable penman, of great integrity, of service to his Prince, and a good husband and father. He was twice married. His first wife was Margaret, daughter of Richard Fanshawe, by whom he had three sons and two daughters. The eldest was married three times and left descendants, but was disinherited by his father for taking the side of the Parliamentarians.

One can well imagine the indignation of the loyal old knight, who could never forgive such treachery to his Sovereign.  John tried on more than one occasion

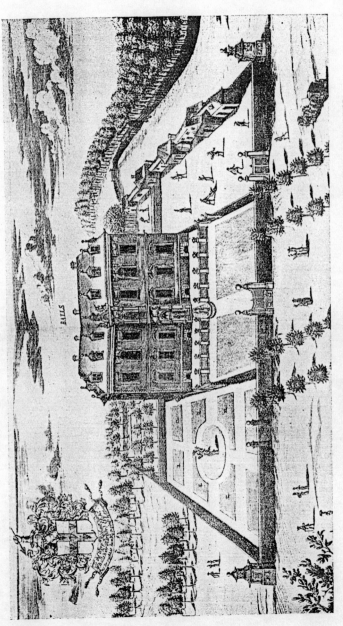

BALLS PARK, HERTS, WHEN IT WAS FIRST BUILT, ACCORDING TO DRAPENTIER

From Dr. Chauncey's *History of Herts*

to be reconciled to his father, and among the MSS. at the British Museum are letters written by him with this object. One dated in 1646 (note, three years before the execution of the King, and when the rebels must have thought that they had gained the day) makes suggestions as to the disposal of the Balls estate. But the old knight was not to be talked over. In his own handwriting he endorsed it as follows: " He understandeth how I have proceeded, and sillily hath invented the weak snare to catch me ".

Another, written by John Harrison to his father's second wife, begs her to intercede for him; and he also wrote again to his father in 1653. But it was all of no avail, and Balls passed away from his line, the only recognition of his family in the old knight's will being legacies of £600 to one granddaughter Ann, and £35 a year between the other two, Margaret and Lettice.

Sir John Harrison's second son William fought as a true son of his father on the side of his King. He died at Oxford early in the war (1643) from a bruise caused by the fall of his horse under him. His sister, Ann Fanshawe, describes him in her *Memoirs* as a " very good and gallant young man as the King said ". Of the third son, little is known except that he died without any offspring: and so Balls came to the family of the second wife of Sir John.

This was Mary Shotbolt of Yardley, a woman of very ancient family, descended from a Ralph Shotbolt (" *alias* Battalion ") who lived in the nineteenth year of the reign of Henry III. The curious name " Battalion " is found later as a Christian name among the Shotbolts. Dame Harrison, *née* Shotbolt, left one daughter, Mary, married to William Lytton of Knebworth, from whom the present Earl of Lytton is descended; and a son, Richard, whose wife was Audrey, eldest daughter of George Villiers, fourth Viscount Grandison in the peerage of Ireland, and therefore first cousin to the notorious Barbara Villiers, Lady Castlemaine, mistress of Charles II., and by him created Duchess of Cleveland. Richard Harrison had a very large family, eight sons and six daughters. His third, but eldest surviving, son, Edward, rose in life by the personal favour of William III., and was successively Governor of Fort St. George, Madras, in the year 1711, M.P. for Hertford in the year 1721, and Postmaster-General in 1726. He married Frances, heiress of Reginald Bray of Barrington in Gloucestershire,[2] and at his death left one surviving child, Ethelreda (or Audrey) Harrison, who became the wife of Charles, Lord Lynn, afterwards third Viscount Townshend.

In the eighteenth century *mariages de convenance* were as much the rule in England as they were, and always have been, on the Continent. A woman who did not marry fairly early, seldom married advantageously and more often not at all. And there was not much place in the world then for an unmarried woman above a certain age. At twenty-five she was looked upon as an old maid, and if not married before she was thirty was condemned to pass her days either as a teacher (for which the education of the time fitted very few) or as "waiting-woman companion" to some lady of title.

Nor were marriages thus "arranged" among the quality alone. There is a vulgar proverb which proves the contrary: "Marry your daughter betimes, for

---

[2] Cockayne (*Somerset Herald*) says she is somewhere stated to be a daughter of one Thomas Wherwood, but there seems to be little doubt that she was a Bray.

fear she should marry herself". Richardson, who is of all novelists the one most concerned with love and lovers, has a preference for this kind of arranged marriage. In No. 97 of the *Rambler* he gives us his beau ideal of a matrimonial transaction. The young man is to see the young woman only at church, where her beauty and pious demeanour will win his heart. He applies to her parents through a mutual friend : they tell her of his offer : she is all resignation to their will : " perhaps " she has also seen him at church : her relations applaud her for her dutiful behaviour : friends meet : points are arranged : hope and fears alternate until the matter is brought to a conclusion. Then, and then only is a meeting arranged. The two principal people concerned never speak to each other till they meet as an engaged couple.

Dr. Johnson had a pet scheme of his own by which couples could be paired and married only by consent of the Lord Chancellor ! I wonder what the young men and women of the present day, accustomed to address each other as " old Bean " and other friendly, if not elegant, names, would say to such an arrangement !

The dullness of the average provincial town in the eighteenth century would have appalled the " old Beans " of to-day ; but, perhaps, Hertford was a little less dull than other places. César de Saussure,[3] a young Frenchman who travelled in England between 1725 and 1736, and wrote an account of his travels in letters admired by no less an authority than Voltaire, speaks of this very town of Hertford in the neighbourhood of which my Lady Townshend passed her early life.

[3] He distinguished himself later in life by being the first man to ascend Mont Blanc.

He describes it as a pretty little place on the river Lea, " where excellent small trout may be caught ". He says that the gentlefolk live in country houses in the neighbourhood, and that every alternate Monday society assembled in a large room hired for the purpose, and dancing went on from seven till ten o'clock in the evening. They must have crammed all the dissipations of the fortnight into one evening, for, after a supper provided in turn by one of the ladies (" the violins, wines and refreshing drinks were paid for by the gentlemen "), dancing began again and was continued until every one was weary. None but the subscribers or their guests could attend these assemblies, which M. de Saussure describes as novel, entertaining and pleasant, and attended by ladies and gentlemen of the best families from the country houses round about, and the town itself.

A young girl living out of London had very few diversions in those days. In the morning she would have a few lessons to do, some writing, and perhaps a little French and Italian. She would be expected to get through a certain amount of needlework, be initiated into some of the mysteries of the stillroom, and in the evening play whist with the parson or any chance visitor, her occupations being thus very similar to those of Lady Teazle before her marriage.

The household at Balls may have been rather less dull than the average country establishment of the day. In the time of Ann Harrison, the well-loved daughter of old Sir John, it was certainly not a bad place for a lively girl. Lady Fanshawe in her *Memoirs* says much on this point :

. . . Now it is necessary to say something of my mother's education of me, which was with all the advantages that time afforded, both for working all sorts of fine work with my needle, and learning French, singing, the lute, the virginals and dancing : and notwithstanding I learnt as well as most did, yet was I wild to that degree that the hours of my beloved recreation took up too much of my time : for I loved riding in the first place, and running and all active pastimes : and in fine, I was that which we graver people call a hoyting girl. . . .

It is quite probable that Balls was every bit as gay under the régime of the spoiled young heiress Ethelreda as it had been in the days of Ann Harrison. Mrs. Harrison, a woman of good family, appears to have been a quiet individual of whom nothing is chronicled in the doings of the polite world, although she lived to the year 1752, long after her high-spirited daughter had so astonished the world of fashion with her brilliant vagaries. But Ethelreda's father, Edward Harrison, had been brought into contact with official people all his life, and the circle of visitors at Balls was undoubtedly a large and distinguished one. Ethelreda was the only child of the house, her brother and two sisters having all died in infancy. Marriageable at fifteen, she would not have been too young to go to those assemblies which were the chief gaieties of the little country town, and she must have been the idol of her parents and somewhat of a spoilt darling, taken about everywhere by them, and often meeting the modish visitors from town.

It is, then, not too difficult to imagine how this marriage originally came about. On the one hand, was my Lord Lynn, heir of an old family, eldest son of " Turnip " Townshend, the great minister of the first George, and Gentleman of the Bedchamber to the King, whose duty it was to marry and marry well. On the other hand, was a very beautiful and very high-spirited romantic young girl, heiress in her own right to a considerable property, who must have found the dull routine of her life irksome in the extreme, and could look forward only to marriage as a means of escape, though, perhaps, she was not so romantic as Biddy Tipkin in Steele's comedy of *The Tender Husband*, who objected to a lover that would have escorted her through a door, preferring to be snatched through a window!

It was a brilliant match for her, placing her at once among the fashionable women of the day, and, if she had so chosen, among the beauties of the Court. It was by no means a bad match for him, considering her beauty, her wealth and her descent from good families on each side. Her father, who, judging from some letters that have come down to us, seems to have been something of a toady, was delighted. Her mother was certainly not displeased that her only surviving child should wed the heir of a viscount's coronet. The marriage was celebrated in 1723, and Ethelreda Townshend at once took her place among the great ladies of society, for, from her first appearance in the world of fashion her salon was frequented by the leading wits of the age, while her extraordinary beauty attracted all alike.

She was but fifteen years of age when she married Lord Lynn, and she developed into a woman exceptionally brilliant in all ways : in beauty, in wit and in that power of dominating all around her which is granted to so few. How beautiful she was may be judged by several portraits of her, especially one by Zincke formerly in the possession of Horace Walpole at Strawberry Hill. Justin M'Carthy, in his *History of the Four Georges*, describes her as carrying her beauty, her insolence and her wit through an amazed and an amused society; and he sums her up, perhaps somewhat charitably, thus :

> She was always entertaining, always alarming, always ready to say or do anything that came into her mind. She lived— a whimsical, spiteful, sprightly oddity to be eighty-seven years of age.

The latter assertion is incorrect; but see Chapter XII. What would be called now, in the Anglo-American slang of the day, the "smart set" in London society was then divided between those who frequented St. James's Palace with its German entourage and dull, heavy routine, and those who hailed the rising sun of the Prince and Princess of Wales at Leicester House.

The dividing line between the two Courts remained marked for many years after the original cause of the quarrel was forgotten. This had been slight enough. Father and son, George I. and George II., had never loved each other, some said because the Prince of Wales resented the treatment accorded to his mother by his father. But the breaking point was reached in 1717 when the old King ordered the Duke of Newcastle to stand godfather to his grandson. The Duke was particularly obnoxious to the Prince of Wales, of which the King was fully aware, and when the younger man expressed his opinion in no measured language, he was actually arrested and confined a prisoner in his wife's bedroom, though she was only just through her confinement. The strongest representations were made to the King that it was impossible to keep the Heir-apparent a prisoner there, especially during his wife's illness, and he was allowed to leave St. James's. The poor little baby, innocent cause of all the trouble, died almost as soon as it was born, and Caroline, Princess of Wales, followed her husband in disgrace, leaving her little daughters, Anne and Amelia, in the charge of their grandfather and his Germans.

The Prince and Princess of Wales went first for a short stay to Lord Grantham's, but finally settled in Leicester Fields in the palatial residence built by a former Earl of Leicester and known as " Leicester House ", or the " pouting place of Princes ", as Pennant wittily called it in after years.

Leicester House was built by Robert Sydney, Earl of Leicester in the reign of Charles I., on ground formerly belonging to the Hospital of St. Giles. It had many royal occupants before becoming the scene of the quarrels between father and son in the reigns of the two Georges. The Duke of Gloucester and his sister, Princess Elizabeth, children of Charles I., were here for some time under the care of the Parliament; Charles II. resided in it for a short time, and then it was taken over by the " Queen of Hearts ", the unfortunate Queen of Bohemia, who died here in the arms of her nephew, Charles II., in 1662. It then became the residence, temporary, of various ambassadors, and finally in 1718 was bought by George, Prince of Wales, and continued a royal residence until the middle of the century. Lever's museum, the " Holuphusikon ", had it for a time till it was demolished to make new streets and, in course of time, become the site of the Empire Music Hall. The experiment of an Opposition Court was successful in every way from an Opposition point of view. Especially did the Prince and Princess reap a substantial advantage from their being able to converse in English, of which the old King hardly knew a word.

It was as lively at Leicester House as it was dull at St. James's. Drawing-rooms were held daily, at which the clever Caroline gathered round her all that was brilliant, witty and renowned in the world of science or letters; and when she was not holding a reception in her own apartment, such women of the bedchamber and maids of honour as were not on duty were entertaining in theirs. Ladies in the Princess's suite who had husbands in the service of the King were commanded to leave her; but some refused to obey and cast their lots with the rebels, among these being the beautiful Mrs. Howard, afterwards Countess of Suffolk.

The early household of the Princess Caroline included the Duchess of Bolton, a natural daughter of the Duke of Monmouth; the Duchess of St. Albans, wife of the son of Charles II. and Nell Gwynne; and the Duchess of Montagu, a daughter of the Duke of Marlborough. The Women of the Bedchamber were Lady Cowper, née Molly Clavering, whose Diary affords much amusing information as to the doings of the Leicester House set; Mrs. Clayton, a clever woman of obscure origin, afterwards created Baroness Sundon; and the three lovely maids of honour—Mary Lepel, Mary Bellenden and Sophia Howe, whose mother was Ruperta, an illegitimate daughter of Prince Rupert.

It is generally stated that Mary Lepel, Lady Hervey, was of the family of the Lepelles or Le Pelleys, seigneurs of Sark. She said herself, however, that those Le Pelleys were no relations of hers, and this has been corroborated by the editor of the Bristol papers. Her father, Nicholas Wedig Lepel, was page to Prince George of Denmark, husband of Queen Anne, in 1684. Her mother was Mary, daughter of John Brooke of Rendlesham in Suffolk. Her father, in his capacity of Brigadier-General, procured for his daughter (through Sarah Duchess of Marlborough) a commission as cornet of horse, the pay for which she drew for many years. Lord Hervey, eldest son of the Earl of Bristol, an intimate friend of the Princess of Wales to the day of her death, married the beautiful Mary Lepel, and Colonel John Campbell, Groom of the Bedchamber to the Prince, married Mistress Bellenden, secretly indeed, in order to check the amorous advances of his Royal master who was perpetually seeking new conquests among his wife's ladies. But while Mary Bellenden was thus enabled to escape the Royal Lothario, Mrs. Howard succumbed to the temptation and became a Royal mistress till she was ousted by Lady Yarmouth and other sirens. The third maid of honour, poor Sophia Howe, came to a bad end, for she was seduced by Anthony Lowther; and he being a mere esquire and not a Prince of the reigning House, she had to hide her head in disgrace and exile.

It would be tedious to give a mere list of the courtiers of the Opposition Court, including, as it would, so many of the best born and most brilliant men and women of the day. One may just mention in passing, Her Grace the Duchess of Buckingham, ever a rebel at heart as became a daughter, though *à la main gauche*, of James II., and many other disaffected dames. Men of science and letters were not wanting: Pope, Addison, Gray, Arbuthnot, and Sir Isaac Newton, Master of the Mint.

The heavy-witted, untidy, beer-drinking old Hanoverian at St. James's, with his retinue of fat and frowsy foreigners, had no chance against the rival Court of his rebel son, brilliant with youth and beauty, sparkling with wit, and presided over by such a woman as Caroline the Illustrious. Only those who feared to offend the reigning Sovereign by their absence put in an appearance at his dull parties, and many of them must have reflected that Kings do not live for ever and have kept in touch with the coming King, as far as possible.

At the time of the marriage of Ethelreda Harrison with Lord Lynn in 1723 the quarrel between the first George and his son had been partly healed, and so her Ladyship had not been one of the courtiers at the Drawing-rooms of the Princess of Wales in the earlier days when the rivalry between the two places had been so marked. But she had certainly nothing in common with the Schulembergs and Kielmansegges of the first George or the Walmodens of the second, and she was assuredly a star at the Leicester House of the younger generation when George II. and his Queen had the same treatment meted out to them as they had served to their own father. Besides being ever a rebel at heart all her life, always " agin the Government ", for which her Irish ancestry may or may not have been responsible, she was one of those fearless individuals who care not whom they offend or how they do it, as long as they please themselves. In both reigns Leicester House was always the livelier rendezvous, the gathering point for youth and good looks. A Court might be very magnificent, and its Sovereign very great, but if it were not a lively Court with an agreeable Sovereign, and if there were no youth, and good-looking youth to boot, it was no place to suit my Lady Townshend.

Her husband was an ungracious, surly individual, cast in a very different mould from that of his lovely wife, and not caring at all for the frivolous things of the world which so amused her.

She, on her side, hated the dull life of the Townshend family in Norfolk, and never lost an opportunity of saying so. In this she resembled her crony, Horace Walpole, who was also of a Norfolk family, but did not care for " Norfolk dumplings, Norfolk ale, Norfolk turnips nor Norfolk turkeys ". Once, when the Duchess of Bedford told her that the Duke was wind-bound at Yarmouth, she said, " Lord ! he will hate Norfolk as much as I do ". In her old age she de-scribed the county as a place where there was nothing to be seen but one blade of grass and two rabbits nibbling at that.

What perhaps gave my Lady extra cause to dislike her husband was a knowledge of the irregularities of his private life. He was not a faithful husband, and whatever her own faults may afterwards have been, his infidelities from the first were of the grossest and most flagrant description, for he maintained one of the Norfolk housemaids as his mistress, eventually leaving her a fortune in his will.

Lord Lynn held a position at Court as Gentleman of the Bedchamber to the King, but nothing is noted to his credit in any of the numerous memoirs of the time, and he was always most eccentric in every way. Witness his conduct with regard to the Militia Bill, promoted by his eldest son George. He opposed it to the utmost. Walpole in a letter to Sir Horace Mann in 1757 says :

> But his father, my Lord Townshend, who is not the least mad of your countrymen, attended by a barber, a parson and his own servants, and in his long hair, which he has let grow, raised a mob against the execution of the Bill, and has written a paper against it, which he has pasted up on the doors of four churches near him.

None of his sons cared for him. There are letters in the Townshend Collection which show that he lived

RAYNHAM HALL, NORFOLK

From a photograph by James Durham, Esq.

a life of his own entirely apart, although he was in fairly frequent communication with them. Besides opposing the Militia Bill of his eldest son, he opposed the marriage of his son Charles with the widowed Countess of Dalkeith, and he does not appear to have been very friendly with his son Roger, while his only daughter Audrey, a beautiful girl, lived almost entirely with her mother in the Privy Garden, Whitehall.

The separation between husband and wife took place early in 1741. For this we have the authority of Mr. Wortley Montagu, husband of Lady Mary Wortley Montagu, who, in a letter dated May 14, informs his wife that Lady Townshend and my Lord agreed to live separately " about a fortnight ago ". " George Paston " mentions this in an account of *Lady Mary Wortley Montagu and her Times*, published in 1907, and adds, rather gratuitously, in a footnote :

The separation was probably due to the indiscreet conduct of Lady Townshend. Her intrigues were a matter of common knowledge.

This is an unsupported assumption. It might be said that her intrigues were a matter of common " talk " among the members of the schools for scandal of the day. That would have been nearer the truth, no one's conduct being safe from the spiteful observation of Mrs. Candour and Sir Benjamin Backbite. In the eighteenth century as in the twentieth, matters of common talk are frequently founded on anything but common fact.

No hint of my Lord's misconduct is put forward as a palliation. The Raynham housemaid, or other similar slight indiscretions of the noble Viscount were of course to be condoned—or ignored. It was no wonder that my Lady was very bitter against her husband for preferring the society of the lower classes to hers, or that she spoke of him in a sharp caustic way, whenever she did allude to him at all.

Once, talking of cures for what used to be called " distempers ", *i.e.* such illnesses as could not be classed under any special name and were probably due to " nerves ", my Lady was wont to reckon that such a doctor had cured so many, and such a medicine so many, but of all the sufferers the greatest number have found relief from the death of their husbands.

On the occasion of the trial of the Jacobite Lords who were " out " in the '45, each peer having to say " Guilty ", or " Not guilty ", as the case might be, " on my honour " — my Lady Townshend hearing her husband vote, said, " I always knew my Lord was guilty, but I never thought he would own it on his honour ".

Again, when the Countess of Pembroke married *en secondes noces*, a Captain Barnard of the Horse Guards, and by so doing had somewhat lost favour at Court, Rigby,[4] in a letter to the Duke of Bedford, says :

My Lady Townshend, whom I saw at Lady Bath's assembly, last night, says more good things upon this event than my paper would hold, if my memory were good enough to remember them. She told me that she had already engaged her Captain against her lord's death, lest they should be all picked up.

As a fact, she hated all the Townshends, and held little, if any, communication with them. Against her husband's half-brother, Augustus Townshend, son of

---

[4] Richard Rigby, 1722–1788, M.P. for Castle Rising, secretary to the Duke of Bedford, and a prominent member of the party. He was Paymaster to the Forces and held other lucrative posts. He left at his death a large fortune, supposed to be chiefly obtained from public money. Mrs. Paget Toynbee, the capable editor of *Walpole's Letters*, states that he was a notoriously unscrupulous and corrupt politician.

the famous Dorothy Walpole (who is supposed to
" walk " the corridors at Raynham from time to time
as " The Little Brown Lady of Raynham ")—who had
remonstrated with her on her close intimacy with Mr.
Winnington of the Board of Trade, she cherished an
especial grudge, and could not express any decent regret at his untimely death. Yet he had been very fond
of her, though only a half-brother of her husband's,
and in a letter to Edward Harrison, spoke of her as
his " dear sister ". He died at Batavia in Java, while
in command of the East Indiaman *Augusta*. Roger
Townshend, my Lady's third son, was with him at the
time.

The faults of the beautiful Lady Townshend have
been laid bare unmercifully for the criticism of the
generations that came after her, and chiefly by members
of her own sex ; but it must be remembered that
whatever her faults may have been, one should always
accept with more than the traditional pinch of salt
what one woman says of another, especially if the
object of the criticism happens to be a very beautiful
woman, and one undeniably popular with the other
sex. Lady Townshend was quite justified in leaving
her husband to his vicious life with his inferiors and
going on her way alone. She was not dependent on
him in any way. As her father's heiress she had
always had her own money, and was indeed a very
rich woman. When her mother died in 1758, she
inherited a further sum of £1000 a year, and never
had any occasion to stint herself or her children in
anything.

There is no doubt that the curiously low tastes and
eccentric doings of Lord Townshend led to her
voluntary separation from him, embittered her outlook

on life, and perhaps caused her to plunge more deeply into the whirl and wildness of a fast life than would otherwise have been the case.

For many years she had no home ties or family cares. There were, indeed, not wanting spiteful persons ready to assert that she never missed them. The fact remains, however, that, whether inclined to home life or not, until her daughter was presented and her sons old enough to make some sort of a family circle, there was no restraining influence to hold her back, nothing to distract her from that continual round of excitement and intrigue which was the daily life of a woman of fashion in her day.

# CHAPTER II

AT THE BEGINNING of the eighteenth century the
aristocratic residential quarter of London was not
confined within the same radius as it continued to
be, later on, for so many years. The West End, as we
know it, was still in process of formation, and to all
intents and purposes finished at Devonshire House
(then just built), while north of Piccadilly and west
of the modern Bond Street was still practically open
country.

Noblemen and persons of note had long lived in
the City itself, and the Strand was almost a continuous
row of splendid palaces. Lincoln's Inn Fields, Bloomsbury, Soho Square—all now in a decadent state—
were occupied by the great families of the day. Now
" The Fields " is, and has been for some time, a

gathering of lawyers' houses, for it will not be forgotten
that the mysterious Mr. Tulkinghorn lived in one of
the houses richly decorated with painted ceilings, on
one of which was the heathen goddess, who with out-
stretched finger pointed to the murdered figure of the
old lawyer while Hortense slunk away in the dress of
Lady Dedlock.

Bloomsbury " Piazza ", Covent Garden " Piazza ",
as the old squares were called, were other aristocratic quarters : perhaps the best known of all, and
the most imposing was St. James's Piazza, laid out in
1677, where lived Moll Davis, the dancer and actress,
mistress of Charles II.; the Herveys, intimate friends
of my Lady Townshend; La Belle Stewart who sat
for the model of Britannia on the pennies; the widow
of the Duke of Monmouth; and many others; and,
in the house now occupied by the London Library,
Edward Harrison, ex-Indian governor and father of
my Lady Townshend herself.

Moving back towards Charing Cross we come upon
the remains of the Royal Palace of Whitehall and the
houses which had sprung up around it. Behind the
Palace, and to one side of it, was the Privy Garden,
the site of which is now occupied by the houses of
Whitehall Gardens and some of the buildings of the
Board of Trade. It was originally a private garden in
fact as well as in name, containing about three and a
half acres and lying between Whitehall Palace and the
river Thames. Pepys walked there in 1662.

In the Privy Garden saw the finest smocks and linen petticoats
of my Lady Castlemaine, laced with rich lace at the bottom, that
ever I saw : and did me good to look at them. . . .

Sir Christopher was ordered by Queen Anne in
1705 to erect a wall to render the spot still more private,

and to enclose that part which contained a fountain, as a pleasure ground to the house occupied by the Scottish Commissioners appointed to settle the terms of the Union of the two Kingdoms. The houses of Privy Gardens were built much later.

Many well-known people of the time lived there or thereabouts at various times. The old house (curiously hidden away at the end of Craig's Court), Charing Cross, belonged to the Earls of Harrington, but Lady Harrington, the cousin and intimate friend of my Lady Townshend, lived, for the most part, in Stable Yard, St. James's, within the royal precincts. The Duke of Portland also lived near by : he had a house formed out of part of the old Palace of White-hall, granted to him by William III. ; the Earl of Loudoun was not far off in 1761 ; and other modish folk in or near the Privy Garden were the Earl of Fife, the Earl of Liverpool and the Duke of Buccleuch. There was certainly no lack of fashion in the vicinity, for just at the back of Inigo Jones's Banqueting Hall was the London house of Ethelreda Townshend during the greater part of her life, her husband, when in town, living by himself not far off in St. James's Street.

Here this brilliant woman held a veritable saloon, entertaining a vast circle of friends with lavish hospitality, and receiving all that was fashionable and select in the society of the day.

From her great friend Sir Thomas Robinson she leased a house which had been part of old Holdernesse House, built in 1718 by the Earl of Holdernesse on a piece of ground within the precincts of the Palace of Whitehall, then covered with ruins. This being afterwards converted into two residences, one-half was taken by Sir Thomas Robinson and the other by my Lady Townshend. After her death it was lived in successively by Michael Angelo Taylor and Viscount Gage, and is now part of the Bankruptcy Department of the Board of Trade.

Ladies of fashion in those days, being on the whole an ill-educated lot, and having few interests outside their own set, lived a most artificial existence, and had nothing much to occupy their time beyond a continual round of excitement. The artificiality of their dress tended also to limit their resources; for who could take proper exercise in hoops, even if it would not have been considered improper to walk about at all! Neither were they very domesticated, the management of their households and children being left a good deal in the hands of servants. They hardly ever read; certainly nothing but the most vapid novels,[1] and their general ignorance goes far to explain the astonishment created by Elizabeth Montagu and her following of bluestockings. Indeed, considering the round of dissipation and excitement in which they passed their days, they would have very little time for reading and none for serious study. The intricacies of a most intricate toilet occupied the greater part of their mornings, visiting and scandal their afternoons, cards and intrigues their nights.

All fine ladies spent their time in much the same way, and the following description may be taken to represent accurately enough a day in the life of my Lady Townshend, if it were not indeed actually written with that intent. It is taken from No. 28 of *The Con-*

---

[1] It will be remembered what kind of book was preferred by Miss Lydia Languish. The list included *The Reward of Constancy, The Fatal Connection, The Mistakes of the Heart, The Delicate Distress, The Tears of Sensibility,* etc. ; but even Miss Lydia Languish probably also read *The Memoirs of a Lady of Quality Written by Herself,* which was quite a different sort of book.

*noisseur* for 1754, a sort of eighteenth-century society journal, almost as transatlantically impertinent in its personal details as are its successors of to-day.

To describe the life of a Fine Lady would be only to set down a perpetual round of visiting, gaming, dressing and intriguing. She has been bred up in the notion of making a figure and of recommending herself as a Woman of Spirit, for which end she is always foremost in the Fashion, and never fails gracing with her appearance every public assembly and every party of pleasure. Though single, she may coquet with every fine gentleman, or if married, she may admit of gallantries without reproach, and even receive visits from the men in her bedchamber. To complete the character, and to make her a Very Fine Lady, she should be celebrated for her wit and beauty, and be parted from her husband : for as matrimony itself is not meant as a restraint upon pleasure, a separate maintenance is understood as a licence to throw off even the appearance of virtue.

There is no doubt but that my Lady Townshend was a very fine lady indeed. She was always ready with an excuse for pleasuring of some kind. Now it is a ball to celebrate the coming of age of her eldest son ; now another for the début of her beautiful daughter ; again, another to welcome the Prince of Nassau-Welbourg, fiancé of a granddaughter of George II., or to entertain some other foreign arrival of note.

With her great personal beauty, her private wealth which kept her independent of her husband, and her success as a leader of fashion, there were of course many spiteful people of her own sex who said hard things about her and her entertainments.

One such was my Lady Mary Wortley Montagu, whose day was a little over. This good lady writes to her daughter, the Countess of Bute, that she was surprised at her mentioning a ball given by Lady Townshend, and that she thought she was parted from her

lord and not in circumstances of giving public entertainments ! This was fairly amusing from one who
lived most of her life parted from her own lord !

" George Paston " quotes the letter, and again over-
flows into a footnote to air his opinion that Lady
Townshend was quite capable of giving a ball without
the support of her husband, " though the company
may not have been very select ". This author, who
has written several very charming books on the period,
makes a slip here. The balls given by my Lady Townshend were the most brilliant of her day, and invitations were eagerly sought by all who were in the
fashionable sets of London society.

She was always a typical lady of quality in the
highest sense of the word. One has only to recall to
mind the reception given by her on the occasion of
the visit of the Prince of Nassau-Welbourg in 1755,
*i.e.* fourteen years after her separation from her husband,
to realise how incorrect is the hint that her entertainments were " not very select ". The footnotes of
" George Paston " betray an almost feminine touch,
that touch which is so seldom absent when one woman
writes about another.

In the *Collection of the Malmesbury Letters* there is
one from Mrs. Harris, mother of the first Lord
Malmesbury, to her son in which she describes a
masquerade given by Lady Townshend in 1772, showing that, in her old age, she continued to be one of the
leaders among persons of quality of her day. Mrs.
Harris writes :

In the evening we went to Lady Townshend's who let in
masques, and a great number she had. Lady Villers was a
Sultana as fine as any Eastern Princess I ever redde of, a most
immense profusion of diamonds all over her. Miss Dutton was

a fine figure in the character of Almeda. There was a most jolly party of milkmaids with the Mayday garland. Sir Watkin Williams Wynne carried the pail, and was a most excellent figure. Lady Williams Wynne, Lady Francis Wyndham and another danced round the pail in the true milkmaid style. Mrs. Stapleton was the old milkwoman and a most excellent masque she was. They had an incomparable blind fiddler, who spoke in a thorough cluck voice: we could not discover who he was. The whole party were the most joyous of any I ever saw.

Mrs. Elizabeth Montagu, the bluestocking, whose friendship for Lady Townshend lasted to the end of a long life, detects in herself the first sign of old age in her sudden resolution not to go to Lady Townshend's ball—" though a new pink silver negligée lay ready for the donning ". " Once ", said she, " her dear friend Vanity would lure her over the Alps or the Ocean to a Ball like Lady Townshend's ".

Horace Walpole, who liked the brilliant woman for her beauty and her wit, though, even in her case, he could not restrain his spiteful pen, went to all these balls we may be sure, and wrote of them to his great friend, the other Horace at Florence. George Selwyn, wit and member of Parliament, would be there; and handsome Harry Conway, the dashing soldier and " military macaroni ", who married the Countess of Ailesbury, widowed daughter of the lovely Mary Bellenden, Duchess of Argyll, and became the father of that Anne Damer [2] whose statue is the first object

[2] Anne Seymour Conway. She married the eldest son of Lord Milton, the Hon. John Damer, who committed suicide, leaving her a widow at twenty-nine. She was a clever sculptress, a great friend of Horace Walpole, who, as is well known, was always devoted to her father, and she stayed much at Strawberry Hill. Horace inscribed on one of her works: " Non me fecit Praxiteles, sed Anna Damer ". In a notebook in the Waller Collection, he records the following facts about her early talent: " Mrs. Damer gave the first symptom of her talent in statuary when she was but ten years old. She was reading Spenser, and with bits of wax candle, and silk and feathers and

to welcome the visitor in the entrance hall of the
British Museum. General Campbell, afterwards fourth
Duke of Argyll, and Sir Harry Nesbitt, another gallant
soldier (killed at the battle of Roncoux near Liége in
1746), were both constant visitors at the Privy Garden,
for my lady, like Gerolstein's Grand Duchess, dearly
loved a red-coat ! [3] My Lord Baltimore,[4] owner of
Maryland, Mr. Winnington, my Lady's political cicisbeo,
the Duke of Newcastle, Sir Charles Hanbury-Williams,
and both the Sir Thomas Robinsons—in short, all the
celebrities, dandies and macaronies of the time flocked
to her assemblies, besides every woman with a claim
to be anybody, from her own cousin Caroline Petersham, afterwards Countess of Harrington, to, in later

tinsel picked out of silks, she made a knight and his esquire, not so long as a
finger, in the perfect costume of the description. A few years after, she made
the portrait of a shock dog in bas relief in wax small : and then heads in
wax in the manner of Gosset." (Fancy a girl of the present day, at ten years
old or even at twenty, reading Spenser ! It is much more likely to be Ethel
Dell !) With all her cleverness, or, perhaps, on account of it, Mrs. Damer
was very peculiar and eccentric in her habits, and was sometimes nicknamed
the " Epicenian ". She was the first woman to wear black silk stockings :
previously, women had always worn white stockings, even when in mourning.
[3] " Fine scarlet shag frocks, no person appearing in them but gentlemen."
Shag was another name for Shagreen, a sort of taffeta. In a copy of *Mrs.
Delany's Letters*, edited by Lady Llanover, which I have seen, there is a note
in manuscript which describes shagreen as " étoffe de soie, qui a des grains
comme le chagrin ". Scarlet was the ceremonial dress colour for all officers,
or so it would appear. Lord Balmerino, a follower of Prince Charlie in the
'45, went to his death on Tower Hill dressed as for a review. Shagreen was
originally made from the skin of the wild ass (cf. Balzac's *Peau de Chagrin*),
the peculiar markings being produced by artificial means.
[4] Charles Calvert, sixth Baron Baltimore, proprietor of the province of
Maryland, who left his name to the capital of it. He was attached to the
Prince of Wales's party as a rule, but was probably only a lukewarm partisan,
and he certainly never allowed politics to interfere with his pleasures or his
vices. George III. spoke of him rather contemptuously as " My lord
Baltimore, who thinks he understands everything, and understands nothing,
and is, *entre nous*, a little mad ". He wanted to marry Mrs. Pendarves (afterwards Mrs. Delany), but she refused him, though she confessed to liking
him, and his name is constantly recurring in her letters.

days, the fascinating Mie-Mie Fagnani, George Selwyn's adopted child.

Sometimes these gay ladies would leave their own houses and hie them to a public masquerade, especially at Ranelagh or Vauxhall, or perhaps organise some sort of a " frolick " to a more out-of-the-way garden of the town.

Our Ladies of Quality, who have at length adopted French manners with French fashions, and thrown over all starchiness and reserve with the ruff and the farthingale, are very fond of a Frolick. I have lately observed with great pleasure the commendable attempts of the other sex to shake off the shackles of custom, and I make no doubt a libertine Lady will soon become a very common character.—(*The Connoisseur*, 1751.)

After all, the essence of the life of the fashionable idler in the eighteenth century was very much as it is to-day. Anywhere and with any one for a frolick ! To any place where fashion leads the way, where there are cards to gamble with, gossips to talk scandal with, and humans to flirt with.

My Lady Townshend was indeed a great flirt. She flung what Walpole called the " broadest Wortley eye "[5] on Mr. Pitt[6] in the park, and she coquetted with Lord Baltimore at Mrs. Boothby's. His Lordship, however, spoke very plainly, not to say brutally, telling her that if she meant anything with him he was not for her purpose, but if only to make any one jealous he would throw away half an hour with her with all his heart !

[5] " Joy lives not here, to happier seats it flies
And only dwells where Wortley casts her eyes."

Horace, we know, hated Lady Mary. So did Pope, latterly.

[6] George Pitt of Strathfieldsave, afterwards created Baron Rivers. Mr. Pitt was very handsome, and Lady Mary Wortley Montagu had liked him extremely when he was in Italy.

According to our ideas she was, to put it mildly, exceedingly indiscreet. According to the accepted code of the eighteenth century she was merely " celebrated for her gallantries and her wit ". Scandal, it is true, was sometimes extremely busy with her name, as, for instance, in 1752, when she was nearly fifty years old, it was spitefully whispered that she " kept a dormitory in her dressing-room at Whitehall for Westminster School boys ",[7] and it had already been openly said that the Ladies Orford and Townshend had exhausted scandal both in their persons and their conversation. Walpole goes so far as to speak of her " libertinism ", but this was very likely a special bit of exaggerated malice on some special occasion.

The Mrs. Boothby referred to above was also a leader of fashion in those days. She was born Anne Clopton, daughter of Hugh Clopton, Councillor of the Middle Temple, and married Thomas Boothby of Tooley Park, Leicestershire. She is alluded to by that most inveterate of all lampooners, Sir Charles Hanbury-Williams, in the satirical poem " Isabella : or the Morning ", in the following line :

> To ancient Boothby's ancient Churchill's flown.

She was also famous for her wit and was a crony of my Lady Townshend's. She entertained at suppers

---

[7] In allusion to a handsome boy, Frederic Campbell, son of John, Duke of Argyll. Though a mere boy, he was a great pet of my Lady Townshend's, who entertained for him more than an ordinary regard. His father was one of her closest friends. (See Chapter XII. for some extracts from his letters to her when hunting the Highlanders.) Lady Louisa Stuart wrote of Frederic Campbell years afterwards to Lady Scott as " a beautiful youth Colonel Campbell's second son, long afterwards known to you as that beautiful old man Lord Frederic Campbell ". This same youth was secretary to my Lady Townshend's eldest son, the first Marquis, when Viceroy of Ireland, and was later appointed to a high post in Scotland. He married Lady Ferrers, widow of the mad Earl Ferrers, who was hung at Tyburn (in a silken suit) for the murder of his servant.

and intimate gatherings the set to which Walpole, Selwyn and my Lady belonged, and was probably one of the Leicester House party on the side of the Prince of Wales.

The truth is that such an age of open gossip, increasing to scandal and culminating in slander, had never been known. The picture of manners drawn by Sheridan in his brilliant *School for Scandal* (produced first in 1777)[8] was not one atom overdrawn. The town was full of women like my Lady Sneerwell, who gives it as her opinion that—

There is no possibility of being witty without a little ill-nature: the malice of a good thing is the barb that makes it stick.

Agents abounded in real life like her agent Snake, earning their living by the invention and spread of scandalous tales for the gratification of a macaroni's spite or a jealous woman's revenge. Sir Benjamin Backbite, the macaroni of the comedy, is a portrait of Horace himself, with his mincing gait, his affected mannerisms, his dilettante attempts at epigrams, and his stinging shafts of malice aimed at the reputations of friends and enemies alike. Bearing all this in mind, and realising that the Sneerwell, Candour, Crabtree and Backbite of the play were but types of persons to be met with in the society of the day, one may believe that many of the spiteful things whispered about the doings of Lady Townshend, either by Walpole or by Lady Mary Montagu, were much exaggerated if not entirely baseless. Such inveterate letter-writers and scandal-mongers, could never resist the temptation of retailing spicy bits of scandal (which probably grew in

---

[8] In the first edition of the play Mrs. Candour was called Mrs. Scandal.

the telling) to their numerous correspondents at home and abroad.

In a letter to the Countess of Pomfret in 1738, some three years before Lady Townshend left her husband to live alone in Whitehall, Lady Mary writes :

Lord Townshend is spitting up his lungs at the Gravel Pits,[9] and his charming lady is diverting herself with daily rambles in Town. She has made a new friendship which is very delightful, I mean with Madame Pulteney, and they hunt in couples from tea-drinking until midnight.

This Madame Pulteney, afterwards Countess of Bath, though very much to the fore in the fashionable world of the day, was a lady of the loosest morals. She was born Anna Maria Gumley, and was renowned for her beauty, her avarice and her corruption. The well-known Lord Chesterfield, and Mr. George Berkeley who married the Countess of Suffolk, the cast-off mistress of George II., were both supposed to have been among her most favoured friends, and the kind-hearted Lady Mary, always so well informed on such points, had written to Lady Mar about her as far back as 1723 as follows :

Mrs. Pulteney consents to be publicly kept by the Earl of Cadogan : whether Mr. Pulteney has a pad nag deducted out of the profits for his share I cannot tell, but he appears very well satisfied with it.

The daily life in town of my Lady Townshend probably differed but little from that of a score of other ladies of quality, except, we may be sure, that whatever her Ladyship did was done more strenuously, more

---

[9] Walford, in *Old and New London*, says that the Gravel Pits was the fashionable resort for invalids from the reign of William III. and Anne to the close of the eighteenth century. The air was supposed to be specially efficacious in the case of lung disease. The site was between the Palace of Kensington and the modern district of Notting Hill Gate.

thoroughly, so to speak, than by any one else : to the end of her long life she was an energetic dame.

Ladies, chiefly without the company of gentlemen, played cards every evening. The lives of ladies, indeed, were so monotonous and dull, that cards became necessary to them. A great lady had none of her husband's company except perhaps at dinner. He had his own pursuits, his own friends, often his mistresses as well ; he was drunk most nights. The lady, for her part, had no intellectual resources whatever. She read no books : she knew nothing that went on, and cared nothing. Her maid dressed her : she had a carriage and four horses : her running footmen before : her hanging footmen behind : she had her town and her country house : her nurse looked after her children : her life was that portentously dull kind of life in which everything is provided and there is nothing left to desire.

The above extract from a work of Sir Walter Besant's, written in his usual rather sweeping style, fits, accurately enough, the life of the modish women of the day, and Lady Townshend among them, but her existence was not quite so dull an affair.

For the greater part of her married life she did not see her husband even at dinner. In her entirely separate establishment she was able to enjoy men's society more than most ladies of her isolated position.

Moreover, far from being outside the interests of the world in general, she was in the middle of everything. Her eldest son was a great soldier, and in later life Viceroy of Ireland : her second son, Charles, was Chancellor of the Exchequer : her youngest son was in the Coldstreamers. Her intimate friends were politicians like the Duke of Newcastle, Mr. Winnington, Sir Thomas Robinson and other members of Parliament. She was more intimate still with gossips like Horace Walpole, George Selwyn, George Montagu, and she was very friendly with Mrs. Montagu, Mrs.

D

Chapone,[10] Mrs. Delany, and other women who were styled bluestockings half seriously and half in derision. It could not have been a dull life with such a circle of intimates. Above all, she was essentially free to do as she liked. Married women, indeed, were as free then as they are now. The protection of a husband's name was sufficient to license the " goings on " that an unmarried damsel could not attempt with equal safety. In this respect the twentieth century has advanced much farther, and it is not now at all necessary to be a wife to have that entire liberty of action which in the days of my Lady Townshend was only accorded to matrons.

What that liberty was may be gathered from the plays of the period. In Vanbrugh's *Provoked Husband*, one of the best of his comedies, occurs the following dialogue between my Lady Townley and her lord:

*Lady T.* Wives have infinite liberties in life that would be terrible in an unmarried woman to take.

*Lord T.* Name one.

*Lady T.* Fifty if you please. To begin with—in the morning, a married woman may have men at her toilette: invite them to dinner: appoint them a party in the stage box at the play: ingross the conversation there: call them by their christian names: talk louder than the players: from thence jaunt into the city: take a frolicsome supper at an India-house: perhaps in her *gaîté de cœur*, toast a pretty fellow: then clatter again to this end of the Town: break, with the morning, into an Assembly: crowd to the hazard-table: throw a favourite levant upon some sharp-lurching man of quality, and if he demands his money, turn it off with a loud laugh and say—you'll owe it him.

In another Act of the same play the vivacious lady exclaims:

[10] Mrs. Chapone, *née* Miss Hester Mulson, one of the coterie who used to sit in an adoring circle round Richardson while he read " Clarissa " or " Pamella " to them. She was a bluestocking, authoress of *Letters on the Improvement of the Mind* and similar boresome didactic works.

BALLS PARK, HERTFORD

I doat upon Assemblies, my heart bounds at a Ball, and at an Opera I expire. Then I love play to distraction — cards enchant me—and dice put me out of my little wits. Dear, dear Hazard—oh, what a flow of spirits it gives one !

Lady Townshend in her later life had also the society of her dear grandson, "Jack" Townshend—afterwards so well known as Lord John Townshend, M.P. for Westminster, Tamworth and other places, the second son of the first Marquis. He and his numerous young friends, including Charles Fox and other gay young men, must have kept the house in the Privy Garden a lively place indeed. Politics, except for her ridiculous excursion into the shallows of a feeble Jacobitism, due to her love of being "agin the Government", did not trouble her much, though she had many intimates among the politicians of the day. Unlike Lady Cowper, and the two beautiful Marys (Bellenden and Lepel), she does not appear to have attended much at either Court, though she was to a certain extent a frequenter of the Princess's circle at Leicester House, where she would come across her brother-in-law and his wife. This was William Townshend, A.D.C. to the King, but, curiously enough, also Groom of the Bedchamber to Frederic Prince of Wales. His wife, Henrietta Powlett, was Lady in Waiting to the Princess of Wales, but not received at the St. James's Palace Drawing-rooms. Their son was the first Lord Bayning.

The friends of my Lady Townshend were not generally chosen from the members of her husband's family. She preferred companions more lively, if possibly less dignified ; so she threw her bonnet " pardessus le moulin ", took up the rôle of a lady of quality on her own account, and played it " con spirito " to the end of her days.

How such a lady passed her evenings may be gathered from a sketch in the *Female Spectator* for 1743, where there is a most amusing account of a visit paid by a lady from the country to an old schoolfellow who had become a great lady of the town such as my Lady Townshend undoubtedly was in that year.

It was between eleven and twelve when I came to her door : where, after knocking a considerable time, a Footman, with his nightcap on, and pale as just risen from the Dead, came yawning forth, and on my asking for his Lady—" Oh Gad, Madam ", drawled he out, " we had a Racquet here last night, and my Lady cannot possibly be stirring these three hours ".

The visitor does not understand what a racquet may be, but thinks it is possibly some accident that has befallen her friend, so she goes for a walk and returns about three o'clock to make further inquiries.

I had the good fortune to be now admitted, and found her at her chocolate : she had a dish of it in one hand, and with the other seemed very busy in sorting a large parcel of guineas, which she divided in two heaps on a table that stood before her. " I am not ", said she, " however, altogether so late as I have been to-day : but you must know, I had a Racquet last night, no less than sixteen tables : and it was towards five before we broke up. I won, tis true, had charming luck : but see how I have been cheated ", pointing to the lesser heap of gold, " all these are counterfeit, not one good guinea among them ". She told me that when the number of company for play exceeded ten tables, it was called a Racquet : if under, it was only a Rout : and if not more than one or two it was only a Drum : she concluded by pitying those of her Acquaintances who could never raise their Drawing-Rooms above the latter.

To the explanation of the town lady it may be added that private balls were also sometimes called drums, and a drum on a large scale was a " squeezer ". There were also drum-majors, routs, tempests and hurricanes—differing only in degrees of multitude and uproar as the significant name of each declares. It may be taken for granted that my Lady Townshend would always be able to command a " racquet " and that her "squeezers" were celebrated. No one gave more splendid balls, and many brilliant assemblies gathered night after night in the house in the Privy Garden.

In the eighteenth century, London society was split up into sets very much as it is now.

Every drawing-room is different in its manners and its modes as it is in its company. One is celebrated for cards, another for wit, a third for beauties, a fourth for coxcombs, a fifth for old maids and scandal, a sixth for fashion, and a seventh for cotillons. —(*Westminster Magazine*.)

At my Lady Townshend's one might find any of these, or, what is more likely, all at one time. Wit there must be where she, Selwyn and Walpole foregathered : beauties could be counted in her salon by the score : coxcombs were assuredly not absent (Horace was there !) : fashion reigned : dancing was continually going on : old maids were perhaps rarer ; but of scandal there was more than enough.

To these circles of Folly, the fine Critics of this tawdry Age repair. Here, Honour is wounded, Virtue stabbed, and Vice Caressed. The formal Divine is here found to keep two mistresses, and though of the Church Militant at Mile-End, appears near Marybone to be the Military *Beau Garçon*. Beaux without estates and Fools with them, cannot pass these circles without a stigma. False hair on false Belles, Warren and Baily's washes [11] Rouge and other Cosmeticks cannot avoid detection. Tis here we know who paints white and red, and what heroes of the Horse and Foot Guards wear chicken-skin gloves. . . . While Luxury and Gaming govern the minds of the Young and Old, these empty topicks will form the theme of polite conversation.— (*Westminster Magazine*.)

[11] Baily, inventor of the " Ess Bouquet ", a perfume much in vogue in early Victorian times and which still survives.

My Lady Townshend was also very fond of organising amateur theatricals at her house in the Privy Garden. Angelo in his *Reminiscences* records that, when he was about ten years old (in 1766), he acted in the tragedy of *Cato* there. Her grandson, afterwards Lord John Townshend, was cast for the title-rôle; Lord Ferrers was Syphax; Lord Harrington, Sempronius; and the Hon. Col. Stanhope, Juba. Sheridan helped in the instruction of these youthful Thespians.

My Lady Townshend was also a great patroness of the Italian singers, who, in her day, were beginning to be all the vogue, and Walpole tells Mann how he took two or three of them to the Privy Garden to one of her parties. Among them were Manzoli and La Zamperini, who created the split in the Opera House that helped to start the rival show at Mrs. Cornelys. She was a fine dancer as well as singer, and was one of old Q.'s lady-loves. Others were La Tondina, Guadagni, La Rena (*chère amie* of George Selwyn), Pacchierotti, Monticelli, Amorevoli, etc.: all much courted by the fashionable world of the day, the male sopranos (or " sopranists ") as much the rage with the ladies as the women were with the gentlemen. Manzoli, one of those now happily extinct animals, was stated by Burney to have a most powerful and voluminous soprano and to have cleared a thousand pounds at his benefit.

This is not the place to enter into a history of the great theatre in the Haymarket, built by Vanbrugh in 1705, when it was called the " Queen's " Theatre in honour of Queen Anne. When George I. came to the throne the name was changed to " The King's " until the accession of Queen Victoria, when, by her special permission, it was known as " Her Majesty's ", which name it bore to the time of her death. Finally it was pulled down in 1892 to make way for the Carlton Hotel and Tree's Theatre (His Majesty's).

In the reigns of the early Georges it was conducted as an opera-house for a long time by Handel and Heidegger—Master of the King's Revels (see Chapter V.), and many of Handel's operas were produced there during a course of twenty years. Most of these are now quite forgotten as operas, though some of the airs survive, sung as solos at concerts, and others were incorporated in his later oratorios. The well-known and hackneyed " Largo " of Handel is nothing but an air from one of his operas.

My Lady Townshend had her own box at the Opera, and in 1781, when over seventy years of age, she was lively enough to organise an opera party [12] for the amusement of Mie-Mie Fagnani, and to see the great dancer Vestris [13] on his last appearance in *Medea and Jason*. On these occasions she surrounded herself, as she loved to do, with young people of both sexes, the friends of her grandson Jack Townshend and of the evergreen Walpole and Selwyn.

In the last years of the eighteenth century, the supreme attraction at the Opera was the ballet. A furore was created by Vestris, but a still more astonishing success was made by the famous *prima ballerina assoluta*, Mlle. Heinel, a sort of Maud Allan or Isadora Duncan of the day.

[12] Correspondence of George Selwyn with Lord Carlisle (Hist. MSS. Comm.).
[13] Walpole thus fantastically describes the appearance of this male dancer : " At the end of the second Act he appeared, but with so much grace, agility and strength, that the whole audience fell into convulsions of applause. The men thundered : the ladies, forgetting their delicacy and weakness, clapped with such vehemence that seventeen broke their arms, sixty-nine sprained their wrists, and three cried ' Bravo, bravissimo ' so rashly that they have not been able to utter so much as ' no ' since ".—(*From a Letter to the Countess of Ossory.*)

One does not like to be always quoting Walpole, but he is the authority on all questions relating to events in the London society of the time. Writing to Lord Stafford in 1771 he speaks of the first appearance of Mlle. Heinel :

There is a fine dancer whom Mr. Hobart is to transplant to London, a Mlle. Heinel, or Ingle, a Fleming. She is tall, perfectly made, very handsome and has a set of attitudes copied from the classics. She moves as gracefully slow as Pygmalion's statue when it was coming to life, and moves her leg round as imperceptibly as if she were dancing in the Zodiac. But she is not Virgo !

And again :

The Town has an idle notion that she made so much impression on a very high heart (*H.R.H. the Duke of Cumberland, one of the sons of George II.*) that it is thought prudent to keep it out of her way. She is the most graceful figure in the world, with charming eyes, bewitching mouth, and lovely countenance : yet I do not think that we shall see a Dame du Barri on this side the channel.

Even staid old Dr. Burney, father of Fanny D'Arblay, has something to say about this prodigy :

" It was at this time ", he writes, " that dancing seemed first to gain the ascendant over music by the superior talents of Mlle. Heinel, whose grace and execution were so perfect as to eclipse all other excellence. Crowds assembled at the Opera House more for the gratification of the eye than the ear : for neither the invention of a new composer nor the talents of new singers attracted the public at the theatre, which was almost abandoned till the arrival of this lady, whose extraordinary merit had an extraordinary recompense : for besides the £500 salary allowed her by the Hon. Mr. Hobart as manager, she was complimented by a *regalo* of £600 more from the Macaroni Club."

Goldsmith, of all people, also alludes to her in the epilogue of *She Stoops to Conquer* :

Doats upon dancing, and in all her pride,
Swims round the room, the Heinel of Cheapside.

On opera nights, fashionable folk were, of course, very late in bed : but on card nights they were up till the early hours of the morning, and at a masquerade it was the same. Walpole complains bitterly how by 1777 the fashion for late hours had increased. He says that everybody tried to be particular by being too late : and as every one tried it no one was too late in reality ! That it was the fashion to go to Ranelagh two hours after it was all over, for the music ended at ten and the company got there at twelve ! He amusingly describes to a friend the troubles of servants on account of their employers' late hours. Having to engage a housemaid, he asked the girl why she had left her last place.

She said she could not support the hours she kept, that her lady never went to bed till three or four in the morning. " Bless me child, why you tell me you live with a Bishop's wife. I never heard that Mrs. North (wife of the Bishop of Worcester) gamed or raked so late." . . . " No, Sir ", said she, " but she is three hours undressing ". . . . The edifice that takes three hours to demolish must be at least double that time in fabricating.

But see Chapter X. for further details on the subject of ladies' dress in the eighteenth century.

One more picture of the daily round of a lady of fashion of that time may be quoted from a skit called *The Hampstead Congress : or The Happy Pair*, and it does not differ much from the round of a fashionable lady of the twentieth century, except that the shopping is now done in the West End and no longer in the City, the " chair " has given place to the motor car, bridge replaces ombre and quadrille, Verdi and Puccini have silenced Handel at the Opera, and the electric light has for ever extinguished the flambeaux of a darker age. The essential features of a lady's life, the Court, the Park, the ring (if it be a betting ring), and the play—and balls, marriages, divorces, news, tea-table scandals and supper parties—remain unchanged and unchangeable for all time.

> Yet what is all your Rural Scene
> And Rustick Sports to those I mean
> With whom the Town in circling Joys
> Each moment of our time employs ?
> The City Jaunt each morning made
> To view the Jar or rich Brocade :
> The Chairs command the yielding Crowd,
> The obliging bow on friends bestowed.
> The Day's yet emptier hours to fill
> With Ombre or at dear Quadrille ;
> At night, the Opera's splendid throng,
> And charming Handel's heavenly Song,
> Round Vauxhall's galaxy to roam,
> Or Ranelagh's stupendous dome.
> The Court, the Park, the Ring, the Play,
> The Flambeaux' blaze that rivals day,
> Assemblies, Masquerades, Reviews,
> Balls, Marriages, Divorces, News,
> Of every kind, till out of breath,
> Tis life with these, without them—Death !

Thus did the ladies of quality pass their time in dressing, shopping, visiting, flirting, intriguing and card-playing. Above all, perhaps, in card-playing. The vice of gambling was one of the curses of the eighteenth century. From Royalty downwards, all gambled. The men perhaps preferred dice—the casting of a main, but the women all played cards. Their reckless gambling was something incredible, carried far beyond the bounds of the bridge and roulette of to-day. Pope, in his *Rape of the Lock*, describes this mania admirably in a wonderful rhyming account of a card-party given by Belinda, the heroine of the Rape, in which the whole game of ombre is described stage by stage. Later on in the cen-

tury, it was the same or worse. My Lady Townshend
gambled like the rest. Lady Mary Coke in her *Diary*
records how she went to Lady Shelbourne's (afterwards
Lady Lansdowne) at seven o'clock and played one
pool of quadrille with Lady Townshend and others,
losing one fish! She then went on to Lady Aylesbury's
and lost fifteen guineas at lu (*sic*) in two hours! The
*Diary* is full of allusions to her gains and losses at
cards, but she was evidently not a heavy gambler.

The fever seems to have reached its climax towards
the end of the century, but for many years previously
it had been the custom for peeresses and other women
prominent in society to hold public card-parties at
their private houses for their private profit, though the
regular leaders of fashion, like my Lady Harrington
in Stable Yard (always on Sunday!), Lady Betty Ger-
maine in St. James's Square, and others doubtless were
too much "grande dame" to make a trade of it. They
all loved cards for the sport, not for gain. "Don't
talk to me about books!" cried old Sarah Marlborough, "the only books I know are men and cards!"

The games principally played were bassett, ombre,
quadrille and faro. The four most notorious women
to make a profit of the gambling craze were my Lady
Buckinghamshire, my Lady Archer,[14] Mrs. Sturt and
Mrs. Duncannon, who were known throughout the
town as "Faro's Daughters".

[14] The allusions in the satirical prints and poems of the day to ladies who
painted their faces, were very numerous, especially with regard to that
particular Lady Archer who seems to have been noted for the practice.

"'A' was an Archer who painted her face."—(Walpole.)

"Lips that made Archer's look too cold in spite of their carmine."—
(Luttrell.)

And a new verse for the Litany: "From beef without mustard, from a
servant who over-values himself, and from a woman who painteth herself,
good Lord Deliver us!"

It was all done in the most open fashion possible. Advertisements were inserted in the daily papers the day before, and paragraphs describing the evenings the next day. In the *Times* of February 5, 1793, one such note states that Mrs. Sturt's house in St. James's Square has been opened the previous evening for the first time for public play, and that visitors had been numerous.

It would seem that money was not always forthcoming for these ladies' banks : advertisements would appear in the fashionable papers offering " a gentleman of unexceptionable character " who would, on receiving an invitation, attend at any of these functions prepared to hold a bank of anything from two hundred to two thousand guineas. The scandal at last became so great, the losses so notorious, that information was laid by the police (led by Townsend the celebrated Bow Street runner) against the ladies mentioned above for playing faro at Lady Buckinghamshire's in St. James's Square : they were eventually condemned to pay a fine of £50 each and their croupier one of £200. Gilray has a print on the subject, in which my Lady Buckinghamshire is represented as tied to the tail of a cart and the Lord Chief Justice (Lord Kenyon) is shown administering a flogging with birch and cat-o'-nine-tails. On the cart is a placard with the words " Faro's Daughters, Beware ". Mrs. Sturt and another woman are shown on one side standing by the pillory. Another print by the same artist shows Lady Archer and Lady Buckinghamshire keeping a faro bank in their old age. Underneath is inscribed :

To those earthly Divinities who charmed twenty years ago, this honourable method of banishing mortifying reflections is dedicated. O Woman, Woman ! Everlasting is your power over us : for as youth you charm away our hearts, and in your after years, you charm away our purses.

By 1800 these noble harpies had disappeared, and with the advance of the new century the gambling mania appears to have gradually become confined to the other sex.

George Selwyn, Lord Carlisle, and Stephen and Charles Fox were among the more reckless gamblers of the day, and it was no uncommon thing for them to sit at a table for hours at a time, losing or winning anything from five to fifty thousand pounds. Almack's the fashionable club, Arthur's, and White's (the lineal descendant of White's Chocolate House) were the best-known haunts of the gambling bloods of the time. Almack's, originally in Pall Mall, was afterwards removed to St. James's Street, and became known as Goosetree's, and finally as Brooke's, and Brooks' it is to this day. It was here that Lord Stavordale lost £11,000 in one night, but recovered it all by one great coup at hazard : upon which he swore an oath, complaining bitterly that if he had been playing deep he might have won millions !

Another form of gambling was rife at the time. This was the mania for betting on any and every subject, sometimes in the biggest sums on apparent trivialities. A few examples will suffice :

Fifty guineas that Mlle. Heinel does not dance at the Opera next winter.

Fifty guineas that 2000 people were at the Pantheon last evening.

Fifty guineas that Lord Ilchester gives his first vote in opposition and hits six out of his first ten pheasants.

Five guineas down to receive a hundred if the Duke of Queensbury dies before half an hour after five in the afternoon of June 27th, 1773.

The duke was dying at the time the last-mentioned bet was made !

Fox and Fitzpatrick played cards on one occasion from 1.0 A.M. till 6.0 A.M., with a waiter standing by to tell the sleepy gamesters whose deal it was ! But Fox (who perhaps does not properly belong to this period) was an inveterate gambler, and a very philosophical one. On one occasion he settled himself to sleep with his head on the hard table on which he had just lost a large fortune : on another, having lost his last shilling at faro, he was found the next morning reading Herodotus.

Brooks, the owner of the club of the name in St. James's Street, made a lot of money out of these gamesters ; but he was always ready to lend money to the losers, who were not always honest enough to repay him.

> Liberal Brooks, whose speculative skill
> Is hasty credit and a distant bill :
> Who, nursed in clubs, disdains a vulgar trade,
> Exults to trust, and blushes to be paid.—(TICKELL.)

He threatened over and over again to resign from the club because he could not get back the moneys he had lent, and finally he did so. He died a very poor man in 1782, and there is a tradition that, to evade the demands of his creditors at a time when corpses commanded a certain price on the market, his body was secretly buried at night in a small opening under the pavement of St. James's Street, close to the club which had borne his name.

But to return to the ladies. Though not such high players as the men, a considerable part of the daily round of a lady of fashion was taken up with cards.

In the early part of the century there had also been much gambling, and stakes had been fairly high, but the ladies, at any rate, did not turn night into day and they got to bed at a reasonable hour. " Clarinda ", who sent a portion of her diary to Mr. Spectator for publication, and who may be supposed to have flourished about the reign of good Queen Anne, accounts for her day as follows:

*Wednesday.*—From 8.0 till 10.0. Drank two dishes of chocolate in bed and fell asleep after them.

From 10.0 till 11.0. Ate a slice of bread and butter, drank a dish of bohea and read the *Spectator*.

From 11.0 till 1.0. At my toilette. Tried a new hood. Gave orders fer Veny to be combed and brushed. (MEM.—Look best in blue.)

From 1.0 till half an hour after 2.0. Drove to the 'Change and cheapened a couple of fans.

Till 4.0. At Dinner. (MEM.—Mr. Froth passed in his new liveries.)

From 4.0 till 6.0. Dressed. Paid a visit to old Lady Blithe and her sister, having before heard they were gone out of Town that day.

From 6.0 till 11.0. At Bassett. (MEM.—Never set again upon the ace of diamonds.)

On another day Clarinda dawdles about at home all the morning, finally gets dressed by three, sees company from four to eleven and goes to bed at twelve. One day she shuts herself up for an hour to practise " Lady Betty Modley's Scuttle ", which is " a pace of affected precipitation ". Another morning she occupied half an hour in shifting a patch about her cheek before settling to fix it above her left eyebrow. She was but one type of a lady of quality of the eighteenth century. My Lady Townshend and my Lady Harrington belonged to quite another.

If, in addition to the amusements of a lady in those

days, one wishes to know what they ate at dinner and other meals, one may turn to a letter written by Lady Mary Wortley Montagu to her daughter the Countess of Bute in the year 1752, in which the elder lady, at that time living on the Continent, thus describes her daily food :

I wake generally about seven, and drink half a pint of warm asses' milk after which I sleep two hours. As soon as I am risen, I constantly take three cups of milk coffee, and two hours after that a large cup of milk chocolate. Two hours more brings my dinner where I never fail swallowing a good dish (I don't mean plate) of gravy soup, with all the bread, roots, &c., belonging to it. I then eat a wing and the whole body of a large fat capon, and a veal sweetbread, concluding with a competent quantity of custard and some roasted chestnuts. At five in the afternoon I take another dose of asses' milk and for supper twelve chestnuts, which would weigh two of those in London, one new laid egg, and a handsome porringer of white bread and milk.

Lady Mary was by way of being something of an invalid when she wrote that letter, but her digestion, at any rate, could not have been much impaired. But every one ate enormously in those days, and continued to do so right up to the middle of the nineteenth century. Here is the menu of a dinner in 1744 at Mrs. Delany's house in Dublin :

| | |
|---|---|
| Turkey | Partridge |
| Boiled Leg of Mutton | Sweetbreads |
| Greens, &c. | Collared Pig |
| Soup | Creamed Apple Tart |
| Plum Pudding | Crabs |
| Roast Loin of Veal | Fricassee of Eggs |
| Venison Pastry | Pigeons |
| | (No Dessert to be had) |

The apology for the absence of dessert has a humour all its own. There are one or two curious points as to the order in which the dishes were served—soup after turkey and mutton, followed directly by plum pudding, and the only kind of fish—crabs! The above menu is copied *verbatim et literatim* from the *Memoirs* of Mrs. Delany. Her letters to her sister abound in similar bills of fare of the same portentous kind. On one occasion she "picknicked" in Ireland off a "swilled mutton", *i.e.* "a sheep roasted whole in its skin scorched like a hog".

In this chapter I have tried to give some idea how persons of quality, such as were the modish crew to which Lady Townshend belonged, passed their time in the round of society in London. I will now endeavour to picture the life led in public by these frolicsome dames when they journeyed for their pleasures farther afield.

# CHAPTER III

## DIVERSIONS OF PERSONS OF QUALITY IN LONDON OUT OF DOORS

The Pleasure Gardens of London : the less fashionable resorts :
Jenny Whim's : the Islington Spa : other Spas in Clerkenwell :
the "Folly" on the Thames : Ranelagh : frequented by all
classes of society : concerts and masquerades at Ranelagh : the
great Regatta : the new Spring Garden at Vauxhall : Lady
Caroline Petersham's supper-party : Betty of the fruit shop :
other Spring Gardens : turtle suppers : derivation of the name
"Vauxhall" : affrays at Vauxhall : Marylebone Gardens :
favourite resort of Macheath, and other highwaymen : Handel
at Marylebone : the Spaniard's at Hampstead : a curious sauce.

TO THE STUDENT of London life in the eighteenth
and early nineteenth centuries few things are more
astonishing than the number of out-of-the-way places
of amusement and pleasure-gardens existing in those
days, now entirely disappeared.

In the never-ceasing expansion of London towards
all points of the compass, and the enhancement of
the value of town land for building purposes, trees
have been remorselessly cut down, meadows have disappeared, and springs have been choked up or built
over. The country suburb of one hundred years ago
is the slum of to-day, crowded with squalid buildings
and teeming with squalid life.

Those pleasure-gardens nearest to the City itself
were, naturally, the first to go. A genteel and pseudo-
aristocratic residential district now covers the site of

old Marylebone Gardens, where Macheath swaggered and kissed the pretty girls, and Handel listened to his own music : the barracks of the Foot-Guards occupy the greater part of the grounds of the modish Ranelagh House, only a small portion being still in the open ; and the engines of the South-Western Railway at the Nine Elms depot hiss and shriek on the spot where Pepys once took " two beautiful ladies " to see the new Spring Gardens of Vauxhall. It would be indeed hard to discover in the near neighbourhood of London any vestige of an eighteenth-century tea-garden, with the solitary exception of the " Spaniard's " at Hampstead, which is still to be found *in situ* as it appeared nearly two hundred years ago.

These open-air places of amusement of the age of wig and powder were, of course, not all of the same distinction, nor, with the exception perhaps of Vauxhall, did they cater for the enjoyment of all classes alike. In the attractions on which they relied for support, and the visitors from which that support was drawn, there could be found every variety, from aristocratic Ranelagh House and Vauxhall Gardens, where, for many years the *beau monde* went every night and Royalty frequently put in an appearance, down to the common public-houses, tea-gardens and tawdry bits of ground clustering round the numerous springs of Clerkenwell and the northern suburbs, and the still commoner low-life haunts south of the Thames.

A letter from a foreigner on a visit to London in 1742 tells a friend in Paris about these gardens:

Every village, of which there are numbers in the neighbourhood of this great overgrown city, is half peopled with publicans who have gardens, walks covered with trees which retain an admirable verdure all the summer long, and are permitted to

further advantage of certain rustic games, to draw in customers
and inflame a reckoning. . . . During the fine season, the
theatres are shut up, but certain places, resembling perhaps
what theatres were in their origin, are then opened at the ex-
tremities of the Town, where the spectators are entertained
with a Medley of Vaulting, Tumbling, Rope-Dancing, Singing
and sometimes Farces, and regale themselves in the interval with
Eating, Drinking, Smoking, or making love to the Ladies of
Pleasure.

By " villages " the writer means, of course, Islington, Clerkenwell, Chelsea and other parts of London
which have long been included in the town itself.
" Ladies of pleasure " were always to be found wherever there was a concourse of visitors, and the swarm-
ing of them at such places was always a prominent
cause of their decline.

Mr. Warwick Wroth, in a delightful book on the
subject of these extinct gardens (*London Pleasure Gardens
of the XVIIIth Century*, Macmillan, 1896), describes no
less than sixty-four different places all well within the
boundaries of the London of the present day. None
of them were outside the four-mile radius from Charing
Cross, and Mr. Wroth treats each one most exhaustively
from Ranelagh House to the notorious " Dog and
Duck " and " Temple of Apollo " on the Surrey side.
There were probably others whose traces, like their
springs, have been covered up. Apropos of " Dog and
Duck " this seems to have been quite a favourite sign.
Besides the very notorious one in St. George's Fields,
somewhere near the site of Bedlam and the Catholic
Cathedral of St. George's, Southwark, there was a
well-known house of this name in Hertford Street,
Mayfair, and another in St. James's Street, two aristo-
cratic thoroughfares in which there is probably no
public-house at all to-day.

Duck-hunting with dogs seems to have been a popular form of "sport" with the aristocratic folk as well as with humbler persons. De Saussure mentions that among the charms of Sir Watkin Wynn's place at Wynnstay was " La chasse délicieuse du canard domestique à la nage ".

It would not be surprising to learn, for certain, that my Lady Townshend had paid visits to more than one of the out-of-the-way gardens at some time or other. We know how dearly she loved a " frolick ", and what better frolic could one ask than a jaunt to some second-rate " spaw ", where the outlandish garb of city madams and the childish diversions provided for commoner folk could be quizzed by persons of quality and fashion ? There is no actual evidence that my Lady went to any but Ranelagh House. But she must often have been at Vauxhall, or else "out of the fashion ", which she never permitted herself to be for a moment, and she probably visited Marybone Gardens as well, what time Mr. Handel produced a new " musick ", or some modish person of her own world organised a " rout ". A somewhat discursive chapter on the pleasure-gardens of the eighteenth century is, therefore, not out of place in writing of the doings and surroundings of a lady of fashion such as was my Lady Townshend.

Putting aside Ranelagh, Vauxhall and perhaps Marylebone, there were other places numbering persons of quality among their regular habitués.

There was, for instance, Cupar's Gardens, where Lord Bath and Lord Sandys once had their pockets picked ! This was a very popular place, described by Jesse as a favourite resort of the gay and profligate up to the middle of the eighteenth century. The site

is now covered by that portion of Waterloo Bridge
Road lying between the river and the Union Jack Club,
together with the land on the left of the thoroughfare.
Some of the trees are still to be seen in the ground
behind St. John's Church, Waterloo Bridge Road, and
the stairs on the Surrey side leading up from the river
opposite Somerset House are still called " Cupar's
Stairs ". Cupar himself, who laid out the gardens, was
gardener to Lord Arundel, from whom he rented the
ground.

Then there was " Jenny's Whim " at Pimlico.
Walpole writes to Montagu that he had picked up
Lord Granby [1]—

arrived very drunk from Jenny's Whim, where he had dined
with Lady Fanny, and left her and eight other women and four
men playing at Brag.

Jenny's Whim was a little red-brick tavern near
Ebury Bridge, Pimlico, at that time a wooden structure
known as " Jenny Whim's Bridge ", where St. George's
Row and the beginning of Sutherland Street now
stand. Not really a fashionable place, it was a very
popular resort for the people. It had a bowling-green,
cockpit and ducking or duck-hunting pond. Its flower-
beds were arranged in stiff geometrical patterns, copied
in the Dutch fashion from more aristocratic gardens.
Art was added to nature in the shape of ponds where
mechanical mermaids and fish bobbed up and down,
and the side-walks were enlivened by the sudden
starting out of harlequins and Mother Shiptons when

[1] Afterwards Marquis of Granby, the hero of Minden, and the original of
so many sign-boards, including that of a famous hostelry at Dorking, where
Weller senior ducked the red-nosed " shepherd " in the horse-trough!
His Lordship's companion, Lady Fanny (whom he afterwards made Mar-
chioness of Granby), was Lady Frances Seymour, eldest daughter of the
proud Duke of Somerset by his second wife, Lady Charlotte Finch.

a hidden spring was trodden on by the unwary visitor.

The lower sort of people have their Ranelaghs and their Vauxhalls as well as the quality, and the royal diversion of duck-hunting may be had into the bargain together with a decanter of Dorchester, for sixpence at Jenny's Whim.—(*Connoisseur*.)

Jenny's Whim was not actually demolished until 1865, but had degenerated into a mere public-house long before that date.

The Islington Spa, or New Tunbridge Wells, which was situated near the site of the present Lloyd's Row in the neighbourhood of Rosebery Avenue, was a resort that at one time had quite a fashionable *clientèle* on account of the strong medicinal quality of its waters. It was in existence as early as the reign of Charles II., but seems to have declined in popularity for some years until about 1732, when its prosperity revived.

As with other similar places, the medicinal waters came to be only secondary attractions as compared with the garden walks, coffee-rooms, music and fêtes. There was always public breakfasting and dancing from 11.0 to 3.0, at which extraordinary care was taken to preserve due decorum.

The Princesses Amelia and Caroline, daughters of George II., came regularly every day to the Islington Spa for the purpose of drinking the waters, and the proprietors would take as much as £30 in one morning, such was " the concourse of the nobility and others ". On the birthdays of the Princesses, as they passed through the Spa Fields, which was generally filled with carriages, they were saluted with a discharge of twenty-one guns, a compliment always paid to them on their arrival : in the evening there would be a big bonfire, and the guns would again be discharged several times.

But towards the middle of the eighteenth century the place had become quite middle-class, and had lost much of its reputation. Ranelagh had arisen and Vauxhall had been resuscitated, and shortly afterwards Islington Spa disappeared altogether from the list of London gardens.

The same neighbourhood could boast of a dozen other spas or wells, many next door or opposite to each other, and all in the immediate vicinity of the modern Rosoman Street, Clerkenwell. Each had its own special spring of curative properties, and the traces of the situation of some are still to be met with in public-houses bearing the old names and built over or near the spot where the water used to flow. There is Sadlers Wells of course, one of the most attractive, whose spring has been rediscovered: there are "London Spa" and "New Merlin's Cave", both in Rosoman Street: there is "Ye Olde Bagnigge Wells" in the King's Cross Road, and there is the "Adam and Eve" at the corner of Euston Road and Tottenham Court Road, and many others. Even on the Thames itself during the early days of the century there was a place of entertainment. This was called "The Royal Diversion", but soon nicknamed "The Folly". It was a timber building erected on a strong barge, moored in the river opposite the Savoy. First opened to the public in the reign of William III., it was much frequented by persons of quality. Later, in the days of the Georges, it became a haunt of the "women of the town" with their attendant followers, and degenerated into a low-class resort. But see the book by Wroth, already mentioned, on the subject of tea-gardens, etc.

It was, however, at Ranelagh House and Vauxhall Gardens that the macaronies and modish women of the set to which my Lady Townshend belonged used chiefly to assemble. Ranelagh House was opened on April 5, 1742, and a fortnight later the ubiquitous Horace Walpole is already breakfasting there.

"I have been breakfasting this morning at Ranelagh Gardens", he writes to Mann. " They have built an immense amphitheatre with balconies full of little ale-houses: it is in rivalry to Vauxhall, and cost above £12,000. The building is not finished, but they get good sums by people going to see it, and breakfasting in the house : there were yesterday no less than three hundred and eighty persons at eighteenpence apiece. You can see how poor we are, when with a tax of four shillings in the pound, we are laying out such sums for cakes and ale."

The Rotunda, the principal attraction of the place, of which many views may be found in contemporary prints, was a huge circular edifice of the same shape and about the same size as the reading-room of the British Museum. Walpole calls it a vast amphitheatre into which every one that loves eating, drinking, staring or crowding is admitted for twelvepence. In 1744 he writes more fully of it to his friend Harry Conway :

That you may not think I employ my time as idly as the great men I have been talking of, you must be informed that every night constantly I go to Ranelagh which has totally beat Vauxhall. Nobody goes anywhere else : everybody goes there. My Lord Chesterfield is so fond of it that he says he has ordered all his letters to be directed thither. If you had never seen it I would make you a most pompous description of it, and tell you how the floor is all of beaten princes—that you can't set your foot without treading on a Prince of Wales or Duke of Cumberland. .The company is universal : there is from His Grace of Grafton down to children out of the Foundling Hospital : from my Lady Townshend to the kitten : from my Lord Sandys to your humble cousin and sincere friend.

It soon became the recognised place for the frolics of the *élite*, whether the frolic was a perfectly innocent one or involved an assignation of a more serious kind.

The highly respectable and learned Mrs. Elizabeth Carter was there in 1748, and did not quite relish the " tumultar torchlight entertainments ". Dr. Johnson praised it highly more than once, calling it rather pompously, and incorrectly withal, " a place of innocent recreation ".

On the other hand, Evelina found it dull! " There's your famous Ranelagh ", says this self-opinionated and rather priggish young person, who surely existed in the flesh as well as in the pages of Fanny Burney's book—" that you make such a fuss about. Why, what a dull place is that ! " *Chacun à son goût*. Ranelagh may have been outwardly more reputable and less raffish than lively Vauxhall. But the habitués of such places had a great deal to do with the making of their own frolics. We may be quite sure that my Lady Townshend and all her numerous following would not have been constant visitors to Ranelagh House if they had found the place in any way dull.

The entertainments at Ranelagh, other than the usual masquerades, balls and special fêtes, varied a good deal. Vocal and instrumental music was a prominent feature. Choruses from Mr. Handel's most admired oratorios were frequently in the programme, interspersed by ballads by Mr. Dibdin, Mrs. Baddeley and other famous performers of the day. Italian singers, so much the rage at that period, would of course be heard from time to time. More notable still is the recorded appearance of a boy of eight years old, one GEORGE MOZART, who played compositions of his own on the organ and harpsichord. This alone for us

RANELAGH

The Jubilee Ball on the birthday of George, Prince of Wales, May 24, 1749.   From an old coloured print in the British Museum

raises the Ranelagh of that day far above the average tea-garden.

The advertisements in the contemporary newspapers were full of thought for the comfort and convenience of folk attending this rather out-of-the-way place of amusement. Cut-purses and foot-pads abounded in the London of those days. Therefore, persons of quality were advised that there would be " a guard on horseback to patrole the road ". In 1772 an additional number of lights were set up along the route, and about the same time, or perhaps a little earlier, we are told that the " footway from Buckingham Gate is lately mended and enlarged so as to make it very safe and easy for chairs ". In one of these numerous notices, the company that come by Hyde Park Corner " are requested to order their carriages to keep the turnpike road by Pimlico to prevent the accidents that must invariably happen by going down the Descent of the New Road " (*i.e.* the modern Sloane Street) " by the Fire Engine ". In almost all the notices it is carefully pointed out that " the Amphitheatre and other rooms are well-aired ". The charge for admission to Ranelagh House on ordinary occasions was half-a-crown, for which you received tea, coffee and bread and butter gratis. On some evenings more was charged, and then it is always pointed out that " the best French and other Wines with a variety of Sweetmeats are provided for the Sideboard and the Beauffets in the Amphitheatre ".

The most popular entertainments were masquerades and ridottos, organised on special occasions from time to time down to the very last days of the gardens.

One such special occasion was the ball on the evening of the great regatta of June 23, 1775. On that night Mrs. Cornelys, of Carlisle House notoriety (see next chapter), had the sole management of the decorations and the supper, but it was stated the next day that, although she had been allowed seven hundred guineas for the supper alone, it was, like most farmed ones, indifferent in quality and the wines very scarce.

On another evening there was also apparently not enough to eat, for Sir Thomas Robinson (the " Long Sir Thomas ", a great friend of my Lady Townshend), manager and general director of Ranelagh House, found himself compelled to invite all the company to have supper with him.

On the whole it may be said that Ranelagh fairly maintained its aristocratic reputation to the last, though at times the company was undoubtedly " somewhat mixed ", and assignations and intrigues not entirely unknown. In the eighteenth century, however, as in the twentieth, there were not wanting numbers of prurient Puritans who could not see any good in amusements of any kind, however well conducted. A group of such people made an attack on the pleasure-gardens of the day, and a pamphlet was published as a sort of apology for and justification of their existence.

This was called " Dame Ranelagh's Remonstrance in behalf of herself and her Sisters, humbly addressed to the G...d J..y of the C....y of M.......x ". This rather amusing skit is signed Ranelagh, Vauxhall, Marybone, etc., etc., and states that complaint has been made that they are " nurseries of idleness and debauchery, schools of impertinence and congresses of vice and impudence, assembled to laugh virtue and modesty out of countenance ". All these charges and many worse ones are boldly admitted, and it is urged that " notwithstanding we are evils, we are at least

RANELAGH : INTERIOR OF THE ROTUNDA
From an old print in the British Museum

as necessary ones as many others which continue to be tolerated under that notion ".

The regatta alluded to above, terminating with a ball at Ranelagh House, must have been one of the most remarkable festivals that London had ever seen.

We are told that the Duke of Richmond, His Grace of Montagu and the Earl of Pembroke had splendid companies on this occasion. Their houses were all in the neighbourhood of Whitehall, and my Lady Townshend was probably at one of their gatherings, unless indeed she had a splendid company of her own at her well-known house in the Privy Garden, the windows of which looked on to the river. Or unless she was out on one of her frolics (she was only sixty-seven years of age, a mere nothing for a woman of her spirit) and made one of the hundred " elegant ladies " in the City Barge !

The Ladies in general, were dressed in white and the gentlemen in undress frocks of all colours : and tis thought the procession was seen by at least two hundred thousand people. In a Word, from the mixed Multitude of Lords and Liverymen, Pinks and Pickpockets, Dukes and Dustmen, Drabs and Duchesses, the whole Scene afforded an admirable Picture of High Life below Stairs and Low Life above.

Besides the crowds in the streets, on the river and on the bridges, there were about five hundred people in the stone and gilt galleries of St. Paul's to see the procession by water. The ball at Ranelagh in the evening was attended by two thousand persons, including the " first persons of distinction ", whoever that might mean to imply.

Ranelagh began to fall upon evil days in or about 1788, the year that saw the death of my Lady Townshend, though its glories were revived, more or less

faintly, at fitful intervals. The last masked ball held
there was in June 1803 to commemorate the installa-
tion of Knights of the Bath. This proved to be one
of the best entertainments ever given there, but it was
the last flicker of an expiring Ranelagh. The Rotunda
was opened for the last time on July 8 of the same
year, though it was not until September 1805 that the
final demolition was commenced. The grand organ
went to the church at Tetbury in Gloucestershire for
a time, and the whole of the furniture was disposed of
by auction. Part of the old ground of Ranelagh is now
open as a garden, where people may walk gratis, but
all that remains of the former apparatus of decoration
are some iron bands attached here and there to trees—
presumably once the supports of lamps or festoons of
some kind.

To enumerate all the people of note who visited
Ranelagh House in the heyday of its glory would be to
give the names of every one of any social importance
in the last sixty years of the eighteenth century. One
was the lovely Emma Hamilton, the ex-scullery maid,
who, when she was Emma Hart and living " under the
protection of " Charles Greville, went with him to
Ranelagh and insisted on singing on the platform,
because she envied the applause bestowed on the
public singer, who, she said, sang out of tune. Her
own performance was anything but a success, and
Greville must have been considerably annoyed, for we
are told he hustled her out of the garden with scant
ceremony. Richardson the novelist, who always had
love or marriage in his mind, looked upon Ranelagh
as a marriage market. It may have been that on
occasions, but it certainly was the place for assignations
—illicit and otherwise.

Masquerade on June 1, 1803
*Design by Cipriani*

Regatta Ball, June 23, 1775
*Design by Bartolozzi*

What wonders were there to be found
That a clown might enjoy or disdain?
First, we traced the gay ring all around:
Ay,—and then we went round it again.

Fair maids who at home in their haste
Had left all clothing else but a train,
Swept the floor clean as slowly they paced,
And then—walked round and swept it again.

(ROBERT BLOMFIELD.)

Amateurs were not unknown at Ranelagh. A skit on the taste for foreign music was composed by Dr. Burney in an adaptation of Thornton's Burlesque Ode on St. Cecilia's Day. It was executed by well-known performers in masks, and the instruments consisted of " the salt-box, the Jew's harp, the marrow-bones and cleavers, the hum-strum (or hurdy-gurdy), etc. It looks like an early example of the toy symphony made popular by Haydn and Romberg.

Sometimes the performances were for charity. In 1791 an entertainment was got up in aid of the celebrated Chevalier D'Eon, who had fallen on evil days and was earning his livelihood as a "female *maître d'armes*" (see Chapter VIII.).

There was an imitation of Ranelagh in Paris, called the Colisée, which existed down to the days of Marie Antoinette and the Revolution; but Angelo says in his *Memoirs* that it was as inferior to the London Ranelagh as Marybone was to Vauxhall.

The garden at Chelsea may have been the resort of fashion, but it was to the garden at Lambeth—the new Spring Gardens of Vauxhall—that London folk, on pleasure bent, betook themselves as a rule. There all classes, from the highest to the lowest, could enjoy themselves freely and have a real good time without too much regard for the proprieties, and indeed with no little looseness of demeanour, if so inclined. Picture to yourself that supper party at which Lady Caroline Petersham [2] cooked seven chickens in a china dish over a lamp. The story as told in Walpole's letter to George Montagu is perhaps a bit stale, but such an account of a Vauxhall frolic will bear repetition :

As jolly and as abominable a life as she may have been leading, I defy all her enormities to equal a party of pleasure that I had t'other night. I shall relate it to you to show you the manners of the Age. I had a card from Lady Caroline Petersham to go with her to Vauxhall. I went accordingly to her house, and found her and the little Ashe [3] or the Pollard Ashe as they call her : they had just finished their last layer of red, and looked as handsome as crimson could make them. . . . We issued into the Mall to assemble our Company, which was all the Town if we could get it : for just so many had been summoned except Harry Vane whom we met by chance. We mustered the Duke of Kingston,[4] whom Lady Caroline says she has been trying for these seven years, but alas, his beauty is at the fall of the leaf : Lord March,[5] Mr. Whitehed,[6] a pretty Miss beauclerc and a very foolish Miss Sparre. . . . We got into the best order we could and marched to our Barge with a Boat of French Horns attending, and little Ashe singing. We paraded some time up

[2] Lady Caroline Petersham, *née* Lady Caroline Fitzroy, daugher of the Duke of Grafton, great granddaughter of Charles II. *à la main gauche*, and cousin of my Lady Townshend through the Villiers blood. She married Viscount Petersham, afterwards Earl of Harrington. Both as Lady Caroline Petersham and as Countess of Harrington she was a leader in the fast set of her day. See Chapter VIII. for a more detailed account of this lady's doings.

[3] A very remarkable young woman, a constant companion of Lady Caroline about this time. She was popularly supposed to have passed through many adventures, including a Fleet wedding and an elopement with the son of Lady Mary Wortley Montagu. She eventually married a Captain Falconer, an officer in the Royal Navy. She was said to have been of high parentage.

[4] He married the bigamist, Elizabeth Chudleigh, Countess of Bristol.

[5] Afterwards Duke of Queensbury—better known as " Old Q.". He lived till 1810, and was buried under the Communion Table of St. James's, Piccadilly.

[6] A friend of Horace Walpole. His real name was Francis Thistlethwaite, but he took the name of Whitehed or Whithed for a Hampshire property. He was M.P. for Southampton and a great patron of literature and art.

the river and at last debarked at Vauxhall : there, if we had so pleased, we might have had the vivacity of our party increased by a quarrel, for a Mrs. Lloyd, who is supposed to be married to Lord Haddington, seeing the two girls following Lady Petersham and Miss Ashe, said aloud, " Poor girls, I am sorry to see them in such company ". . . . At last, we assembled in our booth, Lady Caroline in the front, with the vizor of her hat erect and looming gloriously jolly and handsome. She had fetched my brother Orford from the next box, where he was enjoying himself with his *petite partie*, to help us mince chickens. We minced seven chickens into a china dish, which Lady Caroline stewed over a lamp with three pats of butter, stirring and rattling and laughing and we every minute expecting to have the dish fly about our ears. She had brought Betty the fruit girl with hampers of strawberrys and cherries from Roger's, and made her wait upon us and then made her sup by us at a little table. The conversation was no less lively than the whole transaction. . . . In short, the whole air of our party was sufficient, as you will easily imagine, to take up the whole attention of the garden : so much so that from eleven o'clock until half an hour after one we had the whole concourse round our booth : at last they came into the little gardens of each booth on the sides of ours till Sir Harry Vane took up a bumper and drank their healths, and was proceeding to treat them with still greater freedom. It was three o'clock before we got home. . . .

The Betty alluded to in the above lively account of Lady Caroline's party was Mistress Elizabeth Neale, who for many years kept a fruit shop in St. James's Street, not far from Park Place. She had the first prominence in her profession, and might justly be called the " Queen of Apple-Women ". She appears to have been a woman of pleasing manners and conversation and abounding in anecdote, for she knew everything that was passing in the world of fashion and politics, and was well versed in the family histories of all her patrons. Her company was much sought for by men of the highest rank and fortune, and Christopher Anstey in one of his satirical poems makes a fashionable gentleman say—

F

My Lord Whistlejacket so deep in my debt is,
And Jemmy Blackangle so apt to forget is,
I must seek them at Almack's, at Arthur's or Betty's.

She was at a Pantheon masquerade as Pomona, the goddess of fruit. One of her delights was to attend the House of Commons and listen to the debates, and it was said she was so devoted to London that only twice in her life had she slept out of St. James's Street. When she retired, she lived in a house in Park Place, not far from the jeweller's shop in St. James's Street where Dr. Johnson bought his shoe-buckles. She died in 1767, aged sixty-seven, having lived fourteen years after her retirement, and was honoured with an obituary notice in the *Gentleman's Magazine*, from which some of the above particulars are taken.

Vauxhall Gardens were first opened to the public in 1661, almost directly after the Restoration, and for at least twenty years were known as the " New Spring Gardens at Vauxhall ", there being also an older place of the same name, as appears from an entry in Pepys' *Diary*, dated May 29, 1662, when he records a visit by boat " with my wife and the two maids and the boy " to the old Spring Gardens, and " thence to the new one where I never was before, which much exceeds the other ".

The old Spring Gardens alluded to by Pepys was on the Middlesex side, on the site of the modern Admiralty, the tradition being still preserved in the name of the short turning leading from Cockspur Street into St. James's Park, so long the headquarters of the County Council. This had been formed as a pleasaunce for the use of the inhabitants of the Palace of Whitehall, and took its name from the " trick fountains " which were arranged to splash the unwary visitor who might

VIEW OF VAUXHALL GARDENS

From an old print

tread on a hidden spring. It had a bowling-green and shooting-butts, and places where visitors could drink wine and otherwise refresh themselves. After it had become the resort of " divers ladies ", it was shut up, but the name was preserved for a time in the place at Lambeth, afterwards Vauxhall. It seems " Spring Gardens " was a very common name for a place of this kind. Not far from Jenny Whim's at Ebury Bridge in Pimlico there was another Spring Gardens which had a certain vogue in its day, perhaps for good cooking, for here Lady Harrington once met George Selwyn and other persons of quality " to eat a turtle ". There had been a former Spring Gardens in 1635 in the field at the north-east end of the Haymarket, which was sometimes called " Shavers Hall " from having been built (as a gaming-house) by the barber of the Earl of Pembroke. In the old comedy, *Love for Love*, there is a scene between Mrs. Frail and Mrs. Foresight, in which the former says—

I don't doubt but that you have thought yourself happy in a hackney coach before now. If I had gone to Knightsbridge, or Chelsea, or Spring Garden, or Barn Elms with a man alone, something might have been said.

Knightsbridge Grove mentioned by the frail one was a well-known place for assignations, sometimes also called the " World's End ", near the site of the present Lowndes Square. It was a house with a long avenue of trees, and was much frequented by the ubiquitous Pepys and other gay people. There was another Spring Gardens between Ebury Street and Belgrave Terrace, formerly known as the Dwarf Tavern and Gardens. The one at Knightsbridge Grove was where the Cornelys tried to make money by selling asses' milk in her old age.

There was yet another Spring Gardens where now is the " World's End " public-house in the King's Road, Chelsea ; but this latter was the haunt of the lowest kind of " gay lady ".

Turtles, by the way, were much sought after as a great delicacy in the eighteenth century, and no supper *à la mode* was complete without one. Then, as now, they came chiefly from Ascension Island. In the *Gentleman's Magazine* for October 1753 we learn that the "*Turtler*, Captain Crayton, lately arrived from the Island of Ascension, has brought in several turtles of above three hundred pounds in weight which have been sold at a very high price "; and in a later number it is announced that one weighing 350 lb. " was eat at the ' King's Arms ' Tavern, Pall Mall "—a famous place for suppers—and that this turtle was so large that it was necessary to pull down the front of the oven to admit of its being baked : a sidelight on the method of cooking the beast. Turtles were also sent as presents. One Thomas Bradsley writes to George Selwyn as follows :

I have just heard by accident that you want a turtle for a respectable alderman of Gloucester, and I am happy that it is in my power to send you one in perfect health, and which I am assured by a very able turtle eater appears to be full of eggs.

A French traveller (Moncouys) describes what he calls " Les Jardins du Printemps " at Lambeth in 1663. Evelyn two years earlier spoke in his *Diary* of going to see "the new Spring Garden at Lambeth, a pretty contrived plantation "; and these, with the allusion in Pepys quoted above, are perhaps the earliest references to Vauxhall.

An old pamphlet called *A Sketch of the Spring Gardens, Vauxhall*, sets down the area at about twenty acres and a half, forming " part of a manor belonging to His Royal Highness the Prince of Wales, as Earl of Kennington, the Black Prince having anciently had a Palace there ". The name itself, however, must have had a different origin, and has given rise to much dispute among persons interested in derivations. The celebrated Guy Faux, of Gunpowder Plot fame, certainly lived in a large house in Lambeth called " Faux Hall ", and some genealogists state that he had a manor in those parts and was a descendant of one Fulke, to whom part of the ground had been granted in the reign of King John.

Such a derivation probably involves what Baring-Gould would have called a " curious myth ", and the name is more likely to have been derived from one Jane Vaux, who had a copyhold tenement of Vauxhall in 1615. She was a woman of some pretension to family, and her daughter was married to Barlow, the notorious Bishop of Lincoln, one of the heroes of the story of the " Nag's Head " consecrations. At the death of Jane Vaux the estates were divided between the Bishop's lady and her sister, and eventually Jonathan Tyars, who was to make the gardens so popular, purchased one half of it outright in 1752 from Mistress Elizabeth Masters. At that time it was already a place of amusement for the public. There was a " Ham Room " and a " Milk House " and alcoves to eat in. Tyars added music—that is, an orchestra and an organ—and endeavoured to encourage art by placing statues about the grounds and paintings in the covered parts. Hogarth had pictures here, and Roubillac, who worked in lead as well as marble, made several figures for the gardens.

About the middle of the century Tyars acquired

the whole of the estate, and when he died it was carried on by his son, Tom Tyars, the biographer and friend of Dr. Johnson and the original of " Tom Restless " in the *Idler*.

The Spring Gardens at Lambeth soon developed into a very popular resort, so popular indeed that the name Vauxhall became synonymous with public gardens or grounds, and was adopted even on the Continent. There was a place at The Hague called Vauxhall, honoured by a visit from the Statholder and his consort, and it was a great success. There were also Vauxhalls in Paris, understood to be places where " fêtes were got up by Messrs. Torre, Ruggieri and Others ". There is a little book in the British Museum, published in Paris in 1769, which refers to these gardens. The title deserves to be given in full :

" Le Waux Hall populaire ou les Fetes de la Guingette. Poème Grivois et Poissardi Lyri-Comique en cinq chants, enrichi de Rondes de Table et vaudeviles nouveaux parodies sur les Ariettes les plus jolies. Dedié à M. de Voltaire." At the foot, it was stated to be published " à la Gaité, chez le Compère La Joie : avec permission des riboteurs."

There was a Spring Gardens at Bath, and in 1748 there was an attempt to make a Vauxhall at Bristol. General Howard wrote to Lord Carlisle that " Charles the French Horn, had undertook a grand design, prepared a garden and laid out a great deal of money on it ". But the people, whether from pious or really interested motives, would have no Vauxhall in their midst, and the night before that fixed for the opening they formed a combination against him and had his house " beset with bailiffs in order to stop the diversions ". There was also a Vauxhall at Birmingham, which Mrs. Delany visited in 1749, and there were doubtless many similar imitations in other parts of the country. ✓

Swift tells Stella in a letter that he had been there to hear the nightingale. Sir Roger de Coverley went there in 1712 and looked upon the place as a sort of Mohammedan Paradise on account of the birds that sang upon the trees, " and the loose tribes of people that walked under the shades ". Sir Roger loved the song of the nightingales, but after a lady mask had tried to get a drink out of him (she only asked for a bottle of mead), his virtuous feelings were aroused, and he called her a " wanton baggage " and bid her go about her business : and on leaving the gardens, said to the good woman at the bar—" that he should be a better customer to her gardens, if there were more nightingales and fewer strumpets ".

The good old knight's remark was justified by the presence in the gardens of most undesirable folk, and there is little doubt that, until the place was taken in hand by Jonathan Tyars in 1728, it continued to bear a bad name. There were many dark walks, where the gallants of the town used to take their " ladies ", and it finally became such a scandal that the authorities refused to continue the licence for the gardens until a sufficient number of lamps were erected. Under Tyars matters improved, and respectable people began to go there with their wives and daughters. It never lacked the patronage of the higher classes of society, but was frequented by all alike, and was not as exclusive as Ranelagh House in its more palmy days.

The newspapers, the drama and the novels of the time are full of allusions to Vauxhall. You went there by water for many years, boats being always to be found at the Whitehall or Westminster Stairs. About

1750 it became possible to go by coach, and there was an entrance near the corner of Kennington Lane. The amusements of the place varied, but on the whole were much the same as at other similar resorts. Music, especially ballads of a most sentimental description, occasional masquerades or ridottos,[7] and, above all, private supper-parties, were the chief attractions of the gardens.

There was a monster moving picture, a sort of panorama, similar to that which Pinchbeck and Fawkes were in the habit of exhibiting at Bartholomew Fair, and in one part of the grounds there was an extraordinary representation of a waterfall without a drop of water! Moritz, the German minister, says :

> In a particular part of the garden, a curtain was drawn up and by means of some mechanism of extraordinary ingenuity, the eye and the ear are so completely deceived that it is not easy to persuade oneself that one does not actually see and hear a natural cascade from a high rock.

In the Rotunda were pictures by Hogarth representing Henry VIII. and Anne Boleyn, believed to be really portraits of Frederic Prince of Wales and his mistress, Anne Vane (not the Lady Vane depicted as the " Lady of Quality " in Smollett's *Peregrine Pickle*).

And what could one have for supper? Ham so thin that you could read a newspaper through the slices! It was currently reported that the expert carver at

[7] " They go to the Ridotto : 'tis a hall
    Where people dance and sup, and dance again :
    Its proper name perhaps were a masqued ball,
    But that's of no importance to my strain :
    'Tis (on a smaller scale) like our Vauxhall,
    Excepting that it can't be spoiled by rain.
    The company is ' mixed '—(the phrase I quote is
    As much as saying they're below your notice)."

(*Beppo*, LORD BYRON.)

Vauxhall could cover the entire eleven acres with slices from one ham, and old frequenters declared that they remembered how the waiters had to carry the plates of ham in a certain position to prevent the wind from blowing away the wafer-like slices. Chickens so small that they are described as being no bigger than sparrows (no wonder that Lady Caroline minced up seven for her supper-party), and hung beef such as Sir Roger supped off when he visited the gardens, were the chief items of the Vauxhall menu. The drinks consisted of burgundy, champagne, claret, red port (at 2s. a bottle !), table beer at 4d. for a quart mug, Burton ale (preferred by Sir Roger) and a speciality in the form of arrack (or 'rack) punch, the same kind no doubt of which Mr. Joseph Sedley drank so freely one festal night that green-eyed Rebecca would remember only too well.

Towards the end of the eighteenth century Vauxhall again became a somewhat rowdy place. The last night of the season (as was afterwards the case with Cremorne) was always considered the best night by the young bloods. In *Evelina* we read how young Broughton declared that on the last night " there's always a riot, and there the folks run about, and then there is such a squealing and squalling ! and there all the lamps are broke and the women run skimper scamper ". Henrietta, Lady Luxborough,[8] in a description of an evening at Vauxhall, throws a still more curious light on the rowdy manners of the better classes in her day. In a letter to the poet Shenstone in 1748 she says :

[8] Henrietta St. John, half-sister to the celebrated Lord Bolingbroke. She married Robert Knight (of Barrels), afterwards created Lord Luxborough. Her intimate friendship with the poet Shenstone is a curious episode in the social annals of the time.

There is a party of gentlemen and ladies of Fashion who entertain the company at Vauxhall with the most charming harmony : the ladies crow like cocks, and if any gentleman of the party are within hearing, they answer them by braying like an ass : one Mrs. Woolaston has arrived to the greatest perfection and has the honour of being called the head of the party for her excellence in this art.

" Affrays " were common enough at Vauxhall and always fully reported in the journals of the day. The most celebrated of all Vauxhall " affrays " was that between the Rev. Henry Bate [9] and a Mr. Fitzgerald in July 1773.

The Marybone (or Marylebone) Gardens were perhaps a step lower in the social scale than Vauxhall, or maybe what little vogue they ever had among modish folk lasted a much shorter time. They extended over part of the ground now covered by Beaumont Street, Devonshire Street and Devonshire Place, and originally formed a portion of the grounds of the old Manor House of Marylebone.

In the neighbourhood were several bowling-greens, the best known of which was one attached to the

[9] Afterwards Sir Henry Bate Dudley, Bart., generally known as " The Fighting Parson ". His was a typical personality in that curious age. Born in 1745, son of the vicar of North Farnbridge in Essex, he followed the calling of a journalist, but on the death of his father, took orders and succeeded him in the Essex living. He was best known as a typical " man about town " and as the editor of the scurrilous *Morning Post*, which was founded in 1772. He added the name of Dudley to that of Bate by the will of a relation in 1781, was actually created a Baronet in 1813 and promoted to a prebendal stall in Ely Cathedral in 1817. He died in 1824, aged seventy-nine. Although a magistrate for seven counties in England and four in Ireland, he was essentially an idle man about town, a friend of Garrick and all the wits, altogether a most un-parson like parson ! He married the sister of Mrs. Hartley the celebrated actress. Dr. Johnson would have none of him : as he said to Boswell, " Sir, I will not allow this man to have merit : what he has is rather the contrary ". Without any doubt, he was a most disreputable minister of a decadent Church. A painting of him and his wife by Gainsborough is at Chesterfield House.

" Rose " or " Rose of Normandy ", a tavern in High
Street, Marylebone, on the exact spot where, two
hundred years later, the Marylebone Music Hall stood.
From this green the Marylebone Gardens was
developed. Pepys, with a keen scent for pleasaunces
of all kinds, was there in May 1663 :

> Then we abroad to Marrowbone, and there walked in the
> garden : the first time I ever was there, and a pretty place it is.

At the beginning of the eighteenth century the " Rose "
had acquired a name as a gaming-house, and high play
went on every night. It soon was better known as
" Marybone ", and in those early days may have been
the resort of a certain number of fashionable persons,
for numerous allusions to it are found in contemporary
newspapers and broadsides, showing it to have been
a place frequented by people of wealth, if not of
fashion. In the *Beggars' Opera* Peachum says, apropos
of Macheath :

> The Captain keeps too good company ever to grow rich.
> Marybone and the Chocolate Houses are his undoing. The
> man that proposes to get money by play should have the
> education of a gentleman, and be trained up to it from his youth.

And Macheath himself tells his confederates :

> There will be deep play at Marybone to-night, and con-
> sequently money may be picked up on the road. Meet me there
> and I will give you the hint who is worth setting.

In 1738 Marybone Gardens were opened as a
regular place of entertainment after the manner of
Vauxhall, a charge for admission being made, and the
usual attractions being provided in the form of music
and fireworks, with occasional balls and masquerades.
In 1753 the gardens were enlarged to about eight
acres and opened in the morning for " public break-

fasting " in the great room, with a concert for which the charge was two shillings. Mr. Wroth says that at that period families of good position had country houses near the High Street of Marybone,[10] and probably availed themselves of subscription tickets for the gardens. The same writer tells a good story of Handel, apropos of this place.

Old Dr. John Fountayne, for instance, would stroll in from the Manor House School with his friend Mr. Handel. On one occasion, the great composer begged for Fountayne's opinion on a new composition that the band was performing. They sat down together and after a time the clergyman proposed they should move—" It's not worth listening to : it's very poor stuff ". " You are right, Mr. Fountayne ", said Handel—" it is very poor stuff : I thought so myself when I finished it ".

There is a tradition that Dick Turpin once publicly kissed in the gardens a beauty of the day, who was related to the same Dr. Fountayne. The lady expostulated, but Turpin said, " Be not alarmed, Madam, you can now boast that you have been kissed by Dick Turpin. Good morning."

But the fame of the gardens did not last much more than twenty years. In 1773 they were open for three nights a week only, although the musical attractions were of the same high standard. Handel's " Acis and Galatea ", *inter alia*, was produced here for the first time. But a couple of years later they are spoken of with contempt. It was said that nobody went there, that the tablecloths and other appointments were dirty, and that the gardens themselves had been reduced to two or three grand roads and a few shapeless trees. Twenty years later, in 1793, an effort was made to

[10] " And people of rank, to correct their tone,
  Went out of Town to Marybone."
                    (*The Ballad of Beau Brocade*.)

restore the popularity of the place. A mineral spring was discovered, and the manager boldly advertised " The Marybone Spa " ! but nothing could save them. They were finally closed in 1796, and two years later the site was let for building. As in the case of Ranelagh, some of the old trees still survive, but they are identified with difficulty, and the Music Hall built on the site of the old " Rose of Normandy " is, alas, no more.

Elizabeth Robinson, afterwards Mrs. Elizabeth Montagu, the bluestocking, tells us she breakfasted at Marylebone Gardens at ten in the morning, gave a sitting afterwards to Quirke for her portrait, and spent the evening at Vauxhall. This visit of hers and that of Dr. Johnson, which we know occurred about 1772, besides the performances of Handel's oratorios, dispels the idea that Marylebone was solely the resort of middle-class folk ; but it is certain they never had the mode of Ranelagh nor were as popular as Vauxhall. The entertainments were probably far too prosy and dull—too cheap, as one might say—for the gallants and fine ladies of the town, and if Lady Townshend and Lady Caroline went once or twice, their visits were of the nature of a frolic, and they soon would return to more congenial resorts. I have found no mention of Marylebone Gardens in the letters of Walpole, and that of itself tells a tale.

Probably the only surviving remnant of the eighteenth-century gardens is to be found at Hampstead in the " Spaniards " Tavern. This should be properly spelt " Spaniard's ", for it meant the house kept by an old Spaniard who settled in London somewhere about the end of the seventeenth century. He was celebrated for a " garlic gravy " to be eaten with chops and steaks, and the secret of which was for a long time

with him alone. People would come from far to taste
the Spaniard's sauce. The recipe is still extant. The
inn and gardens, as seen in a little engraving by Chat-
elaine about 1745, were arranged in the Dutch fashion
introduced by William III.; but only the old house
now remains.

# CHAPTER IV

## DIVERSIONS OF PERSONS OF QUALITY IN LONDON
## INDOORS

Court and subscription masquerades : Heidegger, the Master of
the Revels : Elizabeth Chudleigh, the aristocratic go-between :
the great Teresa Cornelys—early life and arrival in England :
organisation of the masquerades and entertainments at Carlisle
House : the clever methods of advertising the new place : the
ball for the Prince of Brunswick : the ball of the Tuesday
Night's Club : " Running Footmen " : funeral elegy at Carlisle
House : funeral customs of the day : decline and downfall of
Carlisle House : " asses' milk at Knightsbridge " : sad death
of the Cornelys : opening of the Pantheon : Sedan-chairs : the
Pantheon masquerades : ball of the Savoir-Vivre Club : Boodle's :
Goosetree's, late Almack's : Almack's Assembly Rooms : the
first " Cock and Hen " Club : the rage for gambling : the
" Redoubt " : other concert halls and entertainments.

A CONTINUAL ROUND of drums, routs and rackets,
or of interminable parties for ombre and quadrille,
must have often proved monotonous to the gay person
of quality, even the most inveterate card-player. Ladies
of fashion, therefore, on the lookout for amusement,
when the season or weather was not propitious for
Ranelagh or Vauxhall, would turn their attention to
the public assemblies and indoor masquerades of the
town.

The Court masquerades were, of course, the most
modish of all. Every one had not the *entrée* to Court,
or the privilege of receiving an invitation for entertainments that Royalty might provide. A very sensitive

lady of the inner Court circle would, therefore, not have to rub shoulders with a number of persons of doubtful standing and morality, who could only attend a public assembly and had not even a good enough position to obtain a voucher for one of the more exclusive entertainments—the Toms, Dicks and Harrys, in short, of the day, with their female companions.

It is true that at Court they were compelled to rub shoulders with many much more doubtful persons than those who had not the *entrée* : for the Court circle of that day was a very large net, sweeping into its meshes a good deal of rubbish. Still, with whatever rubbish there might be, there they were among the *élite*, and that doubtless compensated somewhat for having to meet notorious evil-livers, royal mistresses, or any curious personality that might be basking in the sunshine of the favour of those august dames— the Duchess of Kendal, the Countess of Darlington and the Countess of Yarmouth. It is to be feared that no lady of fashion would have dared to be so straight-laced as to refuse to receive or call upon any friend of a member of the Royal harem. Perhaps in this third decade of the twentieth century we live in an age more openly censorious, more publicly severe on the frailties of human nature than was the case two hundred years ago : but the visiting list of the fashionable world, the real *haut ton*, is still based on the visiting list of the Palace.

Court masquerades in the reign of George II. were very splendid affairs. There was a regular Master of Revels to the King, one Heidegger, a Swiss, said to be the ugliest man of his day. His career had been a remarkable one. He came to London early in the eighteenth century, and at once became the fashion, a position attained, perhaps, by his cleverness, his wit, and his perfect manners. Son of a clergyman at Zurich, he left his native country in consequence of some amour, became confidential servant to a gentleman of good position, and in that capacity visited the chief capitals of Europe, acquiring a taste for refinement and a knowledge of good living. He soon got himself received by persons of fashion in London, and rose to be manager of the King's Theatre in the Haymarket, which stood on the site of the later Opera House and on the spot now filled by His Majesty's Theatre and the Carlton Hotel.

He was generally spoken of as " The Swiss Count ", and in consequence of his extreme ugliness was a constant butt for the wits of the day, but his good-nature triumphed over the sarcasms, and his generosity appears to have so endeared him to every one that no ball or assembly was considered complete without him.

It was asserted that he made a very large income, a good proportion of which went in eating and drinking, but he was of a most charitable nature, and after a successful masquerade was known to give away hundreds of pounds in charity. He must always have been very much before the public, for he has been immortalised by Pope in the *Dunciad*, censured by Fielding in a poem called " The Masquerade ", and caricatured by Hogarth in one of his famous prints. He was probably responsible for establishing the opera in public favour in London, and even wrote an opera himself called *Tomyris*. He lived to be ninety years of age, died in Richmond in a house in Maids of Honour Row, and was buried in the parish church of that little town in 1749.

It was Heidegger who first organised those masquerades to which one was only admitted by a ticket obtained through a voucher from some person of recognised position in society. These tickets were generally procurable, in exchange for the voucher, at White's Chocolate House in St. James's Street. The greatest efforts were always made to keep the company very select, and persons of quality, who were subscribers and had vouchers for distribution, were requested not to lend their names to obtain tickets indiscriminately for others, and if they had any spare ones to send them back, when their cost would be returned.

Heidegger advertised that a sufficient guard was appointed within and without the house to prevent all disorder and indecencies, and strict orders were given not to deliver any bottles and glasses from the sideboards, and to shut them up early. Notwithstanding these precautions the utmost licence and disorder often prevailed among the company. Quarrels and duels were frequent. Bishops preached sermons warning their congregations against them. Poets satirised their follies and vices. But for all this Heidegger and his masquerades, as well as the more public imitations of them, continued to flourish for many a year.

Next in importance to these semi-official masquerades were those organised by persons of quality and known as " Subscription Masquerades ". One such is described by Walpole as follows:

On Monday there was a subscription masquerade, much fuller than that of last year, but not so agreeable or so various in dresses. The King was well disguised in an old-fashioned English habit, and much pleased with somebody who desired him to hold their cup as they were drinking tea. The Duke had a dress of the same kind, but so immensely corpulent that he looked like Cacofogo the drunken captain in *Rule a Wife and*

*Have a Wife*.[1] The Duchess of Richmond was a Lady Mayoress in the time of James I., and Lord Delawarr Queen Elizabeth's porter from a picture in the guard-room at Kensington [2]: they were admirable masks. Lady Rochford, Miss Evelyn, Miss Bishop, Lady Stafford, and Mrs. Pitt [3] were in great beauty, particularly the last, who had a red vail which made her look gloriously handsome. I forgot Lady Kildare. Mr. Conway was the Duke in Don Quixote and the finest figure I ever saw. Miss Chudleigh was Iphigenia but so naked that you would have taken her for Andromeda : and Lady Betty Smithson had such a pyramid of baubles upon her head that she was exactly like the Princess of Babylon in Grammont.

The appearance of the beautiful Elizabeth Chudleigh at the masquerade referred to must have been fairly scandalous, even for that easy-going age, for it seems she was attired in a close-fitting costume of flesh-coloured silk. The Princess of Wales flung her own shawl over her scantily clad maid of honour, and Mrs. Elizabeth Montagu, writing to her sister, describes her appearance in the usual coarsely expressed language of the day :

Miss Chudleigh's dress, or rather undress, was remarkable. She was Iphigenia ready for the sacrifice, but so naked the high priest might easily inspect the entrails of his victim. The maids of honour (not of maids the strictest) were so offended that they would not speak to her.[4]

Bluestocking though she was, Mistress Montagu writes, it will be seen, in the free and open manner of

[1] *Rule a Wife and Have a Wife*, comedy by Beaumont and Fletcher. Cacofogo was the rich usurer of the play, not a captain. But Walpole was no stickler for accuracy in his letters so long as he could round off his periods neatly and effectively.

[2] Afterwards removed to the galleries at Hampton Court.

[3] A celebrated beauty, *née* Miss Penelope Atkins, daughter of Sir Henry Atkins, of Clapham. She married George Pitt, Esq., of Strathfieldsaye, afterwards created Baron Rivers. See also Chapter III., Note 6.

[4] " Summer, in light transparent gauze arrayed
Like maids of honour at a masquerade."
(*Gotham*, a satire by CHARLES CHURCHILL.)

the period. She concludes the same letter by informing her sister that she stayed till five o'clock in the
morning, and was not in the least tired, and had, moreover, better luck than Jenny Conway, who was killed
by a draught of lemonade she drank at the same ball.

This Jenny Conway was the sister of the Lord
Conway who married for third wife Charlotte Shorter,
Horace Walpole's aunt. She was therefore also the
aunt of Harry Conway. In spite of being so closely
connected by marriage, Horace did not fail to seize the
opportunity for a note of scandal, and he says:

Her death was not quite unlucky for her, for she had outlived
the Prince's love and her own face: and nothing remained but
her love and her person which was exceedingly bad.

Her death was commemorated in the doggerel—

Poor Jenny Conway.
She drank lemonade,
At a masquerade,
So now she's dead and gone away.

These subscription masquerades, as well as the more
public ones where any one could go by payment
without vouchers, gradually became, not only the
occasions for all kinds of illicit intrigues, but also
places where high play went on all night, and consequently the resort of sharpers of all sorts.

Sir John Fielding, the celebrated Bow Street magistrate, received information one day in the spring of
1753 that certain well-known highwaymen were to
be at the public masquerade. His officers suddenly
appeared in the gaming saloons at two in the morning,
obliging all the company to unmask and give an
account of themselves. The *Gentleman's Magazine*, in
which the story is told, adds: " It is supposed those
fellows had notice of his coming, before he could get

upstairs, and so made off in the crowd, for none of them were taken. There had been deep gaming that night, and a plentiful supply of bad guineas ".

Contemporary literature, especially the newspapers and those little satirical broadsheets so much in vogue, are full of allusions to the unbounded popularity of these masquerades. Excitement always rose to fever heat when one was announced. In 1763, when an elaborate entertainment of the sort was organised on the occasion of the visit of the King of Denmark, a little jingle appeared :

> A Masque was in return decreed and Ball
> In England seldom seen, but sweet to all.
> "A Masque, a Masque "—ran eager through the streets,
> And every lady tells the friend she meets,
> " Oh, what a charming scene, 'twill be so grand,
> Do step with me, I'm going to the Strand,
> To look at buckles and to buy some hair,
> Jeffrey's, no farther, but shall you be there ? " [5]
> " I fear no, but if possible I can,
> 'Tis so genteel, I love the little man ! "

But Mistress Teresa Cornelys undoubtedly stands out most prominent among those who, in the eighteenth century, arranged diversions for the public in the form of balls and masquerades, which were given in what had been the town mansion of the Earls of Carlisle in Soho Square.

Over a hundred years later, when workmen were digging the foundations for St. Patrick's Catholic chapel in Soho Square, they came upon a small copper tablet commemorating the gratitude of Teresa Cornelys to Elizabeth Chudleigh, the notorious Duchess of Kingston, who was her first patroness in London. Around these two women, the one who " ran the

[5] Jeffrey's, a fashionable jeweller of the day, in Cockspur Street.

show " and the other who gave her patronage to it, circulated some of the most scandalous tales of the eighteenth century. Of Elizabeth Chudleigh many accounts have appeared, but of the life of Teresa Cornelys it has always been supposed that little or nothing is known for certain, though she was the centre of society intrigue and directress of pleasure (lawful and unlawful) for the fashionable world of London for at least fifteen years.

There is, however, no mystery about her at all. Moreover, the celebrated Jacques Casanova in his *Memoirs* gives her away as remorselessly as he gives away so many others.

In such a world of loose morals and debauchery as the London society was for so many years at this time, a mistress of intrigue was an absolute necessity, and Teresa Cornelys appeared in the nick of time to fill the rôle. Her experience of the continent of Europe from her earliest days well qualified her for the work. She had lived in the midst of it all her life, but it was only at Carlisle House, and after reaching middle age, that the seal was set on her fame as a *grande intrigante*, or, in plain English, a great go-between ! She amassed a large fortune in various ways, legitimate and illegitimate, and Casanova says that at one time of her career she had three secretaries, a female confidante, a dumb attendant and thirty-two ordinary servants, a country house at Hammersmith, and six horses. Yet she died in the greatest poverty in the debtors' prison of the King's Bench.

Her maiden name was Imer, and she was born at Venice in 1724. Her father was Giuseppe Imer, a Genoese director of the Teatro San Samuele, a man to whom Goldoni is said to have owed not a little of his earlier success. Her mother was an ex-actress, a curious compound of religious fervour and worldly vice, not uncommon in those times. She insisted on her pretty little fair-haired daughter going to mass with her daily and to confession once a week, and took her regularly every evening to visit the old Senator Malpiero who had fallen very much in love.

This old man of seventy years of age had given up affairs of State for affairs of pleasure, holding every night a reception of charming Venetian ladies. His palace adjoined the building in which the Imers lived, and he was accustomed to amuse himself by gazing into the young Teresa's bedroom while she was at her toilette. He thus became much enamoured, and when she was seventeen years of age made her his mistress. A short time afterwards he found her in a doubtful situation with the celebrated Casanova, then a boy of sixteen. He had young Jacques flogged, and turned Teresa out of the house. This was in 1741, and soon afterwards we hear of her travelling in Germany and settling in Bayreuth, where she first married Pompeati, a dancer at the Court of the Margrave, and then installed herself as the mistress of the Margrave himself—the brother-in-law of Frederick the Great. He was not long, however, in convicting her of infidelity, as she could never remain constant to one man for any length of time. Her next move was to Vienna, where her husband committed suicide by cutting his throat with a razor, not on account of her various amours, for he was a typical *mari complaisant* of the day, but because he was suffering from some very painful disease.

In Vienna she came across Casanova again, who, about this time, acknowledged both her children as his. This may have been about 1753. Then, in trouble with her creditors, she had to sell her jewels and leave the country. About 1758 she was in Amsterdam, and followed her usual custom of becoming the mistress of some one attached to the Court. In this case the happy man was Prince Charles of Lorraine, Austrian Governor of the Netherlands; but though he loaded her with benefits, she got into financial trouble again and fled, having meanwhile married a Dutchman called Cornelis de Rigabos, whose first name she kept for herself during the remainder of her life.

It is quite impossible to guess what was the attraction this woman had for so many different classes of men; but she is said to have had lovers in every town and to have been unfaithful to them all!

London was destined to be the scene of her greatest triumphs, and here she began by aspiring to the rank of singer at the Opera, being engaged to sing at the King's Theatre in the Haymarket in Gluck's *Caduta de' Giganti*. In 1761 she was singing at a concert in Dean Street, Soho, and in 1764 in Dr. Arne's *Judith* at the chapel of the Lock Hospital.

It was about this time that a brilliant scheme took shape in the brain of this arch-intriguer. She conceived the idea of starting an assembly where masquerades could be held rivalling those of the Court, and for all who chose to pay, especially those who were not received at Court. In connection with this she proposed to establish a sort of agency of the confidential kind through which every sort of assignation could be made and every sort of pleasure arranged for those who could, and would, pay enough—from the highest in the land to the rich city madam.

It should be borne in mind that in such affairs a certain amount of veneer of good behaviour had to be arranged, for at any moment some husband might consider that his honour had been outraged a little *too* openly and challenge his wife's *cicisbeo* to a duel. What was therefore needed was a clever, business-like woman with no scruples, with a vast experience of intrigue and a really great talent for organisation, who would take all trouble out of the hands of the ladies and their lovers, and arrange for the safe meeting and parting of those who could not come together in any other way. Women of the highest rank : Elizabeth Chudleigh, Duchess of Kingston ; the jolly Caroline Petersham, afterwards Countess of Harrington ; the Duchess of Ancaster, who loved to dress like a man ; and little Miss Ashe whom Walpole called " the Pollard Ashe ", were one and all often in want of a friendly shelter under cover of which they could carry on their intrigues with such assistance as only a woman can give. The Duchess of Kingston, indeed, was not content with her own escapades, but acted as a sort of aristocratic agent for Royal Personages, and especially needed the help of a Teresa Cornelys. She seems to have been grateful and to have befriended the old Venetian to the end.

Carlisle House, where La Cornelys settled herself, was very suitable for her purpose. It was not very far from Leicester House and other centres of fashionable life and yet sufficiently removed from the busier quarters of the city to serve her ends, and so she spun her multifarious webs on the spot which was in later years to be covered by St. Patrick's Chapel and the warehouses of Crosse & Blackwell.

Teresa started by spending money lavishly on the fitting up and decoration of the place, money which it may be presumed was subscribed by her lady patronesses and those who intended to profit in different ways by the venture, for she never had any money of her own.

She was, moreover, resolved that such persons of quality should come in sufficient numbers to make it profitable for herself from a pecuniary point of view. With this end to be attained, the clever woman in the early days of her venture gave a ball to the upper servants of people of fashion, and entertained them right royally, knowing to what a large extent the success of her assemblies would depend upon their good-will. This particular entertainment is described in the newspapers of the day:

> On Saturday last, Mrs. Cornelys gave a ball at Carlisle House to the upper servants of persons of Fashion, as a token of the sense she has of her obligations to the nobility and gentry for their generous subscription to her Assembly. The company consisted of 220 persons who made up fourscore couples in country dances: and as scarce any one was ill on that occasion, the rest sat down to cards.

Among her lady patronesses, my Lady Harrington, once the gay and naughty Caroline Petersham, was perhaps the chief. When Casanova visited England about 1763 he brought a letter of introduction to my Lady Harrington, and the very first thing she did was to sell him a ticket for a ball at Carlisle House. "Tenez", dit-elle, "il y a encore Jeudi prochain une réunion de la noblesse à Soho Square. Voici un billet d'entrée: bal et souper c'est la bagatelle de deux guinées." He adds, "Je lui remis la somme, et elle écrivit sur le papier—'Payé: Harrington'".

Mrs. Cornelys was an adept at advertisement. Day after day there appeared cunningly expressed paragraphs in the papers, calling attention to some scheme for the comfort or convenience of her patrons, stating what she intended to do in the near future, or describing what had already taken place in the past. No one was allowed to forget the existence of Carlisle House and Teresa Cornelys. At the outset, she was very particular (or pretended to be) as to the maintenance of a select character for her parties, posing as a she-dragon of virtue, a guardian of the unwary and a guarantee for the timid. Thus, in 1764, subscribers were strictly enjoined to write on the tickets the names of those using them, though this rule fell somewhat into abeyance later on, for the place was once raided by Sir John Fielding, the Bow Street magistrate, in search of highwaymen and other notorious folk. She also drew up carriage regulations for the setting down and taking up of her visitors:

Mrs. Cornelys humbly hopes that the nobility and gentry will be pleased to order that their coachmen and chairmen will prudently bring them to the door, for fear of breaking either coach or chair, as she takes as much care as is in her power to prevent any accident that may happen;

and

Coaches and hackney chairs are to stay at the door in the Square all towards the side of Greek Street, to let the passage be free for the Ladies' chairs to go to the door in Sutton Street, and she hopes that the hackney chairmen will make no disturbance.

The names and positions of these streets have not been altered, and it is quite easy to picture to the mind's eye the arrival and departure of the guests at one of her famous routs, only by replacing Carlisle House on the site of St. Patrick's Church.

She aimed at high game, and as often as not brought down her quarry. Members of the Royal Family were frequently present at her entertainments, though there were a very few prudent or would-be prudent ladies, like Lady Mary Coke, who records in her diary that Lady Hertford had asked her to go to Soho, but she had read the invitation with amazement and begged to be excused.

The King of Denmark and his suite were there on one occasion, and in the following year there was a splendid subscription ball got up for the Hereditary Prince of Brunswick, apparently in compensation for certain slights he was supposed to have received at the hands of the King and Queen. De Saussure, the French traveller, writes of the entertainment for the King of Denmark with great enthusiasm.

All the most beautiful and richest ladies in England were there in fancy dresses of singular taste and magnificence. Several ladies, and among them Lady Spencer, one of our acquaintances, wore more than a hundred thousand pounds sterling worth of diamonds. My wife was dressed as a Spaniard in pink and silver, which suited her admirably, I have never seen her look better : and all the sensible (or frugal) men were only in dominoes.

Walpole says that this ball was a most magnificent affair. One hundred and fifty men subscribed five guineas each and had each three tickets. We are also expressly told that there was no " bad company " and that the Prince stayed till five A.M.

From that evening Carlisle House went on from success to success, and in May 1765 Teresa was already advertising the eleventh meeting of that year. In 1766 she organised concerts under the direction of Messrs. Bach and Abel, and her " Society Nights " were so well attended that it was found necessary to make an additional entrance to the house from Soho Square. In 1769 a new gallery was opened for the dancing of cotillons and allemandes. It was, however, in the years 1770 to 1772 that Mrs. Cornelys attained to the highest pinnacle of success in her extraordinary career. Galas, concerts, masquerades and festivals of all kinds succeeded each other rapidly throughout the season. The most notable of these was, perhaps, that which took place on February 27, 1770.

This was given by the gentlemen of an association known as the " Tuesday Nights' Club ", composed of the young bloods of the day, which, like so many clubs of the time had no *habitat* of its own, but met at the " Star and Garter " Tavern, Pall-Mall (probably on Tuesday nights), and organised magnificent balls and entertainments. They were a hard-drinking, high-living lot, headed by the young Earl of Carlisle, George Selwyn and others. Eventually they became too " hard and high " for Selwyn, for in 1774 he wrote to a friend:

The Tuesday Night Club dines at the corner of Half Moon Street, but I will not venture myself among them. If I fall again this year, it shall not be my own conduct.

Seven years later the club was nearing its end, and Selwyn told a friend that the rump of the Tuesday Night's Club was about to meet at the Duke of Buccleuch's.

On the evening of the great masquerade at Carlisle House, Soho Square and the adjacent streets were thronged, nor would the man in the street be done out of his share in the fun. No coach or chair was permitted to pass unreviewed, the occupants being compelled to let down their windows, while lights were held up to show off their figures to the best advantage.

And the world of fashion was there. The event was minutely described in most of the news-sheets of the day, and the names of some of the people who were present will give a good idea of the success attained by Cornelys in attracting the *beau monde* to her parties.

Lady Waldegrave as Jane Shore, Lady Pembroke, the Duchess of Hamilton, the Duchess of Ancaster (as a man of course), Miss Monkton as a sultana, with thirty thousand pounds' worth of jewels, the Duchess of Bolton as Diana, Lady Augusta Stuart as a vestal, the Countess of Pomfret as a sultana, and many other ladies. Among the gentlemen, Mr. Conway as a Highlander, Captain Watson as Adam (in tight-fitting, flesh-coloured silk and an apron of fig-leaves), the Earl of Carlisle as a running footman, very richly dressed, his cap set with diamonds with the words " Tuesday Night's Club " in front, His Royal Highness the Duke of Gloucester in an old English habit, and Lord Edgcumbe as an old woman, with many others of note.

The whole affair was a very notable example of what that brilliant, careless, extravagant set of the eighteenth century could do when it made up its mind to entertain its friends in style. Mrs. Harris, mother of the first Earl of Malmesbury, a gay old lady who went everywhere if she saw any chance of being amused, wrote to her son, " I got home soon after five, and old as I may be, I never left a public place with more regret ".

I may be perhaps allowed a short digression for a few notes on that now extinct animal, the " running foot-man ". There is no trace of them nowadays, save in the word " footman ", which originally meant a male servant who attended his employers always on foot. The latest equivalent for these obsolete servitors were found in the tall liveried attendant with long staves, who used to stand behind a State carriage in Victorian times and, I believe, still does in the case of the Lord Mayor's equipage. Well do I remember the gorgeous turn-out

MISS CHUDLEIGH
(Afterwards Duchess of Kingston) as Iphigenia
From a print in the British Museum

A RUNNING FOOTMAN
From an old print of the tavern sign in Charles Street, W.

of old Margaret, Duchess of Somerset, in the 'sixties, on which there were no less than three of these ornaments, all powdered and nosegayed, hanging on behind.

We have no exact description of the dress of Lord Carlisle on the occasion of his appearance as a running footman at the ball of the Tuesday Night's Club. It was apparently a favourite dress for a masquerade. Old James Gunning, father of the three beauties, went as one to a great masquerade given by the Duke of Richmond in the Privy Gardens in 1763. The attire of a real one has been variously described. One account says that " they wear fine holland drawers and waist-coats, thread stockings, a blue silk sash fringed with silver, a velvet cap with a great tassel, and carry a porter's staff with a large silver handle ".

According to another authority, they wore no drawers, but only a short silk petticoat, kept in place by a deep, heavy gold fringe. But in the account of the wages paid to the servants of the Duke of Somerset in 1726 (given in the *Gentleman's Magazine*) there is a list of articles considered necessary for the equipment of a running footman—" drawers, stockings, pumps, cap, sash and petticoat breeches "—so that they apparently in that household wore drawers and a petticoat too.

The pole was to serve, *inter alia*, to help the carriage out of mud ruts and across swollen streams, and sur-vived in the useless staves carried by the State footmen of the nineteenth century.

A running footman had, of necessity, to be a very strong active fellow, for he may have had to do on foot as much as forty or fifty miles in one day, and there are records of great journeys accomplished extend-ing to seventy miles in a night, and so forth. Those accompanying the private coaches of their employers were not put to very great exertions for the vehicles of the day could not manage more than five or six miles an hour, so that it was not a great matter for the runners to keep a little distance ahead. Their chief duties included pointing out to the coachman the proper turning to take, and making arrangements for the various halts on the road besides helping with the pole on occasions. As accommodation on the high roads improved, a great part of their duties became negligible, and towards the end of the century they were retained only to give an extra air of importance to those who paid them. They could run seven miles an hour or more, were certainly more for country than town use, and were especially required for the more lonely parts of Scotland and Ireland, where means of intercommunication were difficult and rare.

But they were also employed in town for messages requiring a speedy reply, and were very proud of their superior speed. In the *Evening Post* in December 1735, it is stated that Lady Molesworth's " racing " footman had a race with General Churchill's "from St. James's Street to Edgworth (*sic*) Gate ".

The running footman of the Duke of York (brother of Charles II.) was very celebrated for his fleetness of foot, and used to be backed by his Royal master to run races in Hyde Park. They were probably highly paid, for they were not a long-lived race and often died of consumption. One of the last to keep such a servant was " Old Q.", the Duke of Queensbury, better known in the annals of gallantry as Lord March, who died in 1810; but it is to be feared that the messages on which his runners were despatched (they were always in readiness at his door in Piccadilly) were chiefly concerned with his numerous *affaires du cœur*.

There is a signboard representing a "running foot-man" still to be seen near Berkeley Square, over a public-house much frequented by the men-servants of the neighbourhood. Beneath is written "I am the only Running Footman". It may be a portrait of a cele-brated member of the tribe or relate to the superior speed of the original. In this picture, the "drawers" are represented by tight-fitting knee-breeches tied with bows at the knee, and there is no sign of any kind of petticoat. Male servants coming up to London from the country sometimes telegraph here for accommoda-tion or to communicate with friends: it is usual to write the address in full—"I am the Only Running Footman—London", and it never fails to find. But to return to Teresa Cornelys, whose London career was so mixed up with the doings of the gay set to which my Lady Townshend belonged.

The whole life of this extraordinary woman, as well known in the chief cities of the Continent as she came to be in London, was one long drawn-out intrigue. When she settled in England, her past ex-periences in Venice and Vienna, the two most de-praved cities of Europe, stood her in good stead, and a steady flow of visitors from other countries making the "grand tour", either old acquaintances of her own, or bringing letters of introduction, kept up a constant supply of new clients and new sources of gain for Carlisle House. Every visitor to London turned up sooner or later at the Soho Square meeting-place. Alessandro Verri, whose correspondence was edited by Casabe in 1879, alludes in a letter dated February 2, 1767, to "Il Ballo di Giovedi ad una magnifica sala di una Italiana, la Signora Pompeati" (Thursday's ball in a magnificent hall belonging to an

Italian, Madame Pompeati). His mention of her by her old name shows a previous acquaintance with her at either Bayreuth or Vienna.

The attractions provided were not always of the same exhilarating kind. When the Princess of Wales, mother of George III., died in 1772, Mrs. Harris describes a very odd sort of entertainment (if so it could be called) given at Carlisle House :

Madame Cornelys gave a most odd entertainment, a kind of funeral elegy on the death of the Princess Dowager of Wales. A large kind of frame was made round the glasses, and in various parts of the room, with lamps stuck in it, and black crape strained over the lamps to make the light solemn. At the upper end of the room was a black canopy under which was a white tomb with "Augusta " writ on it ; on one side stood a man, on the other side a woman, who sang forth praises of the Princess. A most ridiculous whim of the woman's—window curtains all black, etc.

Absurd as all this may sound to our modern ears, it was quite in keeping in an age when enormous sums were always spent on the draping of houses and furniture with crape and other panoply of woe, whenever a death occurred in the family.[6]

Thus for many years did the wicked old Venetian exploit for her own advantage the foibles and depravity of the eighteenth century. William Combe, the author

[6] In 1704, for example, at the funeral of Lady Mary Coke (not the lady of that name who was so celebrated for her friendship with Maria Theresa, but the daughter of an Earl of Chesterfield) the undertaker's account included £20 for putting the staircase and hall and two rooms in mourning for six months : £5 for pennons in common silk and 24s. for twelve escutcheons in buckram. How Mr. Mould would have enjoyed estimating for and conducting such a funeral ! By the early years of the nineteenth century people had become more sensible; but even I can remember going to a funeral at which there were two mutes with long staves draped in crape standing at the door, and a voluminous garment like a brigand's cloak, together with a long-sweeping hatband, were served out to each gentleman mourner, but afterwards carefully collected by the undertaker.

INTERIOR OF THE PANTHEON
From an old print

of *Dr. Syntax*, in his satirical poem the " Diabo-Lady ",
brands Mrs. Cornelys and the coterie which met at
Carlisle House as one of the chief sources of vice
among the fashionable set :

> At Court, Cornelys and the Coterie
> Where Vice, more vicious by Effrontery
> Fearless, unblushing, braves the eternal laws
> Of God and Man to aid the Devil's Cause.

But it could not last. Evil times were close upon
her. What Sir Walter Besant once called " the usual
invasion of the ladies who spoil all and ruin all, places
as well as men "—set in at Carlisle House.

She was at first accused in the public press of
keeping a common disorderly house, and permitting
and suffering loose, idle and disorderly persons, men
as well as women, to be and remain the whole night
rioting (" and otherwise misbehaving themselves ").
She was then charged with holding public masquerades
without a licence. It was a little late to bring against
her such an accusation, seeing that she had been holding
these masquerades for years past; but the real cause
of the proceedings may well have been that she had
most imprudently got into collision with the authorities of the Italian Opera House (who held a sort
of Government monopoly under the Hon. George
Hobart) by annexing Guadagni, one of their chief
singers, and opening a rival harmonic meeting in Soho
Square with him for the principal attraction.

Other causes, as we shall see later, combined to
bring about the final downfall of Carlisle House. First,
the Pantheon in Oxford Street, and then Almack's in
King Street, St. James's, started in opposition and
took away the most respectable and most influential
part of her patrons.

Faint-heartedness was never one of her weaknesses, and she struggled on, organising the " Coterie ", an Association of her Lady Patronesses, headed of course by Lady Harrington, now getting old, which met ostensibly for intellectual recreation, but in reality for the carrying on of their own intrigues, and arranging more masked balls, almost as splendid as the old, in competition with her rivals. It was of no avail. In November 1772 her name appeared in the list of bankrupts in the *London Gazette*, and in 1773 she was sold up by auction. The description of a supposititious auction at Carlisle House, published in the *Westminster Magazine* for January 1773, gives some idea of the estimation in which the good Cornelys and her goings on were held by the general public. I have alluded to it at greater length in a chapter on satires and lampoons, but it is too outspoken to be quoted in full.

Somewhat crushed, but not entirely defeated, she is again advertising in 1774 as Directress of Masquerades in the same old place. The funds were probably provided from other sources, for in the May of that year a hotel at Scarborough, " formerly in the possession of Mrs. Cornelys "—is put up for sale, and in the meantime she may have catered for the public in some other way. In 1775 she gives a " Rural Masquerade ", and Carlisle House apparently starts on a new lease of life on the old lines, the sinews of war being without any doubt provided by the notorious ladies who had a personal interest in the continuance of such a resort. In 1777 and 1778 she is still carrying on, though her company has become far less choice, and there are frequent paragraphs in the press about disreputable fracas and low disputes at Carlisle House. In 1779 she again has to disappear for a time, and the place is advertised as being " under new management ". About this time " Schools of Elegance ", a sort of high-class debating society, alternated with masked balls and Sunday evening promenades, and one of the subjects of debate (for ladies only !) was " Is not the hope of reclaiming a libertine a principal cause of conjugal unhappiness ? "

In 1780 or thereabouts William Hickey notes in his *Diary*, there was an Assembly started at Carlisle House by Mrs. Cornelys, known as " The Promenade ", this may have been the same as the Sunday evening promenades referred to above. Hickey says that every one of any consequence attended it, " as did the whole beauty of the metropolis, from the Duchess of Devonshire to the little milliner's apprentice from Cranbourne Alley ". But the character of the visitors to these promenades, whether they were on Sundays only or every day in the week, became very mixed and they ceased rather abruptly. She had had her day, and a very brilliant day it had been at times. The ball given by the Tuesday Night's Club was, for example, one of the most brilliant functions of the whole century ; but some of her later shows had not gone off so well, and there is no doubt but that Carlisle House became in the end a centre of fashionable dissipation and vice. Mrs. Cornelys, a past mistress in the art of illicit arrangements of all kinds, reaped rich rewards for her exertions, either offered by grateful clients or, perhaps, extorted from unwilling victims. But she spent all she made and more, and towards the end of the century had to remain in hiding from her creditors. In 1795 the indomitable old soul reappeared under the name of Smith (a very old woman by that time), and opened an establishment at Knightsbridge House in Porter's

Lane, near the site of the present Wilton Crescent, as a vendor of asses' milk to royal patrons and a provider of public breakfasts. Fashion would, however, no longer follow her lead. Though she managed to find the money to decorate her Knightsbridge House with huge mirrors and other garish effects, and tried to make as brave a show as of old, the gay world found no amusement in breakfasting in public in Porter's Lane, or drinking asses' milk there. Mrs. Cornelys was well over seventy by that time, and the Spirit of Intrigue, so necessary for ventures of this kind, hobbled on ungainly crutches or stayed away altogether. She failed again, and was received into the Debtors' Prison of the Fleet. One of the old intrigante's most intimate friends all her life was a certain Mrs. Betty Sumbel-Wells, *née* Davies, an actress, and in the account of her own life she relates that when Mrs. Cornelys was taken into custody at Knightsbridge House, she hit her breast against the door of the hackney coach and developed a virulent cancer which was the real cause of her death. The women of the ward at the hospital to which she was removed would not allow her to dress it. She got worse and was transferred to the Fleet Prison. Mrs. Wells describes her at this time as " a neat little old woman with hair as white as snow, with a pleasing address and affable manners ". When she realised she was dying, she sent for her actress friend, who found her sitting up in bed, in a sort of delirium, with a large crucifix before her, crying out that the devil was dragging her down. She died in 1790, apparently in the most dreadful agony.

I have, perhaps, lingered too long over the life and death of the famous Cornelys, but she was the chief caterer for the amusement of the fashionable world for many years and could not be dismissed in a few words in any account of the diversions of the quality of her day.

In the latter years of the eighteenth century manners of London society much improved for a time, but an open disregard for the common decencies of life set in again during the worst years of the Regency and the reign of the fourth George. After the accession of Queen Victoria a more sober, if somewhat hypocritical, period supervened ; but in the post-War days of these modern Georgian times, notorious night-clubs have taken the place of the Carlisle House and Redoubt of the eighteenth century, and some future social historian will doubtless search newspaper files and the blatant memoirs of to-day for some account of the weird resorts concentrated within a quarter of a mile of Piccadilly Circus, whose ultimate objects are, though unacknowledged, identical with those of Teresa Cornelys' place.

The first cause of the downfall of Carlisle House was the building of the Pantheon in Oxford Street in 1770. This was originally intended to be a sort of winter Ranelagh, where masquerades and all other kinds of Ranelagh diversion and Ranelagh intrigues could be carried on, whatever the weather might be. It soon superseded Mrs. Cornelys' establishment, which had become a little too loose even for the loose ladies of that very loose age, and it was far more conveniently situated for fashionable folk than either Ranelagh or Vauxhall, for it could be reached comfortably in one's own chair, still the most popular way of going about for persons of quality, and being within the boundaries of the town proper, could be visited without any extra guard against footpads or other ruffians. Sedan-chairs, or " chairs " as they were always called for short, were the private cars and taxis of the eighteenth century. Even the nobility and richer folk who had their own coaches had also their own chairs, or hired public ones when occasion required.

They were introduced into Western Europe some-time in the sixteenth century, but were first brought into England by Sir Sanders Duricombe in 1581, though not in general use here till about fifty years later. Persons of quality always kept at least two—a plain one for general use, and a highly decorated and luxurious one for attending the Court, or great recep-tions, which was accompanied by two, three, or even four running footmen or servitors before and behind.

These chairs were often fitted up in the most gorgeous style, elaborately ornamented with paintings by artists of note, panels of Vernis Martin and the like, and lined throughout with rich silks or satins. Lady Mary Coke says she spent "£32 : 11s. on her new sedan-chair". Some cost much more. The one be-longing to Sarah, Duchess of Marlborough, was once stolen while she was in church, for the sake of its crimson cushions.

Chairs were the usual vehicles for women as long as Bloomsbury and Whitehall were the farthest points to which they had to be carried. Maiden ladies and those not very well off had no mode of conveyance other than the public chairs, and as a general mode of locomotion in London they lasted well into the nineteenth century. Dr. Pusey's mother always went to church in a chair, and they were to be seen for hire in London on a stand in St. James's Street as late as 1830, if not later. They must have lingered much longer in the provinces in places like Bath and Chelten-ham, and were certainly known in Bath in Pickwick's

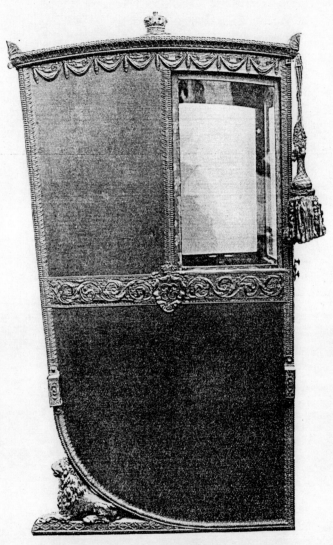

A SEDAN-CHAIR
In the South Kensington Museum
(*By kind permission of the Director*)

day, for is it not recorded that, after a most disastrous rubber of whist, Miss Bolo went home " in a flood of tears and a Sedan Chair ".

The use of the Sedan-chair died hard. Mr. Appleton, in one of his chatty books, says they were to be seen in Peterborough in 1860, and in Exeter in 1870. There appears to have been one for hire in Newcastle in 1885, and in Bury St. Edmunds in 1890. On the Continent they may be possibly found to this day in Genoa and Seville, to mention only two European towns, while in Brazil they are still common, the bearers being stalwart negroes. I have been told there is still a Sedan-chair standing in the hall of No. 6 St. James's Square, the town house of the Earl of Bristol. The comfort, or reverse, of chairs must have depended a good deal on the skill and sobriety of the bearers.

The Pantheon [7] was started on the most lavish scale, for it cost £60,000 to build, a very large sum in those days. Walpole, gossiping to Mann in 1770 in his usual newsy style, writes :

The new winter Ranelagh in the Oxford Road is nearly finished. It amazed me myself. Imagine B . . . . . . (query *Babylon*) in all its glory. The pillars are of an artificial *giallo antico*. The ceilings, even of the passages, are of the most beautiful stucco, in the best taste of grotesque. The ceilings of the ball-rooms and the panels are painted like Raphael's loggias in the Vatican, a dome like the Pantheon glazed.

[7] The Pantheon had its worthless imitators. Just as there had been a host of Vauxhalls springing up all over the place in imitation of the fashionable one at Lambeth, but with no pretension to the same class, so directly the Pantheon in Oxford Road was started, some wag opened a little place in the Spa Fields, Bermondsey, which he called by the same name. In the *Macaroni and Theatrical Magazine* for 1773 there is a notice as follows :

" Pantheons : The Nobility, Oxford Road.
The Mobility, Spa Fields."

I have not come across any particulars of this resort, which must have been of the commonest description, something like its near neighbour, the " Dog and Duck " in Lambeth.

The building, when not being used for an entertainment, could be seen at any time, on payment of five shillings, a charge later reduced to half-a-crown. The attractions were the same as in similar resorts, viz. subscription concerts and masquerades. The former were generally in two parts, one English and the other Italian. In 1783 a Handel Festival was organised, which was a great success and attended by the King and Queen. Promenade concerts were also given in the declining days of the Pantheon, the charge of admission only three shillings, tea and coffee included. It is rather amusing to note that these cheap concerts were kept as " dressy " as possible, gentlemen being requested " not to come in boots ".

But in the heyday of its prosperity, the masquerades were the glory of the Pantheon. The number of tickets sold was always very great, though there was supposed to be a limit. The crush, however, was such that an extra door was opened in Poland Street for ladies only. On no account was money taken at the doors.

Sometimes the masquerades were less brilliant. In April 1773, only three years after the starting of the place, a magazine of the day noted that the masquerade at the Pantheon was as solemn and full as dull as if it had been at the Tabernacle at Tottenham Court. (This was the Meeting-house of Wesley and Whitfield, and its successor still occupies the same site half-way up the Tottenham Court Road on the left.)   The account went on to say that there were many " Jew character dresses and none well supported. The wine was good but champaign (*sic*) could not exhilarate the spirit of the group ". In the following month of the same year it was not much better, if one may credit the account given in the *Town and Country Magazine. Inter alios,* the writer notes " Mother Phillips with a parcel of advertisements denoting her MODEST commodities and the place of their sale " !

These gatherings seem, indeed, to have been often used for the purposes of legitimate advertisement, as for instance that of—

Patty Duggs, the milkwoman, takes this method of informing the public in general that she had just opened for the summer the " Lactarium " near the new erection in the centre of St. Georges Fields. Whipped and Unwhipped syllabub and milk fresh from the cow every morning and evening.

But there were occasions on which the company was the most brilliant the town could show. For instance, the clubs of the day vied with each other in organising lavish entertainments in the form of masquerades, and the " Savoir-Vivre " (or " Scavoir-Vivre ") Club, afterwards known as Boodle's at 28 St. James's Street, gave what was perhaps the most magnificent of these at the Pantheon on May 18, 1775. This was supposed to be a private affair, but, as so often happens, tickets found their way on to the market. An advertisement appeared a day or two before, offering tickets at ten guineas each, to be had of one Mrs. Lewis, a milliner of Beak Street? One may be permitted to wonder how they got into her hands !

Even Gibbon the historian alludes to this masquerade and to the large sums expended on the decorations and supper. Cascades and bowers ornamented the niches of the ballroom and trees of orange and myrtle were disposed at frequent intervals. The supper was of the best and the wine the costliest. The ballroom was not entirely cleared of guests before ten the next morning. The admission ticket was designed by Cypriani and Bartolozzi, and represented a naked cupid

with a bandage over his mouth, and the motto " Muto
non ciecho " (" Dumb, not blind "), signifying that
Love was to see and admire the Fair, but was to hold
his tongue as to what he saw !    ✓

After the Savoir-Vivre Club had become Boodle's
it seems to have made the experiment, in a mild way,
of an early Ladies' Club. Mrs. Harris, in a letter to her
son, dated May 12, 1770, whom she kept informed of
all that was passing in the London gay world, says :

A new assembly or meeting is set up at Boodles, called
Lloyd's Coffee Room, Miss Lloyd, whom you have seen with
Lady Pembroke, being the sole inventor. They meet, every
morning, either to play cards, chat, or do whatever else they
please. An ordinary is provided for as many as choose to dine,
and a supper to be constantly on the table by eleven at night :
after supper they play loo : . . . I think there are twenty-six
subscribers : others are to be chosen by ballot : my intelligence
is that the Duchess of Bedford and Lord March have been black-
balled : this I cannot account for. . . .

The proprietor of Boodle's for many years was a
Mr. Gaynor, a large-hearted man, to whom many
members owed not a little assistance. He always had
a large amount of ready-money handy, and at his death
is said to have been owed ten thousand pounds. By
a clause in his will this was not to be asked for from
the debtors. There is a very old-established merchant
in St. James's Street, who has always followed the
same plan of never suing a customer for his bill. He
just stops the account. It is a system that probably
pays well in the end.

There must have been a Willy Clarkson and a Ben
Nathan in those days, for dresses for the masquerades
were hired out for the evening much in the same way
as they always have been in all countries for similar
occasions. Jewels, also, were easy to get for the night

RANELAGH ADMISSION TICKET
Masquerade, June 14, 1776
*Design by Cipriani*

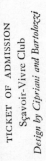

TICKET OF ADMISSION
Sçavoir-Vivre Club
*Design by Cipriani and Bartolozzi*

only. George III.'s mother, the Princess of Wales, on one occasion went as Mary Queen of Scots covered with diamonds, forty thousand pounds worth of which she had hired from a jeweller, who refused to be paid for them, only asking that she should tell every one where they came from. In these rather degenerate days, when caterers have so largely taken the place of private servants, it is always ascertainable from the carefully worded notices in the daily papers where the pastry and ice-creams came from !

After the masquerade at which the Miss Chudleigh had so shocked every one by the scantiness of her attire, an advertisement, not without a touch of sarcasm, appeared in the papers, worded as follows :

Whereas there will be a very splendid appearance at Ranelagh Jubilee, C. Richman takes leave to inform the nobility, AND NO OTHER, that he can furnish them with new invented masks, for those who are ashamed of their own faces, or have no face at all. Naked dresses in imitation of their own skin, and all other natural disguises.

The Duchess of Ancaster generally appeared at the masquerades as a man. She was the second wife of the third Duke, and was of mean birth, her father being Thomas Panton, said to be a Newmarket jockey, who was, however, promoted later on to be " Master of the King's Running Horses ", or as we should now say, " Trainer to His Majesty ". She must have been a sort of eighteenth-century prototype of those women who, in our day, love to cut their hair short like a man, don the collar, tie and shirt of a man, stalk through the streets with manly stride, and stand with their legs apart and their arms akimbo on every available opportunity. Lady Mary Wortley Montagu, who, with all her faults, was essentially a feminine woman,

writes of this same Duchess of Ancaster as " one of
a party of Amazons who on one occasion stormed the
House of Lords and disturbed the debate by their
rowdy behaviour ".

In spite of her peculiarities this same Duchess of
Ancaster, *née* Panton, was Mistress of the Robes, and,
accompanied by the lovely Duchess of Hamilton, *née*
Gunning, was sent to Germany to escort to England
the Princess Charlotte on the occasion of her marriage
to George III.

The gentlemen of Goosetree's Club gave an entertainment at the Pantheon in February 1775, and in
1779 there was a very magnificent subscription ball,
where the company was similar to that to be found at
the Opera balls or at Carlisle House in its best days.
Among the revellers were to be seen H.R.H. the Duke
of Gloucester, the Duke of Devonshire, the Duke of
Queensbury, Lord Townshend (eldest son of my Lady
Townshend), General Conway, and all the ambassadors.
It is quite possible that to these names would have
to be added that of Ethelreda, Dowager Viscountess
Townshend, who, old as she was, would never miss
any kind of frolic.

Goosetree's Club, in Pall Mall, was originally
Almack's, founded in 1764 by a clever Scot whose
name, some say, was McCall. He and his wife, *née*
Elizabeth Cullen, lady's maid to the Duchess of
Hamilton, also a shrewd Scot, were first of all proprietors of the Thatched House Tavern in St. James's
Street. That prospered so well that he was able to
take the premises in Pall Mall (now the Marlborough
Club) and start the first Almack's, really a gaming-club,
but started under the best auspices with such influential people as the Dukes of Roxburghe and

Portland, Lord Strathmore, Charles James Fox, etc. It was originated in frank opposition to Carlisle House in order to prove that an Assembly need not be degenerate and loose. It afterwards became Goose-tree's, and in 1774 Brookes's, and was moved to St. James's Street in 1775.

Almack's Assembly Rooms, better known to posterity than the club itself, were back to back with the Pall Mall premises, with the entrance in King Street, St. James's, then communicating with St. James's Street by a narrow passage only. These Assembly Rooms were opened in 1775, when, as Walpole said, they were hardly ready and the ceilings dripping with wet—one of his usual exaggerations probably. The subscription was fixed at ten guineas a year, for which you could have a ball and a supper once a week for twelve weeks. The bishops of the day opposed the holding of masquerades, and it appears that they were successful in the case of the King Street Rooms. But they also opposed the masquerades at Carlisle House : La Cornelys took no notice of their opposition, and at her next masquerade the wives of four of the opposing bishops were present.

Almack hit on the idea of having an Assembly governed by a committee of ladies of high position in London society, without whose permission no one could be present, and at first these ladies were very strict (to show their power one supposes), and many prominent persons were blackballed, including Lord March (Old Q.), Sir Brooke Boothby, Lady Holdernesse, Lady Rochford, Lady Harrington, etc.

The new Brooks' Club in St. James's Street was also very particular about this time, and blackballed several friends of the Prince Regent. On this account a Mr. Weltzie, of St. James's Street, who was the Prince's house steward, factotum, etc., started a club in opposition, and the supper of the great ball given at the Opera House by the Knights of the Bath in May 1779 was provided by him ; but he does not appear to have made any notable success with his rival establishment.

One Willis had succeeded Almack as the proprietor of the Thatched House Tavern, and he married the niece of Almack, who had inherited the goodwill of the King Street Assembly Rooms. After the death of the Almacks they were known as Willis's Rooms, and were the usual place for bazaars, concerts, etc., in mid-Victorian days. Later they became a fashionable restaurant, and now the great room where all the big balls used to be held is the auction mart of Messrs. Robinson & Fisher. Other portions of the original Almack's have been transformed into a restaurant and a few shops between the auction mart and the Orleans Club.

But I have strayed too far into the nineteenth and twentieth centuries. Selwyn in 1781 described Goosetree's as a small society of young men in opposition, and he added, " As they discourage gambling as much as possible, they will not do much harm, and probably not persist a great while : it seems to be formed on the model of the Tuesday Nights Club ". In the following year he again alludes to the club as a society of young ministers formed by young Pitt, " who were to fight under his banner and who assemble at Goosetree's ". The masquerade at the Pantheon in the same year (1781) was a smart affair as regards the company, which included the Prince Regent, Mr. Pitt, Charles Fox, the Townshends, the Cavendishes, etc. ; but though the company was smart, the dresses were not. Newspaper accounts sum up the gathering as composed generally of " Turks who never heard of the Koran, Jews who knew nothing of the Talmud, nuns without even the decency of demurity, Cockney dairymaids who hardly knew a cow from a bull, and a drunken oyster-woman who was *up to anything* ".

In 1788 admission to the Pantheon masquerades had been reduced to one guinea, a sure sign of decline, and the story of its remaining days may be told in a few words. The place was turned into a theatre for performances of Italian opera and *ballets d'action*. It was burned down in 1792, but rebuilt on the model of La Scala at Milan, and reopened in the early years of the nineteenth century as a grand opera house. It lasted only a few years, and the materials were seized by the creditors of the impresario, even the curtains of the boxes and the seats of the pit being torn up and carried away. This was in 1814, and what remained of the building was used for a short time for various exhibitions, such as Miss Linwood's Needlework, etc.

In 1834 it became a bazaar and continued as such for many years, certainly down to the 'sixties, and it is still standing with its façade as it actually was 150 years ago—a storage for the liquor of Gilbey & Co.

What was derisively called the " Cock and Hen Club ", which was instituted by the clever Almack in King Street, was perhaps the development of a club for both sexes which had used to meet in a tavern,[8]

---

[8] Perhaps the " Star and Garter Tavern ", in Pall Mall, a well-known meeting place for clubs of all kinds. The Jockey Club used to gather its members there regularly, and the Tuesday Night's Club has already been mentioned. It was famous for its choice cooking, especially of turtle; but it was also noted for its exorbitant charges. We read that : " My Lord Sir John, after whiling

I

according to Mrs. Boscawen. Lady Pembroke objected to the tavern as being considered low, so it took possession of the premises provided by Almack's, and, as we have seen, became a most autocratic affair. The *entrée* to it was a passport to the highest society of the town. It was under the sway of a committee of six ladies whose fiat as to admission within its sacred precincts was absolutely final.

The ladies nominated and chose the gentlemen and *vice versa*, so that, as pointed out by Mrs. Boscawen, no lady could exclude a lady and no gentleman could exclude a gentleman. Yet much heart-burning must have been caused by the blackballing that went on.

I think it is a mistake of Mrs. Boscawen to say that Sir Brooke Boothby and Lord March were black-balled at first, for there are indications that both these gentlemen were among the original members. Boothby especially was a shining light at all the quality clubs. He was a particular friend of Lady Townshend's, and, among other things, a minor poet of the Lichfield set who shocked Anna Seward, the " Swan of Lichfield ", by his extravagances, his perfumery bill in one year alone amounting to £200.

Almack's Club proper, for men only, was a most exclusive little club, allowing its members to belong to no other except White's. Among its earlier members were Edmund Burke, Sir Joshua Reynolds, David Garrick, Hume, Walpole, Sheridan, Old Q., and

---

away an hour or two at the Parliament House, would drive to the ' Star and Garter ' to regale with macaroni or piddle with an ortolan ". Another club meeting here was the " Je ne scai quoi " club. This was rather an exclusive affair. Among its members were the Prince of Wales, the Duke of York, Duke of Clarence, and the Dukes of Orleans, Norfolk and Bedford. This tavern has a unique interest for sportsmen, for here in 1774 first met a committee of noblemen and gentlemen to revise the laws of cricket, and they were then cast in the form in which they are now known.

Selwyn. Brooke was a wine merchant and money-lender and, like Gaynor, a very confiding person in so far as his more aristocratic clients were concerned. He suffered for it in the end, dying a comparatively poor man. On the occasion of a lunch given by Charles Fox, Tickell sent the following lines to Sheridan :

Derby shall send, if not his plate, his cooks
And know, I've brought the best champagne from Brooke's.
From liberal Brooke, whose speculative skill
Is hasty credit and a distant bill :
Who, nursed in clubs, disdains a vulgar trade,
Exults to trust and blushes to be paid.

Selwyn said Brooke was " the completest composition of knave and fool that ever was, to which I may add liar " !

Another way of spending the evening in these extraordinary times was to go to a prize fight—not a mere boxing contest with gloves and time limits, etc., which are to-day held in the great Hall of Arts and Sciences called after the worthy Prince Consort, but real fights, sometimes with knives or other sharp weapons, where blood flowed freely, doubtless to the great delight of the spectators. These fights were not only between man and man but also sometimes between woman and woman. César de Saussure in his account of England in the times of George I. and II., describes such an one. The gladiators he saw were brawny women, one English and one Irish, clothed scantily in a little bodice and very short petticoats of white linen. The Irishwoman had blue ribbons on her head, waist and right arm, the Englishwoman red ones. The weapons were a sort of two-handed sword three to three and a half feet long, with a blade three inches wide, six inches of which was sharp as a razor. The spectators were numerous and the wagers high. On each side of the combatants were stationed men with long staves to separate them if blood should flow.

Before the fight the two women talked loudly and amicably to each other, boasting what they could do. One regretted that she had not been born a man, for then she would have got very rich by her great strength : the other declared she beat her husband every night " to keep her hand in ". The Englishwoman drew first blood, giving the other a nasty cut on the forehead, which had to be plastered up, during which operation she drank large glasses of spirits " to keep up her pecker ". In the second round they had a dagger in each hand to ward off blows. In the third, they had wicker shields for defence. The Irishwoman was defeated after a deep wound in her throat and neck, and both retired dripping with sweat, and the Irish with blood ! Advertisements in journals of the period show that these fights between women were quite common in the eighteenth century.

Another place of indoor amusement, concerning which I have not been able to gather much information, was " The Redout ". This appears to have been a sort of eighteenth-century Argyll Rooms, frequented by women of the town, who went there purely for the purposes of their profession, but also attended by perfectly respectable persons of both sexes as onlookers only. De Saussure notes in his *Diary* :

Went to the ball at the " Redout " with the eldest Miss Blount. Ladies pay half a guinea : men a guinea. Fine rooms, fine company. Girls escorted by their " abbesses " : youths accost them in passing, everything well conducted with a singular air of propriety. Talked to Lord Palmerston, who explained to me the customs of the company.

This must have been a very singular place. Miss Blount was a lady of the highest respectability, whose sister married Sir Joseph Banks, the great entomologist. But the " abbesses " were ladies of Mrs. Warren's profession, and the " girls " they escorted were there in open market !

For an evening's amusement there were also the theatres of the day Covent Garden, Drury Lane—and the Little House in the Haymarket, not to mention Astley's towards the end of the century, where every one went. Besides the theatre there were other centres of amusement in London of a more staid and respectable kind. Among these were Festino's Rooms in Hanover Square, Mrs. Stewart's New Rooms in Tottenham Street, near the scene of the Bancroft triumphs of the mid-Victorian era, and numerous Concert Rooms. At a well-known one in Brewer Street, Golden Square (now a rather disreputable narrow thoroughfare, but then the very centre of the fashionable world), Mozart himself appeared. The Rooms of Bach and Abel in Hanover Square were followed on the same site by the celebrated Hanover Square Rooms of Victorian days, where I can remember the great Giulia Grisi as a very old woman sing, appropriately enough, the " Last Rose of Summer ". These rooms were later turned into a rather rowdy club, which Trollope has immortalised as the Beargarden Club in his novel *The Way we Live Now*.

But that set of lively ladies to which my Lady Townshend and my Lady Harrington belonged would have found such places as concert rooms prodigiously dull, and would have always preferred a " racket " at their own or their friends' houses. When too old for the intrigues of Ranelagh House or the orgies of the

Pantheon, it is not to be supposed that these ladies with a rather flamboyant past could console themselves with exhibitions of needlework or the harmonies of Bach. They probably fell back upon cards, their " dear ombre " or quadrille or whist, and " sweetened their tea with scandal " what time they discussed the madness of the King, the wild doings of the Prince Regent's crew, or the horrors of the French Revolution's early days.

Peace be to their ashes ! With all their faults they always remained true to their sex—women to the end ! It remained for the twentieth century to produce, with all its vulgar vagaries, the new sexless type !

# CHAPTER V

## DIVERSIONS OF PERSONS OF QUALITY AT THE COUNTRY SPAS

Origin of Bath : the Road to " The Bath " from London : " The Bath " and its Entertainments : ballroom regulations at " The Bath " : fortune hunters : " The Wells " at Tunbridge : Samuel Richardson : Epsom Wells, Cheltenham and other minor Spas.

WHEN LADIES AND GENTLEMEN of quality in the eighteenth century got weary of life in London with its round of pleasure, and wanted a change, they usually went to Tunbridge or Bath—especially to " the Bath ", as the famous West-country resort was generally called. In like manner, the springs at Bristol were called " The Hot Wells ", thus differentiating them from those at Tunbridge, which were known simply as " The Wells ". Lady Mary Wortley Montagu in her letters always spoke of the Somersetshire watering-place as " The Bath ". Whether these various springs had any real medicinal value or not, it was good for the jaded persons of fashion to go there. A few weeks of a comparatively quiet life, early hours and bathing in the hot springs, must have had a wonderful effect on people worn out by the continual racket of the daily London round, and who did not wash themselves as we of the twentieth century understand washing to mean.

The springs of Bath had been famous for many years, even if we reject as mythical the story of Prince Bladud, father of King Lear of Britain, who, earning his livelihood as a swineherd, caught the leprosy and then cured himself by plunging into the hot waters of the district as he observed was the custom of his swine when similarly affected. There is another story of Prince Bladud which makes him out to have been a skilled magician, who, having enchanted a stone, cast it into the waters, making them hot and healing for any sick folk bathing therein. He is also said to have made wings with which he flew to London, but was dashed to pieces on the Temple of Apollo—that same temple, may be, which Dr. Phené, the eccentric Chelsea antiquary, declared he had located underground in Whitehall somewhere near the site of the Royal United Services Institution. Bladud lived sometime in the ninth century B.C., and a statue to his memory was erected in the Pump Room at Bath two thousand five hundred years afterwards to prove the truth of the old legend!

The Romans, who, as we are taught, occupied England early in the Christian era, had a great city on the site of modern Bath, which they called " Aquae Solis ", and which lasted for at least three hundred years or more. There they erected magnificent baths on the model of those at Rome and built sanatoria on the surrounding downs for the soldiers who had been invalided in their various wars with the wild tribes of the North. The Roman bath, excavated for the wonder of posterity, is still to be seen.

But when they left Great Britain early in the fifth century, and were succeeded by the rude tribes from the German forests and coasts of the North Sea, all these vestiges of a past civilisation were wiped out. It would seem as if the barbarians from central Europe, the Huns as we have learned to call them, have always destroyed for the mere pleasure of destroying. The wars they waged were always wars of extermination. They never spared people, however innocent, not even women and children, and they took the greatest delight in levelling beautiful cities to the ground. After accomplishing the ruins of a district they generally left it alone, fearing, perhaps, the vengeance of the spirits of the place. But the waters of Bath seem to have struck them as having a certain value, and we find an Anglo-Saxon town rising on the ruins of Aquae Solis, which was given the name of Akemanceaster, meaning, possibly, " The Camp at the Waters ", but the derivation is uncertain.

It could not have been a very important place in times when no one travelled unless they were obliged, and what importance it acquired later was perhaps due to the great Benedictine Abbey which arose in the neighbourhood in early Norman days, near the site of the present Bath Abbey.

Lepers probably continued to go there for what relief they could get, till there were no more, or very few, lepers left in the country; but in spite of the curative renown of the waters the place does not seem to have attained to any particular distinction until Royalty took it in hand and made it a fashionable resort. Anne of Denmark, wife of James I., was there in 1616, Henritta, wife of Charles I., in 1644, the Queens of Charles II. and James II. later, and Queen Anne in 1702. After the visit of that good and gouty Queen, Bath gradually became a rendezvous for all persons of quality in the fashionable world.

Previously to that Pepys went there as he went everywhere. His visit was in 1669, and he notes in the *Diary* :

> Up at four o'clock, being by appointment called to the Cross Bath, and by and by, though we had designed to have done before company come, much company came.

With his usual keen eye for the fair sex, he contentedly notes the presence of " very fine ladies and the manners pretty enough " ; but he adds, thoughtfully, " only methinks it cannot be clean to go so many bodies together in the same water ".

The Bath continued to be a very dirty place for many years after Pepys's visit. Sarah, Duchess of Marlborough wrote to Lady Cowper in 1716 that she—

> never saw any place abroad that had more stinks and dirt in it than Bath, but I am willing to bear it all with patience if I think the Waters do the Duke of Marlborough any good.

For some years the name of the Bath was a byword for disreputable doings and immoral intrigues ; and then we find that extraordinary individual, Richard Nash, better known as Beau Nash, established as an autocratic ruler over all the doings of the society there.

His reign was absolute. He was deferred to by all persons on every question, and seems on the whole to have exercised his power for the best. He was a fop, a gambler and a libertine. By his portrait he appears to have been a heavy, common-looking person. But he had a magnificent talent for organisation, and he converted the dirty, rowdy, ill-kept country town of the later Stuarts into a well-built, tidy and fashionable watering-place, a rendezvous for all persons of quality from London, their followers and hangers-on. Such it continued to be through the reigns of the first three Georges, and early in the nineteenth century developed into that centre of refined and intellectual society immortalised in the pages of Fanny Burney and Jane Austen. The curious as to the doings of Beau Nash may be referred to his *Life* by Oliver Goldsmith, or to a comparatively recent work by Mr. Lewis Melville.

All sorts and conditions of men and women flocked yearly to the Bath. Mr. Austin Dobson, in his entertaining preface to a translation of Barbeau's delightful book on the subject (*Life and Letters at Bath in the XVIIIth Century*, 1904), describes the crowd there as—

A medley of notables and notorieties, members of Parliament, chaplains and led-captains, noblemen with ribbons and stars, dove-coloured quakers, duchesses, quacks, fortune hunters, lackeys, lank-haired methodists, bishops, and boarding-school misses. Ferdinand Count Fathom will be there as well as my Lord Ogleby : Lady Bellaston and Mr. Thomas Jones : Geoffrey Wildgoose and Tugwell the cobbler : Lismahago and Tabitha Bramble : the blushing Miss Anville and the caustic Mrs. Selwyn. Be certain too you will encounter Mrs. Candour and Lady Sneerwell, Sir Benjamin Backbite and his uncle Mr. Crabtree, for this is their fitting environment : in fact, they were born in Bath.

It will not be forgotten that Lady Bellaston has generally been thought to be a portrait in words of my Lady Townshend. Here then, we shall meet not only Lady Townshend but Lady Harrington, Lady Vane and Lady Orford, and other modish folk of the day in all the pride of their hoops and toupees : and here once, but only once, Horace the tattler.

A poetaster, the Rev. Mr. Dalton, in one of his effusions addressed to the Countess of Hartford in 1744, sings :

> She that at Bath so debonair,
> Sung gallant Damon and his fair,
> To beauteous Townshend tuned her lyre.

But my Lady Townshend went to many spas. She was certainly very often at Tunbridge, and it was at those famous wells that took place her quarrel with Mistress Kitty Edwin, which gave rise to so many scandalous satires and lampoons. The gaieties of Tunbridge were not on the same level with those of the Bath. The card parties, the intrigues and the balls did not reach the same standard of distinction, and all such diversions were as much the concern of my Ladyship at the watering-places as they were in the whirl of London life. Bath was her favourite spa. She was there in 1738, for in that year my Lady Wortley Montagu wrote to my Lady Pomfret that Lord Townshend was at his house in Grosvenor Street, and that his good lady "is coming from the Bath to meet him with the joy you may imagine", a characteristically spiteful way of saying that they did not agree. This was, however, three years before the actual separation took place.

Let us, in imagination, accompany her Ladyship on one of her annual visits to the Bath.

It was the most fashionable place outside London during the whole of the eighteenth century, though the journey thither could have been no light matter or to be undertaken without much forethought and due preparation against all misadventures. Yet every one went there who could go, or thought that they had a good reason for taking the cure. Persons went for gout, for "the vapours", for all sorts of real diseases, or, as my Lady did, because it was the thing to do, if one wished to remain in the fashion. Some went by stage-coach, some on horseback, some in their own carriages. All invalids went there, and those who were mad were sent there. "Go to Bath" meant "You are mad ". There were plenty of beggars, for there were hosts of rich people to beg from, and the high road thither must have been filled with as motley a crowd as the Dover Road to Canterbury in Chaucer's day. In the days of good Queen Anne, when the Bath first began to be fashionable, the coaches left the " Belle Sauvage " on Ludgate Hill every third day and (God permitting) reached there in three days. From April to Michaelmas the journey was advertised to be done in two. The fare was 25s., to which had to be added many vails for the driver and guards and refreshments and expenses for sleeping *en route*. In 1716 a daily service was started, and coaches went from various points in town besides the " Belle Sauvage "—from the " Three Cups " in Bread Street, from the " Black Swan " and the " Black Bull " in Holborn, from the " Bell " in the Strand, from the still more famous " Old Bell " in Holborn, from which as many as twenty-one coaches left daily for various destinations, and from a house that lasted for many years—the " White Horse " in Fetter Lane, which was only demolished at the close of the nineteenth century after having served as a common lodging-house for many years previously. There was no regular mail as yet. Letters were carried by post-boys on horseback, and often lost or stolen on the way. Not till the close of the century (1784) was the first mail coach put on the road to carry letters, between London and Bristol via Bath. By the opening of the nineteenth century the stage coach went to Bath in one day, and to carry on a little further still, in 1832 it started from the " White Bear ", a queer old wooden inn occupying almost the exact site of the present Criterion in Piccadilly Circus. This inn lasted till 1860, and must have seen the

laying-out of Regent Street by Nash and the construction of Piccadilly Circus. Though the building is gone,
the white bear itself is said to be still in existence in
the garden of a little public-house named after it at
the village of Fickles Hole, near Croydon.

In the eighteenth century the fares were 4d. a mile
by mail; 3½d. or 4d. a mile by stage coach inside and
2d. outside; or by night, 2½d. inside and 1½d. outside,
all plus tips to guards and drivers, and beds, food and
drink on the way. For the poorer classes and those
who were not so pressed for time, there were stage
waggons for under one penny a mile. These did only
four miles an hour and stopped at every village *en
route*.

Posting to the Bath in your own private carriage
was only for the well-to-do. One could hardly get
there in a post-chaise and pair under eleven pounds,
taking into consideration the cost of the carriage, the
stoppages on the way, the cost of refreshments for all
concerned, and the tolls, which formed a considerable
item. But the privacy of the post-chaise must have
made up for a good deal of extra cost and some
discomfort.

The lively Lady Townshend would doubtless travel
in her great private carriage, with smart postillons [1] to
ride the thoroughbred horses, and running footmen
to clear the way; with perhaps a companion of her
own sex (besides her faithful maid, Johnson), and, we
may be sure, with at least one of the other, to beguile
the tedium of the journey; besides a retinue of extra
servants to guard her party from attacks by the

---

[1] The proper dress of a postillon was " a narrow-brimmed hat with gold
cording, a cut ' bob ', a decent blue jacket, leather breeches and a clean
linen shirt, puffed above the waist-band."

" Knights of the Road " and to see that everything was made as comfortable and as easy as possible along the different stages *en route*.

Mrs. Elizabeth Montagu took four days on the road, " arriving a good deal tired ", as she said. My Lady Townshend could do no better : it was Hobson's choice. She would certainly stop several times, and the inns in those days were built and provided for the comfort of travellers on long journeys.

From Hyde Park Corner to Bath is about 105 miles.

Beyond Hyde Park Corner the road was for many years one of the very worst leading out of town. Not only was the actual condition of the highway a disgrace, but the danger from highwaymen and footpads, even at that short distance from London, began to be considerable, and travellers always, when possible, made up parties to journey in strength for mutual safety. At a point in the road opposite to which the Exhibition Road now runs south to Brompton, was an old inn, a rendezvous for many dangerous folk, and not till 1780 or thereabouts was it made safer by the apprehension of some of the worst of the desperadoes. This inn stood *in situ* till 1848. As late as 1864 there was a toll-gate at the beginning of Kensington, near the site of the Victoria Road, which was known as the " Halfpenny Hatch ", and many others existed in the neighbourhood well within the recollection of living travellers. The last one in Middlesex appears to have been removed in the early 'seventies, about 1872.

After Kensington was passed, the road to the Bath was open country till one reached the village of Hammersmith at the sign of the " Red Cow ", an old-fashioned inn more than three hundred years old at the time of its demolition, where the horses of the Bristol and Bath coach were generally first changed, having probably come all the way from Ludgate Hill or some other part of the City. ✓

The "Red Cow" has disappeared now, but there are still some inns along the road surviving from coaching days. Such is the "Old Pack Horse" at Turnham Green, where the conspirators who were plotting the murder of William III. met to mature their plans, and where the notorious "Sixteen String Jack" was wont to stop for a final glass.

But a traveller to the Bath in the eighteenth century entered on what was perhaps his most dangerous stage when he started to cross Hounslow Heath. Here was the scene of the exploits of the polite Claude Duval, who, as every one knows, induced a fair lady to tread a coranto with him on the heath; of the great Mall Cutpurse, the female highwayman, who wore breeches and pursued a successful career till she amassed a fortune and retired to don petticoats in which to spend it; of the Bishop of Raphoe, who turned high-wayman in 1752; and of many others. No wonder that the "quality" of those times would provide well-armed escorts when they journeyed far afield.

Another reason why Hounslow was considered the most dangerous of all lay perhaps in the fact that the more daring highwaymen always preferred to operate as near to town as possible, so that they might, in their unoccupied hours, enjoy the pleasures (and also may be the profits) of Ranelagh, Vauxhall and Marylebone, and frequent the gaming-hells with which the town abounded. For they were all inveterate gamblers, as we know from the story of Macheath!

Past Reading and Tyford and other less important places, the traveller to the Bath reaches Newbury,
scene of two of the earliest battles of the Civil War,
and which also includes a place called Speenhamland,
at which there was a famous coaching - house, the
"Pelican", which Quin the actor has immortalised
in his epigram :

> The famous inn at Speenhamland,
>     That stands beneath the hill,
> May well be called the " Pelican "
>     From its enormous bill.

By Hungerford, through Savernake Forest to Marlborough, and so to Beckhampton, where the London
folk always stopped to eat ; through Calne, Chippen-
ham, Corsham and Box, all places where there were
good inns in the coaching days, but which have now
dwindled in importance, except where, as at Marlborough, there is a great public school to keep the
name alive, or, as at Beckhampton and others, there
are racing establishments harbouring great possibilities
of possible winners of the Derby or Leger. I am much
indebted to one of Mr. Harper's enchanting road
books (*The Bath Road*) for some of the statistics and
details given above.

After Box we are soon at the Bath, where the loud
ringing of bells will announce to all and sundry the
arrival of my Lady Townshend and suite to take the
waters.

All visitors were received in the same way,[2] and
whatever may be said against the pernicious habit of
making hideous jangling noises on the least excuse,

---

[2] " The bells rang so loud that we could not hear one another speak, for the
honour of Mr. Bullock, an eminent cowkeeper of Tottenham, who has just
arrived at Bath to drink the waters for indigestion."—(SMOLLET, *Humphrey
Clinker*.)

K

the custom had the one merit of announcing new arrivals : for "invalids are fond of news, and upon the first round of the bells everybody sends out to inquire for whom they ring ". New arrivals were also visited at their rooms by " waits " with fiddles and other music, and lest we should be under the impression that such delicate attentions were merely acts of polite greeting, we are told that the ringers got half-a-guinea and the waits half-a-crown !

Bathing commences at an early hour, so my Lady Townshend must find herself at either the King's Bath or the Cross Bath (the two baths used by persons of quality) not later than nine in the morning. She may go as early as six if she chooses, and perhaps may do so at first, but the card-parties drums, routs and racquets will soon compel her to lie in bed a little longer.

The baths were small and not over clean, but it was the gayest crowd that filled them, men and women all bathing together in most primitive costumes and in hats ! Ladies usually went to the baths ready dressed for the ceremony. Citizen Chartreau, speaking of the Bath, says :

Les femmes arrivent aux bains dans des chaises à porteur, qui sont hermétiquement fermées lorsqu'elles sont laides, vieilles ou prudes : et artisquement pénétrables à l'œil lorsqu'on a de belles formes à lui offrir. J'en ai entrevues de charmantes, et l'habillement de bains qui consiste en une espèce de chemise étroite ou serrée sur la taille, leur étoit extrêmement favorable.

The good citizen must have been lucky in what he saw. As a matter of fact, the bath costume for the ladies was hideous and unbecoming in the extreme. They wore jackets and petticoats of brown linen and ordinary chip hats, in which they fixed handkerchiefs

THE " KING'S BATH " AT BATH

From an old print

to wipe the sweat from their faces. It was surely a very queer sight, for they were all immersed up to their necks and nothing could be seen but perspiring faces and chip hats.

Another account says :

In the morning, the young lady is brought in a close chair, dressed in her bathing cloaths, to the Cross Bath. There the music plays her into the bath, and the women who tend her present her with a little wooden dish like a bason, in which the lady puts an handkerchief and a nosegay, and of late years, the snuff box and smelling-bottle are added and some patches : tho' the bath occasioning a little perspiration, the patches do not stick as kindly as they should.—(DEFOE, *Tour Through Great Britain.*)

Yet another account speaks of the ladies who, " with their floating Jappan bowles freighted with confectionery, knick-knacks, essences and perfumes, wade about like Neptun's courtiers ". A few years later the Abbé Prévost notes the rosewood tray, tied to the waist with a ribbon, which floated in the water.

The cost of the actual bath was little enough. In the *Prose Bath Guide* for 1778 it is stated that the bathing guide—" who is to find bathing linen, is entitled to one shilling each time, and the sergeant and the cloth-woman 3d. each time : this is the whole expense at the King's Bath, the water being the GIFT OF GOD ".

My Lady Townshend, probably without a guide, will walk about the bath with her gossips of both sexes, listening to the music and exchanging jests, perhaps not always of the most refined kind. In an hour's time she will return in her chair to her private lodgings, to reappear in the Pump Room (*en déshabille*, be it noted) to drink the waters, talk scandal and quiz the dress and appearance of the motley, untidy-looking crew.

The original idea of Sheridan was to set one of his scenes in the *School for Scandal* in the great Pump Room at Bath, and there can be no doubt but that much evil speaking, lying and slandering went on there from day to day. After breakfasting in public at the Rooms or in private at home, these astonishing folk went to a daily service at the Abbey ! It was as much part and parcel of the routine as drinking the waters or stewing in the bath. My Lady Townshend, ever in the mode, goes too, and if she does exchange sly looks with her many admirers, who shall say that she is alone in so doing ?

> Now for pure worship in the Church design'd
> O that the Muse could say to that confin'd !
> E'vn there by meaning looks and cringing bows,
> The Female Idol her adorer knows.
>
> (*A Description of Bath*, 1734.)

Dinner was generally taken in the afternoon, so my Lady had ample time after church to stroll about the city, perhaps pay a visit to Sally Lunn's famous bun-shop in Lilliput Alley, or to some " toyshop " (where one of the principal articles on sale appears to have been " hair-rings "), or do some other necessary shopping, or in her later visits, sit down to write to her dear grandson, " Jack Townshend ", or his father the Colonel. Visits were paid in the evening after tea, and the day always wound up with cards, dancing or a visit to the local playhouse. As in London, among the persons of quality, cards were always the principal attraction ; and it was wittily said that the mornings at the Bath were taken up with saying " How d'ye do ", and the rest of the day in asking " What's trumps ? "

The ball was, however, the principal event of the

day, and the most precise regulations were laid down and insisted upon by Beau Nash for the conduct of these assemblies—regulations from which there was no appeal possible, no matter who the appellant or what the nature of the appeal. Before the coming of Nash, Lord Chesterfield at Bath wrote to his son in one of those inimitable letters which read so curiously in these days, complaining of the strange mixture of company which included bucks, bloods and bumpkins. He says of these three categories that—

the two first are offensive by their ill manners, the latter are only ridiculously awkward. They hunt all the morning, and appear often in the Publick Rooms in their boots and spurs, their leathern caps and deerskin waittescoats. . . . How glad I am to be convinced that you will never appear anywhere in any of these ridiculous and offensive characters, and to know that you have already a just contempt for them all.

All this irregularity so deplored by the affected Chesterfield was changed by Nash, and, for the balls at any rate, the severest sumptuary laws were enacted. No boots for the gentlemen! No aprons for the ladies! These aprons seem to have been peculiar to England. In Angeloni's *Letters* there is one to an Italian Countess in which he speaks of the part of apparel which is called an apron and which he has no way of describing. Sometimes these aprons were of the most gorgeous and expensive kind. The Duchess of Queensberry (Prior's Kitty) came to a ball at Bath in an apron worth five hundred pounds. King Nash tore it off and threw it contemptuously aside, with the remark that such things were for abigails only. Her Grace bore the treatment good-temperedly and said no word of remonstrance—marvellous to relate, considering who

she was ! [3] As for the men, not only were their boots
taboo, but later on their swords also. There was a
good reason for this, in that, prior to this regulation
being enforced, quarrels had been frequent and swords
drawn on the slightest excuse.

On great ball nights, the minuets were always
danced first, and by one couple at a time : it must have
been a very solemn moment for any young *débutante*
who might be led out to dance under the quizzing
eyes of the more experienced performers of her own
sex. There is a famous caricature by Bunbury of the
Long Minuet as danced at Bath, which bears underneath it the following obscure inscription :

Longa Tysonum minuit, quid velit et possit rerum concordia
discors.

This solemn succession of minuetting couples went
on for about two hours, and then came the country
dances, in which a due precedence was also observed
—the ladies of rank dancing first. By the rules, all
dancing had to finish precisely at eleven o'clock, even
if the dancers were in the middle of a set; and Beau
Nash on one occasion refused the request of Her Royal
Highness the Princess Amelia, who had begged for
" an extra ".

According to our notions, it was a queer way of
enjoying a ball, but was probably the best adapted to
the age of wig, hoop and powder, which would have

[3] She was the Lady Catherine Hyde, second daughter of the fourth Earl of
Clarendon, so related to the Stuarts in no distant degree. She was noted for
her beauty and her eccentricities, which occasionally bordered on insanity.
She maintained a close friendship with some of the leading writers of the
Augustan Age of English Literature, such as Congreve, Pope, Thomson,
Gay and Prior. She said once to Quin the actor, " Pray, Mr. Quin, do you
ever make love ? " (alluding to his acting, for he generally played either the
heavy lead or the comic characters). " No Madam," replied Quin, " I always
buy it ready made ! " She died an old woman in 1777—beautiful to the last.

A LONG MINUET AS DANCED AT BATH

From the drawing by H. Bunbury

all been sadly disarranged if the dancers had attempted anything resembling, say, the " Kitchen Lancers ! "

Society at the Bath was like one united family. Every one met everybody else every day. People who in London would have found themselves in totally different cliques, mixed on a footing of perfect equality, and it was not at all necessary to know people " on the Mall " because one had perhaps exchanged courtesies with them in the Bath ! In fact, as was remarked by Ferdinand Count Fathom, " two persons who lived in the most intimate correspondence in Bath or Tunbridge shall, in four and twenty hours, so totally forget their friendships as to meet in St. James's Park without betraying the least token of recognition ".

Horace Walpole, who went everywhere, of course went to the Bath, but he seems to have spent a very short time there and to have hated it. He had lodgings in Chapel Court, a very fashionable quarter, and the day after his arrival writes peevishly to Harry Conway that he dislikes the place exceedingly and is disappointed in it.

Their new buildings that are so admired look like a collection of little hospitals : the rest is detestable : and all crammed together and surrounded with perpendicular hills that have no beauty. The river is paltry enough to be the Seine or Tiber. Oh ! how unlike my lovely Thames !

It was not from want of companionship that Horace so hated the place. He met plenty of his own set at the Bath, and, in fact, speaks of Lord Camden the Chancellor, Lord Northington, Lord and Lady Powis, Lady Malpas, Miss Rich and Lady Vane. The last-named he went to see " open the ball and glimmer at fifty-four ". My Lady Townshend could not have been there at the time, or, being a much greater lady, would have opened the ball instead of my Lady Vane. But he grumbled all the time he was there. To Lady Suffolk he wrote, after a stay of a few days only:

I am tired to death of the place and long to be at home . . . as I shall not stay above a fortnight longer, I do not propose to learn the language . . . the Bath is sure of doing me some good, for I shall take great care of myself for fear of being sent hither again.

He told George Montagu two weeks after he had got back to his dear Strawberry Hill, that it did one ten times more good to leave Bath than to go to it.

Methodism had quite a vogue at the Bath for a short time. The Countess of Huntingdon had two chapels in the city, and Wesley himself preached there in 1739, but apparently only twice. On the first occasion, recorded in his own journal, he had an audience of four thousand; on the second, but one thousand; and on a third sermon being announced, Nash interfered in his autocratic way and questioned the legality of the conventicle.

The truth was, the old Beau was jealous and hated anybody or anything which, by bringing something new to notice, lessened the number of his own followers; or, as in Wesley's case, brought a more sombre outlook on life in a city where pleasure was the aim of all.

But my Lady Huntingdon was a much harder nut to crack than Wesley. She was really a great lady, a distinguished person even among countesses. Arch-snob that he was, Nash could not bring himself to oppose a countess ! much less when it was a question of an intimate friend of such notable and modish people as Sarah, Duchess of Marlborough, the Duchess of Ancaster and my Lady Townshend. He therefore once visited Lady Huntingdon in her own house to hear

a preaching, but was so mercilessly satirised by the
habitués of the Pump Room that he seems never to
have had the courage to go there again.

Walpole, cynical as ever, describes Wesley's services
as an opera where boys and girls with charming voices
sing hymns in parts to Scotch ballad tunes. He says:

> Wesley is a lean elderly man, fresh-coloured, his hair smoothly
> combed out, but with a soupçon of curl at the ends. Wondrous
> clean but as evident an actor as Garrick. He spoke his sermon,
> but so fast and with so little accent that I am sure he has often
> uttered it, for it was like a lesson.

Religion, however, was not of much consequence
to the visitors to the Bath. They went to church daily,
it is true, but hardly took the trouble to disguise the
fact that it was in order to see their lovers, make
assignations and pass *billets-doux*.

Neither was the main object of their stay in the
place to do a cure by bathing and taking the waters.
The real reason of their visits was pleasure in all its
forms. The whole of the society at the Bath danced,
intrigued and gambled day and night. In addition, it
was a matrimonial market for such slightly tarnished
goods (what the French style *Pêches à quinze sous*) as
had not succeeded in finding purchasers elsewhere.
Fortune-hunters flocked thither in search of a wife:
maids and widows in search of a husband. It was all
done and arranged above board. Even Dr. Johnson
wrote to Mrs. Thrale that " Bath was a good place for
the initiation of a young lady ", and many marriages
were regularly brought about as a result of the annual
visit to the Bath.

Some people went to the Bath for yet another
reason. In those days, as now, fortunes were made
by speculation, by trading, by usury. Folk of no birth

and less breeding found themselves suddenly possessed
of the means to mix equally with the best in the land,
but without the power of obtaining introductions into
sets far more exclusive than those of our own day.
The great army of snobs flourished in the eighteenth
century as it did a hundred years later in Thackeray's
day, and as it does more than ever before in ours.
Wealthy parvenus abounded then, as fond of a title and
as anxious to rub shoulders with the great, and shine
in the best circles as any ennobled contractor or grocer
of to-day. Smollett recognised the position, and in
*Humphrey Clinker*, which affords a perfect picture of the
Bath of that time, he speaks of these *nouveaux riches*
as knowing no other criterion of greatness but the
ostentation of wealth. They pour their affluence without taste or conduct through every channel of the most
absurd extravagance ; and all of them hurry to Bath
because here, without any further qualification, they
can mingle with the princes and nobles of the land.
Even the wives and daughters of low tradesmen who,
like shovel-nosed sharks, prey upon the blubber of
these uncouth whales of fortune, are infected with the
same rage of displaying their importance ; and the
slightest indisposition serves them for a pretext to
insist on being conveyed to Bath, where they may
hobble country dances and cotillions among lordships,
squires, counsellors and clergymen. These were the
days long before the time of Herr Baedeker or the
great Mr. Murray ; but shoals of publications of all
sorts—handbooks, guides and pamphlets—were issued
to advertise the attractions of the Bath and induce
persons of quality to go there instead of to the Wells
at Tunbridge, which had so long held the lead with
London folk of rank and fashion.

A writer in the *Prose Guide to Bath* relates from his own knowledge the sad story of a young lady member of a family who had used at one time to go regularly to the Bath, but one year went instead " to a lonesome house in a bad neighbourhood ". There she meets with a " married coxcomb " and is persuaded to " take a moonlight walk " in her father's garden. Her absence being at once discovered, the young lady (though nothing seems to have taken place over and above the moonlight walk) casts herself into the fish-pond and is drowned. The writer adds that he used every argument in his power " to *convince* the *Villain* who betrayed the Lady with such *Indiscretion* to expiate his *Sins* by putting himself at the *Bottom* of the *same Pond*", but without effect. He sums up with the moral, that if the young lady had continued her usual visits to the Bath, she would have " declined a Walk by Moonlight with the Man ", which indeed seems very probable.

Impostors of both sexes were numerous at the Bath, the Wells and all similar places.

> The London Pastry-Cook, his money gone,
> Comes down to Bath, and styles himself Sir John :
> Creates himself a knight or Baronet,
> And, like a Lord, contracts, but pays no Debt.

Professional gamesters and cheats, professional duellists and bullies, parasites and flatterers, thieves and blackmailers, and the whole tribe of Moll Flanders and her kind, flocked to the Bath to meet those on whom they preyed. Comedies of the day are full of allusions to the vices of the various watering-places. Jane Austen shows the other side of the picture in *Persuasion* and *Northanger Abbey*, etc., but she would never have permitted herself to allude to anything so foreign to her as " watering-place vices ", even if she had known all

about them ! Her books are for the " young person ",
though, indeed, the young person of the twentieth
century would find them very dull after Miss Dell and
Mr. Arlen.

In the time of my Lady Townshend and my Lady
Vane the fribbles, beaux or macaronis were there in
full force. Here is a rhyming sketch of an individual
described as being at Bath in 1748, whose prototype
is to be found in all lands at all times, and who may
still be seen lolling away his time, perfumed, bejewelled,
*fainéant*, in the bow-window of some West-End club or
sucking his cane in the stalls at the performance of
some decadent comedy of modern manners.

> Meanwhile Sir Simon Trifle rushes in
> Stroking his Fore-Top and his beardless Chin.
> But why SIR Simon ? for 'tis hard to tell
> Whether he be a gentle Beau or Belle :
> Trips to the Glass his Features to survey,
> Then, turning half-way round, he blows away
> The *filthy* Powder which had chanced to fall
> From his shook Wig well whitened for the Ball.
> He smooths his Neck, and his stiff *Pasteboard* hides
> And to their Places erring Hairs he guides :
> Admires the Lustre of his Diamond Ring,
> And to his Solitaire cries " *Pretty Thing !* "
> Viewing the Whole, till he the Whole approve,
> Smiles like *Narcissus*, with Himself in Love.

When he had lost all his money at the gaming-table,
or spent it in fine clothes, fine servants, and the
dissipations of town, the macaroni in his old age would
return to the Bath, hoping that he would not be
allowed to starve. For Bath was famous for its charity.
Nash, fop and gamester as he was, gave away large sums
and got them out of other people for the same objects,
so that a poor macaroni would stand a better chance at

the fashionable Spa than by hanging around the Park or haunting the precincts of Almacks and other clubs.

Some people, like Walpole, went to the Bath really because they were ill and had been ordered thither by their doctor. Such visitors did all the prescribed routine for the prescribed time, generally three or four weeks, and were glad enough to get home again. Invalids who came lame with rheumatism or gout or similar complaints, hung up their crutches or sticks as a sign of their recovery, just as is done at Lourdes and in many other votive chapels of the Madonna.

For Londoners who could not leave their business or afford to take the journey, the waters were bottled and went to town, and extraordinary care seems to have been taken that the proper stuff, and no other, was delivered to the customers.[4]

In the *Daily Journal* for October 1739, the public are informed that " Fresh Spa and Pyrmont Waters, also Bristol and Bath Water are sold and delivered to any part of the Town from Mr. Richard Bristow's, Goldsmith, at the ' Three Bells ' in Fleet Street, the former at six shillings and the latter at seven shillings and sixpence per dozen, bottles and all ". It is somewhat gratifying to one's patriotism to find that British mineral waters were valued at a shilling a dozen more than those brought all the way from the Continent. Ten years later, a notice appeared in the *Evening Post*, giving a list of places where *genuine* Bath water could be obtained, and stating that the penalty for adulteration was a fine of a hundred pounds.

Bath, as known to my Lady Townshend, lasted to

[4] Nivernais, when over here on a special mission from the French King, was charged with the commission of sending Bristol water to the French minister, Choiseul. Bristol water seems to have been sent about much more than the water from Bath.

nearly the date of her death in 1788, but for a few years before that a change had taken place almost insensibly in the social atmosphere of the city which would have made it very difficult for the habitués of the previous thirty or forty years to recognise the Bath they had known. It was no longer mainly the resort of Londoners anxious for a change, nor the country headquarters for gambling and other vices. An intellectual set had arisen which settled permanently in Bath for its own sake, and for reason wholly unconnected with the Pump Room or the Bath itself.

The old autocratic rule of Nash, of his successor Derrick, and of the weaker fry who took their place, disappeared altogether. Private parties, as distinct from the public assemblies in the Rooms, and which had always been absolutely forbidden, became the general rule among the higher ranks of Bath society. Moreover, the advance of Cheltenham for drinking purposes endangered the former ascendancy of the Bath. Such changes do not, however, belong to the eighteenth century.

Tunbridge Wells was the predecessor, and for some time the rival, of the Bath, though finally outshone by the western city. Its reputation as a spa died hard, and Walpole in one of his letters at the close of the eighteenth century mentions several well - known people as going to or coming from the Wells. The spring was accidentally discovered, it is said, about the end of the reign of Queen Elizabeth, by Lord North, who, having hurt his constitution " by living too gayly and freely ", came down to a hunting-seat belonging to Lord Abergavenny, near Tunbridge, in order to repair his broken state of health by a more retired and regular life.

He appears to have noticed casually the mineral scum on the surface of some waters, and their chalybeate taste, and, taking a bottle to his London physician, was soon convinced of their medicinal qualities.

Life at the Wells must have been very similar to life at the Bath, all the more so as the great Nash himself assisted in organising the entertainments and assemblies, which were modelled on the style of the western spa.

A contemporary guide informs us that the morning was passed "in an undress"[5] in drinking the waters, in private or public breakfasting, in attending prayer at the chapel, in social converse on the parade, at the coffee-house, in the public rooms or at the booksellers' shops on the Pantiles ; in raffling for, and cheapening, goods at the milliners', turners' and other shops ; in billiards, cotillion dances, private concerts, cards, or some adventitious or extraordinary curiosity or novelty such as a painter, a musician, a juggler, a fire-eater or a philosopher. After dinner, all went (" dressed " this time) to the Parade again, and to the Rooms to take tea : at night to the ball or assembly and sometimes to a play. A few minutes of the day were spent by some in making verses "as the waters, or the genius of the place, or as Love, might inspire ".

It is not to be supposed that my Lady Townshend ever wasted her time in making verses, even with ample love and leisure to inspire her, but she was a good deal at the Wells, probably every year for a short time. It is therefore most disappointing not to find her repre-

---

[5] "But to see the fine ladies in their deshabille,
A dress that's sometimes the most studied to kill."
(*Tunbridge* : a poem. 1726.)

sented among others in the very quaint coloured print, showing some remarkable characters who may have been at the Wells at the same time as Mr. Richardson, the novelist. A copy of this print forms the frontispiece to a little book called *Tunbrigalia, or the Tunbridge Miscellany*, and was added to the volume after its publication in 1740; but it is a reproduction of a water colour which had belonged to Richardson himself; and another copy is found in Mrs. Barbauld's *Life* of the author of "Clarissa." The original was in the possession of the descendant of the novelist for some time.

The persons in the drawing, a dainty one of its kind, each figure being correctly drawn and coloured, are all numbered, and the references to their identity given at the foot in Richardson's own handwriting. These include the following: Dr. Johnson talking to Dr. Gilbert (Bishop of Salisbury), Lord Harcourt, Mr. Colley Cibber, Mr. Garrick and Beau Nash, Miss Giulia Frasi ("La Frasi", an opera singer whose morals left much to be desired), the famous or infamous Elizabeth Chudleigh, Duchess of Kingston, Mr. Pitt (Earl of Chatham), A. Onslow, Esq. (Speaker of the five Parliaments of the reign of George II.), the Earl of Powis (formerly Lord Herbert of Cherbury), the Duchess of Norfolk, Miss "Peggy" Banks (Margaret Banks, a celebrated beauty, married Henry Grenville, son of Countess of Temple, a great friend of Walpole), Lady Lincoln (*née* Lucy Pelham, married Lord Lincoln, afterwards second Duke of Newcastle. Walpole once said of her, "Lord! How ugly she is!"). Mr. (afterwards Lord) Lyttelton, whom Chesterfield dubbed a "respectable Hottentot", "The Baron", a German gamester, "Anonym" (meant for Richardson

THE PANTILES AT TUNBRIDGE WELLS

From a coloured print once the property of Samuel Richardson, which bears his business stamp

himself), Mrs. and Miss Onslow, Mrs. Johnson, wife of the Doctor, Mr. Whiston, and, in conversation with the " Woman of the Wells ", the artist himself, Loggan the dwarf, who had made several similar drawings at other watering-places.

The background of the picture shows the Parade on the left, the old houses and shops with the colonnade (the " Pantiles ") in front, where the visitors would walk in wet weather; on the right the Grove. One feels so certain that my Lady Townshend ought to have been of this company that one resents the fact she happened to be absent what time " Mr. Loggan the artist " was making his interesting little sketch.

She was, however, there in 1738 with Mistress Kitty Edwin, at one time her inseparable friend and companion, and we get from Lady Mary Wortley Montagu some account of the quarrels between these two friends in that year.

Tunbridge battles which served for the entertainment of the public. The secret cause is variously guessed : but it is certain Lady Townshend came into the great Room gently behind her friend, and tapping her on the shoulder with her fan, said aloud, " I know where, how, and who ! " These mysterious words drew the attention of all the company and had such an effect upon poor Kitty, she was carried to her lodgings in strong hysterics. However, by the intercession of prudent mediators, peace was concluded : and if the conduct of these heroines was considered in a true light, perhaps it might serve for an example even to higher powers, by showing that the surest method to obtain peace is to begin with vigorous war.

In the eighteenth century, if you did not go to the Bath or the Wells for a change, there were but few places where you would be likely to be amused. Seaside resorts, as we know them—Brighton, Folkestone, Hastings, Torquay, Eastbourne or Bournemouth —were practically unknown. Weymouth only came into fashion when Farmer George took his Royal Court there. Bath, Tunbridge, Bristol, and perhaps Harrogate and Scarborough, remained for a long time (with the possible exception of Epsom Wells) the only really fashionable centres at any distance from town where you could get the needful change and at the same time not altogether lose your friends, your card-parties and your intrigues.

A very quaint periodical called *Le Pour et le Contre* appeared in Paris from 1733 to 1740. The contents were principally from the hand of the witty Abbé Prévost, and consisted of articles of the *Spectator* type. Among them is a description of the British spas in 1734.

The worthy Abbé says that there were twelve or thirteen of these spas—all about equally celebrated. But when he goes on to enumerate them as Bristol, Bath, Tunbridge, Scarborough, Epsom, Acton, Islington, etc., we may be allowed to wonder at the Acton and the Islington, speculate as to what were included in the etc., and conclude that he obtained his information second-hand; for, with the exception of the first three named and Epsom, there was not much to be said for the Abbé's celebrated spas. Scarborough was just beginning to be frequented in the eighteenth century. There is a short satire extant, called *Scarborough Wells*, which was printed in 1735, and we know that Mrs. Cornelys ventured as a speculation to take some houses at Scarborough, which were sold when she got into financial difficulties. It was a very small spa in those days; and the waters, collected in a cistern, were said to form the " usual physic of the inhabitants ".

Visitors also bathed in the sea, the first thing in the morning, after which—

> Hence to the Spaw in groupes they march along,
> Matrons antique and nymphs as fair as young :
> Spruce beaus, decrepit rakes, and scoundrel Jews,
> Here make promiscuous and ungoverned crews.

It does not sound a very promising mixture, and was never a really fashionable resort—for London folk anyhow.

Epsom had a well-known spring of strong waters, and modish company gathered there in the seventeenth and early eighteenth centuries. The races may have been an additional attraction. There are records of Charles II. and his mistresses and Queen Anne paying it a visit, and the Virginian made friends at Epsom with Beatrix, Baroness Bernstein. The references in Evelyn and Pepys are scanty. Macaulay, enumerating the chief watering-places under the Stuarts is silent as to Epsom ; but one does not go to Macaulay for complete or accurate information. Walpole, I think, never mentions it as a spa at all. Perhaps by his time it had degenerated into a third-class resort, whatever it was before. Its visitors were probably largely of the class of the successful merchant and City madam. Acton Wells was a popular, but never a fashionable, spa from about 1750 to 1790. Its site may be made out in the kitchen-garden of a farm-house near the Great Western Railway, not far from Wormwood Scrubbs and the White City of these days.

Islington was not a country spa at all, but near enough to the centre of the town to have been treated of in an earlier chapter.

The good Abbé, however, puts them all on the same

level and speaks of them collectively and impartially thus :

All rich people desiring to enjoy themselves, visit them yearly, one after the other : and to be in the fashion one should have completed the tour of this round of pleasures, etc.—*Translation*.

He goes on to mention the various classes who frequent the watering-places, winding up with " des marchands de toutes sortes de bijoux, de délicatesses et de galanterie ".

Cheltenham may be dismissed in a few lines. Its time did not come till later. Although the spring was discovered as early as 1718—in this case it is said to have been the daily use of it by flocks of wild pigeons which led to the examination of its properties—it attained no real vogue until after the visit of George III. in 1788, when a medal was struck in commemoration of that auspicious event. Previous to that date it had been reported as " avidiously resorted to by respectable companies " ; but it was never the mode in the eighteenth century and was much too near to the Bath, to say nothing of the Hot Wells at Bristol, to be a serious rival to the leading spas.

Unfashionable and out of the way as it was, we may be pretty sure that my Lady Townshend was never there.

# CHAPTER VI

## THE "ECCENTRICITIES, GALLANTRIES AND WIT" OF THE LIVELY LADY TOWNSHEND

Smartness at repartee of my Lady : the two Sir Thomas Robinsons : her dislike of the Germans at St. James's : Augustus Townshend and Mr. Winnington : her curious passion for my Lord Kilmarnock and her feeble Jacobitism : her alternate fancies for Catholicism and Methodism : Selina, Countess of Huntingdon.

IT HAS BEEN SAID more than once that my Lady Townshend was noted for her "eccentricities, Gallantries, and Wit". Eccentric she certainly was, like so many of the Townshends before and since. Her "Gallantries" were probably just the gallantries of the time indulged in more or less openly by every person of quality. Her widespread reputation for wit which has survived to our own day was well established in hers. She lived up to it by all means in her power, and it is recorded of her and Lady Aberdeen [1] that each, resolving to be recognised as having the most wit of any one in the room, chose different parties or different ends of the room.

To the end of her long life she was welcome wherever she went for her bright conversation and cheery manner. When quite an old woman, fifteen years after the death of her son Roger, she was to be found at Mrs. Montagu's at a time when that lady was

[1] Wife of third Earl of Aberdeen, *née* Catherine Hanson; died 1817.

ill and only receiving intimate friends, " in her best way—very chatty ", as was reported by Mrs. Boscawen [2] to Mrs. Delany the following day.

" Very chatty " describes her well. She was indeed an inveterate newsmonger, though without the deliberate malice of Lady Mary Wortley Montagu or the childish spite of Horace Walpole. Lady Mary Coke used to declare that there was no news to be had when Lady Townshend had none, and that she never failed to be entertained by her.

This Lady Mary Coke was intimately connected with the Townshends. She was a sister of the widowed Countess of Dalkeith, who married, *en secondes noces*, Charles Townshend, the second son of my lady, and she had the care of his children after his death. Her father was John, Duke of Argyll and Greenwich ; her mother, his second wife, *née* Jane Warburton. She herself married, in 1747, Edward, only son of Thomas Coke, afterwards Earl of Leicester. She was considered a great beauty, but was generally known as " The White Cat " on account of the dead whiteness of her skin, the absence of eyebrows, and her very fierce eyes.

It was a most unfortunate marriage. Lady Mary seems to have been a kind-hearted creature and might have made him an excellent wife, but his conduct was insupportable, and they were separated almost at once. She was a woman of very conceited and self-satisfied ideas, generally under the impression that some illustrious personage was in love with her, such as one of the German princelings who was over in England on a visit, or even one of the sons of George II., on whose death, she went into deep

---

[2] Widow of an Admiral Boscawen, who had seen much active service and defeated the French at Lagos Bay and Luisberg.

mourning. She quarrelled with nearly everybody sooner or later : with the good-natured Princess Amelia the unmarried daughter of the King, and with the Empress Maria Theresa, who had treated her as an intimate friend. But she was a soured woman ; the tragedy of her unhappy marriage had spoilt her life.

The great kindness of heart and overflowing good-humour of my Lady Townshend found her many friends and made her immensely popular with all sorts of people. The Princess of Brunswick, visiting the wife of Charles Townshend, said she didn't expect to find so many people and had hoped to find only Lady Townshend. Mrs. Harris, on another occasion, wrote that she was blessed with a most excellent neighbour in Lady Townshend, who carried her out every day in her coach.

Some specimens of my Lady's smart repartee and caustic comments have come down to us in the letters and memoirs of her contemporaries. Especially did Walpole, ever on the lookout for something with which to fill his letters, love to retail all her best sayings to Mann, Montagu and Selwyn. Many of her witty remarks are of course lost, and the charm of manner which, in her case, must have greatly enhanced all she said or did, is absent from a mere recital, but it is still possible to realise to a certain extent how quick she was in lively sally and ready retort.

Walpole, speaking of certain scandals in which the name of Lady Grosvenor had been coupled with that of a Duke, said there was none of that kind of proof which my Lady Townshend had once said existed in another case, when, being asked for proof, replied, " Lord, child, she was all over proof ! " She was particularly fond of sharpening her wit on those of her own set. Of the two Sir Thomas Robinsons, one of whom was very tall and thin and the other very short and plump, and who had both offended her, she said, " I can't imagine why one should be preferred to the other: I see but little difference between them: the one is as broad as the other is long ".

Sir Thomas Robinson, " the long ", first baronet of Rokeby, Yorkshire, Commissioner of Excise, and Governor of Barbados from 1742 to 1747, was a great friend of my Lady. He was celebrated for the magnificent private balls he gave, at which all fashionable London was present. He spent large sums in building and furnishing, but recovered a good deal by becoming the proprietor and director of Ranelagh House, the modish rendezvous of persons of quality at Chelsea. He died at Ranelagh, blind, in 1777, at the age of seventy-six. At the coronation of George III. he was selected to impersonate a mock Duke of Normandy, to indicate that the King of England was also King of France—Dei gratia !

Sir Thomas Robinson, " the short ", was British Minister at Vienna, and was afterwards created Baron Grantham. He held several important posts under Government and died in 1770.

Another of my Lady's intimate friends was old Lord Bath. He once complained to her of a pain in his side ; but she told him that was impossible, as " he had no side ". When her husband died, leaving her a very rich widow, this same old Lord Bath proposed to marry her, though he was then eighty years of age.

Very little is heard of my Lady Townshend in connection with the Court of the Georges. On her marriage to Lord Lynn, afterwards third Viscount Townshend, in 1723, she must have been presented

ETHELREDA (OR AUDREY), VISCOUNTESS TOWNSHEND

After the portrait by Van Loo, now the property of Lord St. Levan,
at St. Michael's Mount

to George I. and his German mistresses, who ruled as queens of a sort, and perhaps she attended the Court functions occasionally as long as her husband held an official position; but, ever a rebel at heart, she was certainly one of the entourage of the brilliant Caroline, Princess of Wales, at Leicester House.

She walked at the coronation of George II. when about nineteen years of age—that is, in 1727—and again at that of George III. in 1761, when she was past fifty. On the latter occasion a party was made up, consisting of Lady Hervey, Lady Hertford, Lady Anne Conway, Mr. Chute, Kitty Clive, the actress, and her brother, Mr. Kafter, Miss Hotham and her maid, and my Lady Townshend with her grandson Jack (then a little boy of four years old), who was in after years to be better known as Lord John Townshend, M.P. They all went to the house of a Mr. Bedford in Palace Yard for the occasion. It is quite likely that my Lady made up this party herself, for she had told Walpole she would much like to see a coronation.

" Why, Madam," said Horace, " you walked at the last ! "

" Yes, child," said she, " but I saw nothing of it : I only looked to see who looked at me ".

She always dearly loved sights and shows and frolics of all kinds, and classed a coronation under the category of a jaunt of sorts.

The dull routine and tiresome etiquette of a Germanised Court must have bored her to tears, and gay, frivolous woman though she was, she always remained indisputable *très grande dame*, with a supreme contempt for that very curious horde of fat foreigners so highly favoured by the first two sovereigns of the Hanoverian line.

She lost few opportunities of saying bitter things

about the Royal circle, and it was probably this contempt for the Georgian Courts which caused her to drift into the currents of a lukewarm Jacobitism. So she easily gained a reputation for hostility to the reigning line. One of her friends rebuked her sharply for abusing the Royal family, adding, " It was very well when you were only affected, but now you are disaffected, it is intolerable ". But she could never restrain her caustic remarks about the Georges and their wives and mistresses, even after Jacobinism had gone out of fashion, and the virtuous, domestic and supremely dull household of the third George and the good Charlotte left nothing to be desired from a moral point of view. Alluding to that Royal Family's habit of going out a great deal to public shows and private suppers, she declared it to be the cheapest family to see and the dearest to keep that ever was !

She would often have a sly hit at any member of the Court circle whom she did not like, or who perhaps did not approve of her, as on the occasion when a friend expressed her surprise that Lady Northumberland should have been made a Lady of the Bedchamber. " Surely ", said my Lady, " nothing could be more proper : the Queen does not understand English, and can anything be more necessary than that she should learn the vulgar tongue ! "

My Lady Townshend, as might be expected from her Irish blood, had a great respect for birth, and the dignities of her position as fine lady, and when Mr. O'Brien was created Earl of Thomond she rejoiced. " For ", said she, " he has family enough to re-establish the dignity of the Irish Peerage to which of late nothing but brewers and poulterers have been raised."

Peers were indeed being created in batches about that time, and my Lady said she expected every day to receive a bill from her fishmonger's headed " Lord Mount-Shrimp ". She also protested that she dared not spit out of window for fear of spitting on a lord! Strange glimpse into the everyday manners of a lady of quality living in a fine house in the Privy Garden, Whitehall.

In later life she seems to have been imbued with something of the same sort of morbid taste that was so curiously developed in her friend George Selwyn— a taste for grim sights and ghastly experiences. She took " a strange little villa at Paddington near Tyburn ", and when her friends wondered at her choosing such a situation, and asked what sort of a neighbourhood she had—" Oh," said she, " one that never tires me for they are hanged every week " !

This may have been in allusion, not to the executions of ordinary malefactors at the Tyburn gallows, but to the military executions which were many after the '45 rebellion. The scene of all such military executions was just inside the railings of Hyde Park, near the site of the present Cumberland Gate.

Perhaps not very brilliant any of this, according to our modern notions of wit, but ready and amusing in an impudent sort of way, as all her sallies were. Her reputation of saying smart things, well established as it was in that society of wits, did not, we may be sure, rest only on such scraps as have come down to us in the pages of Walpole and others. Much of her talk was doubtless very outspoken stuff, only suited to a very outspoken age ; but it was always uttered in a fresh, natural manner that would take the edge off any offence due to crudity of expression.

She was always abusing the Government. Gilly Williams wrote to George Selwyn in 1764:

My Lady is creaking along in her old coach between London and Paddington for ever. Between the King's ministers that ruin her country and the late lord's executors that plunder her jointure, she is in one constant alarm, and her conversation an uninterrupted thread of abuse.

She was a masterful woman and never allowed herself to be imposed on for a moment. In 1865 she was arrested in the streets at the suit of a house-painter whose bill she refused to pay in consequence of it being double the estimate given her. The attorney who had given the order for her arrest had evidently not known what sort of lady he had to deal with. He was afterwards arraigned at the bar of the House of Lords for seizing the person of a peeress, but was dismissed with a severe reprimand on his making a humble submission and paying the fees. Lady Townshend wished to employ the Duke of Newcastle and Lord Cornwallis to make her complaint, but said one was too old and the other too young, so asked Lord Winchelsea to make it for her.

In a letter dated 1745 Walpole told Montagu that Wit and Beauty remained in town in the persons of my Lady Townshend and my Lady Caroline Fitzroy; and he added:

But such is the want of taste of this Age, that the former is very often found to wrap up her wit in plain English, before it can be understood, and the latter is almost as often obliged to have recourse to the same artifices to make her charms be taken notice of.

Perhaps one of the latest examples of her ready wit was what she said about the famous pagoda erected in Kew Gardens. This had been put up by the Princess

Dowager of Wales, whose intimacy with the Earl of Bute was the talk of the town. Some one told my Lady Townshend that the pagoda was of exactly the same height as the monument of the Fire of London. "Yes," she replied, "and like that, it is erected in the very spot where the fire began."

The gallantries of my Lady Townshend were as much the talk of the town as her wit. How far those gallantries went, and to what extent, if at all, she actually transgressed the seventh commandment, will never be known. Sinner or not, she had the reputation of one, and her name was frequently coupled with several of the best-known rakes of the day.

Walpole, who wrote (and copied) his letters for posterity, has placed on record opinions of his own, and some reports of the town, which are too gross for repetition, and which the editors of his *Letters* have sometimes thought better to represent by dotted lines. But it is pretty certain he never hesitated to cross the boundary between innocent gossip and malicious slander, if by so doing he could spice his letters more highly : much of what he said about my Lady Townshend and others is of course untrue.

It was indeed, *par excellence*, the age of satires and lampoons. The only methods of dealing with these was either to challenge the authors to a duel (if they could be identified), or absolutely disregard what was said, or laugh with the lampooners against oneself.

My Lady Townshend always went her own way, not caring the least bit what was said about her right and left, enjoying life to the utmost in her own fashion, doing exactly as she liked, knowing those she wished to know and snubbing those she did not wish to notice, or who were not amusing folk themselves.

Real lovers, or those who wished to be considered as such, no doubt appeared at the house in the Privy Garden. It must be remembered she was a very beautiful woman, entirely independent of her husband, who was notoriously unfaithful, hardly ever left his Norfolk home, and was considered by many people not a little mad! Besides, the moral code of that day permitted a married woman to have one or two lovers openly dangling at her skirts, after the fashion of the Continent. Sheridan explains this clearly in the *School for Scandal*.

> *Lady Teazle.* You know I admit you as lover no farther than Fashion requires.
> *Joseph Surface.* True : a mere Platonic cicisbeo : what every London wife is entitled to.
> *Lady Teazle.* Certainly one must not be out of the Fashion.
> (*School for Scandal*, act ii., scene 2.)

Lady Teazle, we know, never exceeded a certain limit. Nor, probably, did my Lady Townshend. Assuredly neither of them was ever out of the fashion. The sins of that day were committed pretty openly, and not covered with a veneer of respectability and Grundyism as in the Victorian age. How far my Lady permitted her admirers to go we cannot say. The nasty mob of lampooners were ever busy with her name; but it cannot be too often repeated that much that has been said against her comes to us through the spiteful tattle of Walpole, Lady Mary Wortley Montagu and the like. One man whose name was often associated with hers was a certain Mr. Winnington, a bluff, good-humoured official of a mediocre type, who filled successively the positions of Lord of the Admiralty, Lord of the Treasury and Paymaster to the Forces. My Lady Townshend, it was said, had for a long time the greatest influence over him, and induced him to decline to visit Sir Robert Walpole when that minister had lost his power.

Many stories were told at different times about the two. Some of them reached the ears of her husband's half-brother, Augustus Townshend, son of the second Viscount's second wife, Dorothy Walpole, the " Little Brown Lady of Raynham ". Augustus Townshend was very fond of his half-sister-in-law and ventured to expostulate in a letter on her intimacy with Winnington; but it is to be feared that, as might have been expected, he had very much the worst of it; and there was actually a duel of sorts. The incident is best related in the words of Walpole, who of course wrote all about it to Mann in his exaggerated feminine style :

Do but think on a duel between Winnington and Augustus Townshend ! the latter a pert boy captain of an Indiaman, the former declared cicisbeo to my Lady Townshend. The quarrel was about something that Augustus had said of them : for since she was parted from her husband she has broke with all his family. Winnington challenged : they walked into Hyde Park last Sunday morning : scratched one another's fingers, tumbled into two ditches (that is, Augustus did) : kissed, and walked home together.

In another letter to Mann a little later Walpole accused my Lady Townshend of influencing Winnington in his political and official acts, and he declared that Winnington had no principle himself, and that those " no principles " were governed absolutely by hers, which were " no-issimes ".

It was certainly rather unfortunate for any one who might chance to offend Horace and come under the lash of his spiteful pen !

In the British Museum there is a copy of the *Odes* of Hanbury Williams, which was once the property of

Horace Walpole and which is plentifully sprinkled in the margins with notes in his own handwriting. One such note is worth quoting :

Winnington had been bred a Tory, but had left them in the height of Sir Robert Walpole's power. When that minister sunk, he had injudiciously and to please my Lady Townshend, who had then the greatest influence over him, declined visiting him in a manner to offend the steady old Whigs : he had a jolly way of laughing at his own want of principles : he had more wit than any man I ever knew, and it was as ready and quick as it was constant and unmeditated. He died by the ignorance of a quack who blooded and purged him to death in a few days.

Winnington died at the age of fifty. He was well known and liked in the social as well as the political world, and was an intimate friend of such men as Lord Hervey, Henry Fox (Lord Holland), and Sir Charles Hanbury-Williams. The quack alluded to by Walpole in his note was a Dr. Thompson.

The Winnington-Townshend alliance seems to have come to an end in 1746, for in a letter from Conway to Walpole (written at the time he was out against the Highlanders of the '45, and preserved in the *Rockingham Memoirs*), he says : " I hear that there has been fifty quarrels between Lady T——d and Lady Car (*i.e.* Lady Caroline Fitzroy) : between the latter and his Grace (*i.e.* Duke of Grafton, her father) : and an irreparable breach between Lady T——d and Mr. W. These things are all very diverting and I am really glad to hear the town has so much spirit ".

Among those spoken of by Walpole and other gossipers as being favoured by my Lady Townshend were Sir Harry Nisbett (a well-known handsome soldier, killed at the battle of Roncoux, near Liége, 1746), the Duke of Cumberland (" Butcher Cumber-

ETHELREDA (OR AUDREY), VISCOUNTESS TOWNSHEND
From a portrait in the Stone Parlour at Raynham Hall
Photograph by Nicholas Durham, Esq.

land ", son of George II.) and Lord Kilmarnock, the Scottish laird who was " out in the '45 ".

For the last named she conceived a curiously sudden but apparently violent passion which, from the very circumstances of the case, should be classed with her " eccentricities " rather than her " gallantries ". At one time in her life she espoused the Jacobite cause with some warmth and more or less openly (though at the same time among her special friends were " Butcher Cumberland " and that Duke of Argyll, who commanded the English troops against Prince Charlie, not to speak of Conway, who was with Argyll). A reason for this outward show of sympathy with the " rebels " may have been that her husband's people had always been strongly Hanoverian ! With his usual want of delicacy, Walpole hints that another reason may have been one of spite because some " overtures of civility " which she made to the Duke of Newcastle had been rejected by his Grace.

When Lord Kilmarnock was put on his trial for open rebellion, my Lady Townshend was present and fell in love with him on the spot. In a letter to Montagu, written shortly before the execution of the rebel lords, Walpole tells the tale :

It will be difficult to make you believe to what heights of affectation or extravagance my Lady Townshend carries her passion for my Lord Kilmarnock, whom she never saw but at the bar of his trial, and was smitten with his fallen shoulders : She has been under his windows : sends messages to him : has got his dog and his snuff-box : has taken lodgings out of town for to-morrow and Monday night and then goes to Greenwich : forswears conversing with the bloody English and has taken a French master. She insisted upon Lord Hervey's promising her he would not sleep a whole night for my Lord Kilmarnock and in return says she " never trust me more if I am not as yellow as jonquil for him ". She said gravely t'other day : " Since I saw

M

my Lord Kilmarnock, I really think no more of Sir Harry Nesbitt than if there was no such man in the world ". But of all her flights, yesterday was the strongest. George Selwyn dined with her, and not thinking her affliction so serious as she pretends, talked rather jokingly of the execution. She burst into a flood of tears and rage : told him she now believed all his father and mother said of him : and with a thousand other reproaches flung upstairs. George coolly took Mrs. Dorcas her woman, and made her sit down to finish the bottle. "And pray sir ", said Dorcas, " do you think my Lady will be prevailed upon to let me go and see the execution ? I have a friend that has promised to take care of me and I can lie in the Tower the night before." My Lady has quarrelled with Sir Charles Windham [3] for calling the two lords malefactors.

Of the four Scottish peers condemned to death for participation in the '45, Lord Cromarty was eventually pardoned ; Lord Lovat was executed in 1747, and Lord Kilmarnock and Lord Balmerino were beheaded on Tower Hill in 1746. The scaffold was erected in front of No. 14 Tower Hill, and it was said that for a long time afterwards a trail of blood was visible along the hall of that house, and up the stairs where their headless bodies were taken prior to being buried in St. Peter Vincula within the Tower. A very vivid account of the last moments of Lords Balmerino and Kilmarnock has survived. Just before they came out of the Tower, Lord Balmerino drank a bumper to King James's health. On the scaffold Kilmarnock appeared all in black, his hair unpowdered and in a bag : he was supported by a Presbyterian and a young clergyman. Balmerino, on the contrary, walked alone, in a blue coat turned up with red (the regimentals of the rebels), a flannel waistcoat and his shroud underneath. Their two hearses followed behind.

[3] Fourth Baronet. Succeeded his uncle as the second Earl of Egremont. Was Secretary of State in 1761. Died 1763.

Kilmarnock seemed in fear, shedding tears all the time. His head was cut off at once, only hanging by a bit of skin : it was received in a scarlet cloth and laid in a coffin at once.

Old Balmerino followed, treading with the air of a general. He read the inscription on his coffin, looked round on the crowd, read aloud a treasonable speech, and said the Young Pretender was so sweet a Prince that flesh and blood could not resist following him. Lying down to try the block, he said : " If I had a thousand lives, I would lay them all down here in the same cause ". He also said that if he had not taken the sacrament the day before, he would have knocked down Williamson, the Lieutenant of the Tower, for his ill-usage of him. He then took the axe and felt it, and asked the headsman how many blows he had given Lord Kilmarnock, and then gave him three guineas. After taking off his periwig he put on a night-cap of Scotch plaid, pulled off his coat and waistcoat and lay down. Being told he was on the wrong side, he vaulted round, and immediately gave the signal by tossing up his arm as if giving the signal for battle. On his way to the scaffold he had pointed to the crowd, saying : " Look, look, how they are all piled up like rotten oranges ".

A little while after the letter quoted above had been sent to Montagu, Walpole writes to Mann that my Lady Townshend, who had fallen in love with Lord Kilmarnock at his trial, will go nowhere to dinner for fear of meeting with a rebel pie, for that she says every one is so bloody minded that they eat rebels ; and, thinking this an exquisite joke, he brings it up many years afterwards in his correspondence when he had practically ceased to chronicle the tittle-tattle of the town.

There was a scurrilous little society paper at that time, very much on the style of a horrible kind of journal that has a great sale in New York. It had a very good name, the *Parrot*, and alluded to the Kilmarnock story as follows:

I hear by the bye that a certain English Lady of Quality was so much charmed with the Person and Deportment of the Lord Kilmarnock at his Trial, that finding all the intercession that could be made for him was ineffectual, has ever since his Death avoided company : and it is apprehended will never touch a card again to the great mortification of Mr. Hoyle, who has long been her master in the art and mystery of the game of whist. If this be true, somebody however, will be the gainer.

This odd sort of passion for the Scottish laird, whom she does not appear to have known before his apprehension for rebellion, and with whom she could not have carried on a serious amour, must have lasted for some time. Nearly a year after the trial she picked up a little stable boy in the Tower, whom the warders palmed off upon her as a natural son of Lord Kilmarnock, and took him into her own house.

She was but a half-hearted Jacobite after all, and in spite of her great social position, was never looked upon in the light of a dangerous conspirator. Indeed, she always remained on the best terms with the members of the Hanoverian Government, who must have had many a quiet laugh over her eccentric " playing with rebellion ". As we have seen, some of her most intimate friends were " hunters of Highlandmen " in those days.

Her highly excitable and eccentric nature impelled her to the commission of many extravagances. On the occasion of her son George embarking for foreign service (it was just after the Battle of Fontenoy) she seems to have shown her grief in parting from him in the most extravagant manner. Walpole wrote to his dear Conway in May 1745 all about it.

The day the young volunteer departed for the army (unluckily indeed it was after the battle), his tender mother Sisygambis [4] and the beautiful Statira,[5] a lady formerly known in your history by the name of Artemisia from her cutting off her hair on your absence, were so afflicted and so inseparable that they made a party together to Mr. Graham's (you may read "Iapis"[6] if you please) to be blooded. It was settled that this was a more precious way of expressing concern than shaving the head, which has been known to be attended with false locks the next day.

Walpole probably did not intend to hide the identities of persons by the silly habit of giving them classical names. The tale may have been true or an absolute invention of the gossip-monger.

So excitable a nature as was my Lady Townshend's would be sure to be affected by the religious controversies of the time. On the one hand, there were the Roman Catholics, persecuted at that period, not indeed with the torturing and maiming they underwent in the days of Good Queen Bess and of James the "Wise Fool", but at any rate with such severe penal laws that only in the private chapels of the ambassadors of Catholic sovereigns, or in carefully con-

[4] Lady Townshend. The allusion is to Sisygambis, mother of the warrior king Darius. There was a craze about this time for giving all one's friends classical pseudonyms. Even the serious Elizabeth Montagu, Mrs. Boscawen and Mrs. Delany were bitten by this affected mania.

[5] Mrs. Paget Toynbee says that this is probably meant for Lady Caroline Fitzroy, who had been very much in love with Harry Conway, to whom this letter is addressed. Statira was a stock name in those historical romances which represented the fate of empires as turning on the effects produced on a crack-brained lover by some charming "Statira". In Cunningham's edition of the *Letters*, "Statira" is said to be meant for Audrey Townshend, daughter of my lady, but this, I think, is manifestly an error.

[6] Iapis was the mortal who received the gift of healing from Apollo. Dr. Robert Glynn, a famous apothecary in Pall-Mall, was known as "dilectus Iapis", or sometimes "the loved Iapis on the banks of Cam".

cealed holes and corners, could they carry on their form of worship.

On the other hand, the blasphemous acts of Sir Francis Dashwood, John Wilkes, and others at Medmenham Abbey, were allowed to pass with a smile, and even George Selwyn, educated gentleman that he was, seems to have been astonished that the university authorities should send him down for the perpetration of blasphemies on the subject of the Mass. (*See* next chapter.)

At one time my Lady Townshend affected a leaning towards Catholicism. Horace heard of it, and, faithful gossiper as usual, immediately sent off an account to Mann.

Have you heard the great loss the Church of England has had ? It is not avowed, but hear the evidence and judge. On Sunday, George Selwyn was strolling home to dinner at half after four. He saw my Lady Townshend's coach stop at Carraciolo's chapel.[7] He watched her go in : her footman laughed : he followed. She went up to the altar : a woman brought her a cushion : she knelt, crossed herself and prayed. He stole up and knelt by her. Conceive her face if you can when she turned and found him close to her. In his most demure voice he said—" Pray Madam, how long has your Ladyship left the pale of our Church ? "

She looked furious and made no answer. Next day he went to see her and she turned it off upon curiosity : but is anything more natural ? No, she certainly means to go armed with every viaticum : the Church of England in one hand, Methodism in t'other, and the Host in her mouth !

Walpole's allusion to Methodism may be explained by the fact that eighteen years prior to that visit to the Portugal Street Chapel, my Lady Townshend had

[7] The chapel attached to the Neapolitan Embassy in Portugal Street, leading off Lincoln's Inn Fields. For a long time this was one of the few places in London where Catholics could hear Mass. It was demolished in 1908 and rebuilt in Kingsway, not far from High Holborn.

INTERIOR OF THE SARDINIAN R.C. CHAPEL IN LINCOLN'S INN FIELDS—
OTHERWISE KNOWN AS CARACCIOLO'S CHAPEL

From an old print in the British Museum

made sundry appearances among the worshippers at the Countess of Huntingdon's services, where Wesley and Whitfield used to preach. Lady Jane Coke [8] gives this bit of news in a gossiping letter to a Mrs. Eyre:

Of all the news I have heard from London, at least the most extraordinary is Lady Townshend's being much with Lady Huntingdon. Wesley preaches at her house every Thursday and Sunday and, as Lady Huntingdon gives leave to everybody to come, who send to desire it, it is now the fashion to go, and Lady Townshend never misses.

If it were really the fashion to go to Selina, Countess of Huntingdon's to hear Wesley and Whitfield preach, my Lady Townshend would be there. Her visit to Caracciolo's chapel had, perhaps, more the appearance of sincerity. Like many of her sex before her day and since, she took her religion in doses by fits and starts. In the year of her husband's death she seems to have inclined to the Methodists. That was the year in which she was robbed of five hundred pounds in bank-notes by Molly, niece of her own maid Dorcas, in conjunction with one of her footmen. Gilly Williams, a member of the Strawberry Hill coterie, tells the story in a letter to Selwyn, July 10, 1765:

Lady Townshend was yesterday robbed of £550 in bank-notes. She kept them in the drawer of a little table and in a room to which nobody had access but Molly the niece of Dorcas, and the upper footman who used to pay the bills, and by that means knew where she kept her money. It seems that these two have kept up a constant correspondence with Draper, her old thief who lives now in Ireland, and to whom, without the least doubt, they have remitted the money. You would like the house at this time better than ever. Methodists, constables, Fieldings, [9]

[8] Lady Jane Wharton, elder daughter of the Marquis of Wharton. Married twice: (1) John Holt; (2) Robert Coke, of Longford, Derbyshire.
[9] Men of Sir John Fielding, the celebrated magistrate of Bow Street and related to the author of *Tom Jones*, whom he succeeded in the magistracy.

turnkeys, etc: she sleeps with one of Fielding's men in the next room.

It is certain that however sincere her religious feelings might be, or the reverse, and in whatever direction they may have inclined, her own Church at that time would have done nothing for her.

Astonishingly quiescent was the Church of England throughout the great part of the eighteenth century. Rome, ever on the lookout for a fresh opening to recover the place she had lost, worked incessantly, making many converts. The Methodists under Wesley, Whitfield and the Countess of Huntingdon were building chapels all over the country, and attracting thousands to their side by the fervour of their preaching and the purity of their lives.

And the Church of England, as by law established, with its easy doctrine of compromise and its parsons of the Barlow type, peacefully slumbered between the two extremes.

# CHAPTER VII

## TWO OF MY LADY TOWNSHEND'S INTIMATE MEN FRIENDS—WALPOLE AND SELWYN

Lady Townshend's circle of friends a wide one : the Walpoles : the " Little Brown Lady of Raynham " : spiteful character and effeminate nature of Horace Walpole : his malicious scandal-mongering : La Marquise du Deffand : George Selwyn : his blasphemous conduct at Oxford University : the Monks of Medmenham and the Hell-Fire Club : Charles Churchill : Mie-Mie Fagnani : the Chevalier D'Eon de Beaumont : devotion of George Selwyn to my Lady Townshend : his delight in death, burials and corpses.

A MAN IS SAID TO BE KNOWN by the company he keeps. Similarly a woman may be judged to a great extent by her friends and the people she chooses to number among the more intimate of them.

My Lady Townshend knew every one worth know-ing, both men and women, in the world of fashion for more than sixty years of the eighteenth century. Her intimates included her cousin, the notorious Countess of Harrington, and most of the fast set of the day, but she was also known and loved by such a different type as Elizabeth Montagu and Mrs. Bos-cawen, two famous blue-stockings ; Mrs. Delany, the friend of " Good Queen Charlotte " ; and Selina Ferrers, the Methodist Countess of Huntingdon.

She mixed in the world of beaux, fribbles and macaronis from her marriage in 1723 to her death in

1788. One can, then, only give a sketch of one
or two of her intimates—men or women, selecting
some who made their mark in the social world of
her day.

We have seen how lavishly she entertained in the
Privy Gardens, Whitehall, and how she was always to
be found at all public assemblies and at the great
routs and balls given by persons of quality.

Though doubtless occasionally present, with other
women of fashion, at the Queen's Drawing-room and
at the Leicester House parties, her lively character and
the freedom, some said licence, of her manners,
rendered anything like a strict observance of the
etiquette of a Germanised Court extremely distasteful
to her. She was of far too independent a type to loiter
about the corridors of St. James's or Leicester House,
or to fawn on royalty of any kind. So her name is
conspicuously absent from the memoirs of the time,
while it is constantly cropping up in the gossiping
correspondence of Walpole, Selwyn, Montagu and
others.

The Walpoles had always been closely connected
with the Townshends. They were next-door neighbours in Norfolk, where the Raynham and Houghton
lands run side by side. Horace himself was a godson
of his aunt Dorothy Walpole,[1] who became the second
wife of the second Viscount Townshend, and he had

---

[1] I have already alluded to the ghost of this Dorothy Townshend, who is
said still to haunt the galleries and rooms of Houghton and Raynham. She
is known as " The Little Brown Lady of Raynham ", and is one of the best
authenticated of all family ghosts. More than one person has stoutly testified
to the reality of the " Brown Lady ", whose appearance is supposed to
presage the death of some member of the family. She was seen by a Colonel
Loftus (whose mother was a Townshend) and by Lady Anne Sherson,
daughter of the fourth Marquis and great-great-granddaughter of Ethelreda
Viscountess Townshend, and also by Lady Caroline Dawson Damer, afterwards the wife of Admiral Sir George Duckworth King.

"THE LITTLE BROWN LADY OF RAYNHAM"
Dorothy Walpole, second wife of the second Viscount Townshend
From the portrait by Jervas

for school-fellows at Bexley four Townshend cousins,[2] sharing also, in the winter, their tutor at Raynham itself. It was therefore but natural that as he grew up he should become very intimate with the wife of the eldest brother of his former school-fellows, more especially as in London they all moved in the same set.

The mother of Horace Walpole was a Miss Catherine Shorter, of whom little is known save that she was a granddaughter of that Lord Mayor of London who was arbitrarily appointed to the position by James II. just before his flight. His reputed father was Sir Robert Walpole; but there is a story, supported by the authority of Lady Louisa Stuart (granddaughter of Lady Mary Wortley Montagu), that he was in reality the son of Carr, Lord Hervey, elder brother of " Lord Fanny ". He certainly was born eleven years after all the other children of Catherine Shorter, and in every respect, both in appearance and in character, was as much like a Hervey as he was unlike a Walpole.

Mr. Peter Cunningham, first editor of the *Letters*, believes that he was of Hervey blood. He recalls the observation of Lady Mary Wortley Montagu, who was wont to divide the human race into " Men, Women and Herveys ",[3] and adds that Walpole was certainly of the " Hervey " class.

In appearance Horace Walpole is said to have been

---

[2] George, a Rear-Admiral, *ob.* 1762; Augustus, captain in the mercantile marine (my Lady hated him), *ob.* 1746; Horatio, *ob.* 1764; and Edward, Dean of Norwich, *ob.* 1765.

[3] In allusion to the astonishing effeminacy of the Lord Hervey, so bitterly attacked by Pope under the soubriquet of Sporus. Sarah, Duchess of Marlborough, and others of her set always spoke of this same Lord Hervey as "Lord Fanny", and the nickname has stuck to him ever since. Perhaps the severe strictures on Lord Hervey were only partially deserved. He was of a very sickly nature, could digest no solid food, and had to paint his face to hide its corpse-like pallor. Pope was certainly no unbiassed critic, and where personal feeling was concerned was probably incapable of impartial judgment.

slender, but compact and neatly formed, with a high forehead and a pale, almost sickly, complexion. His laugh was forced and uncouth and his smile unpleasant.

For many years he was one of my Lady Townshend's most constant companions and closest friends ; but, unlike George Selwyn, who proved her really faithful admirer to the last, he seems to have gradually dropped out of the habit of meeting her often for discussing the latest scandal, or to talk over the events of the day. The truth is, she never flattered him in his later years as did the Misses Berry and others. She was far too outspoken a lady, too independent to flatter any one. On the other hand, he had perhaps ceased to find her amusing, and when anybody or anything ceased to amuse Horace Walpole, he, she or it at once dropped out of his ken.

But at one time Lady Townshend and he were constantly together. She went down to inspect Strawberry Hill before it was quite completed, and her criticism of the pseudo-Gothic monstrosity was characteristic enough.

" Lord God Jesus ! " she cried out, as she rustled up the staircase, probably sweeping aside many an ornament with her ample silk petticoats. " What a house ! It's just such a house as the parson's, where the children all lie at the foot of the bed ! "

In 1759, on the occasion of the marriage of his niece Maria with Lord Waldegrave, my Lady Townshend was entrusted with the task of choosing Walpole's dress. This is how he whimsically describes the affair in one of his letters :

" Our great match approaches. I dine at Lord Waldegrave's presently, and suppose I shall then hear the day. I have quite reconciled my Lady Townshend to the match (saving her abusing us all) by desiring her to choose my wedding clothes, but I am to pay the additional price of being ridiculous, to which I submit : she has chosen me a white ground with purple and green flowers. I represented that, however young my spirits may be, my bloom is rather past. But the moment I declared against juvenile clothes, I found it was determined I should have nothing else ; so be it ! "

This niece Maria was an illegitimate daughter of Walpole's brother, Sir Edward Walpole, who died unmarried in 1784, but left behind him three daughters and one son. The mother of these children was Mary (or Dorothy) Clement, an apprentice of the Pall Mall tailor over whose shop he lodged. Horace calls her "a little milliner ", but it was also stated that she had once been the inmate of a brothel; and Lady Louisa Stuart wrote that, "according to common report, the keeper of some infamous house, descrying her uncommon beauty, had beckoned her in from the top of a cinder-cart ". Whoever their mother may have really been, the three girls all made great matches. Laura, the eldest, married Keppel, Bishop of Exeter, brother of the Earl of Albemarle ; Maria, the second married, firstly, James, second Earl of Waldegrave, and secondly, H.R.H. William Duke of Gloucester, brother of George III. ; Charlotte, the youngest, married Lionel, fourth Earl of Dysart. They were all three celebrated for their great beauty, especially the Duchess of Gloucester. The son won some distinction as a soldier, but died young and unmarried.

Selfish throughout his early life, Horace Walpole grew more and more selfish as he grew older. He found it increasingly difficult to tear himself away from his beloved Strawberry Hill, its paintings, its precious rubbish and, above all, its private printing press ; on the rare occasions when he alludes to my Lady Townshend, in his later letters, it is but to recall a witty

saying already recorded by him in earlier correspondence.

He was a curious type of that very curious age.
His name was never coupled with that of any woman:
and this, considering the looseness of morals and
general conduct of the period, is odd, to say the least.
His pleasure in the society of women was purely of
the "tame cat" order. He was never in love with
any one but himself. Mistress Kitty Clive, the old
actress, a neighbour of his near Twickenham, kept a
handsome tiger (or possibly leopard) as a pet, which
Horace admired in his dilettante way; and my Lady
Townshend once sarcastically declared that this beautiful animal was the only thing he had ever wanted to
kiss! One can well imagine the disdainful scorn with
which such a remark was uttered by the lady who so
thoroughly appreciated all that was manly in a man,
and who, it is said, knew so well the pleasures of
kissing! But Walpole tells the tale against himself with
a delight all his own.

Eliot Warburton, in an introduction to his memoir
of Walpole, says that, according to his own showing,
he lived for himself alone; that no sentimental interest
in the welfare of his fellow-men, no restless aspirations
to promote the good of his country, disturbed his
polished leisure. His ambition was bounded by the
narrow, though brilliant, society of which he was
alike the idol and the worshipper. Like Voltaire, he
was essentially " L'enfant gâté du monde qu'il gâta ".
Yet in some ways he must have been an interesting
companion; and the Miss Berrys, for whom he wrote
some reminiscences, had a chance that fall to few when
they were his privileged guests at Strawberry Hill and
could listen to his tales of the past. For at the beginning

of the nineteenth century he formed an extraordinary link with a past which stretched back to the beginning of the eighteenth century and beyond.

He knew the members of the broad Bolton and Coalition ministries. He had seen, or known (certainly knew a great deal about), the many mistresses of the four Georges, from the Duchess of Kendal to the Countess of Suffolk, from Miss Vane to Mrs. Fitzherbert.[4] He was known to two kings and their children. He lived through a long life in the best society and the best clubs. His means were ample, and every reasonable desire he seems to have gratified. As a boy he kissed the hand of George I., and as man in years he conversed with two young men [5] who, long after his own death succeeded George III. on the throne of England. He had seen in the flesh two of the heroines of De Grammont and the Restoration (La Belle Jennings and Arabella Churchill) and lived long enough to offer his coronet to two ladies (Mary and Agnes Berry), who lived far into the reign of Queen Victoria.—(Introduction to Cunningham's edition of *Walpole's Letters*.)

Though he wrote a great deal himself, much of which was printed at his own private press at Strawberry Hill, he had the curious affectation of pretending to despise authors, and asserted that he did not regard himself as one. Some say he had a dread lest his reputation as a fine gentleman should suffer by association with that of the inhabitants of Grub Street, and this very unworthy snobbish feeling seems to have obsessed him and involved him in many curious inconsistencies.

Sir Benjamin Backbite, in the *School for Scandal*, who was drawn from Walpole, is made to have the same affectation with regard to authorship. He says to Lady Sneerwell:

[4] It may be noted that Mrs. Fitzherbert was really married to the Prince of Wales (George IV.) according to the rites of the Church, though, legally, only his mistress on account of the Royal Marriage Act.

[5] George Prince of Wales and William Duke of Clarence.

To say truth Ma'am, it is very vulgar to print ! and as my little productions are mostly satires and lampoons on particular people, I find they circulate more by giving copies in confidence to the friends of the parties.

Sir Benjamin was a portrait of the literary macaroni, and the affectations of walk and demeanour which belong to the rôle seem a part of Walpole himself. We are told that he made his entrance into a room in that style of mincing delicacy which fashion had made almost natural : *chapeau bras* [6] between his hands, as if he wished to compress it, or under his arm ; knees bent and feet on tiptoe, as if afraid of a wet floor. That is Walpole by one who knew him : it is also the affected fop of the plays of Sheridan and his contemporaries. Another of his affectations was a pretended dislike of everything English and a preference for all that was foreign, more especially Italian. His friend, Sir Horace Mann, kept him supplied with every sort of curio, real or fictitious, and he was, or imagined himself to be, a connoisseur of the artistic and the antique.

In the British Museum there is an amusing little skit on the manners of the time. It is called *Ranelagh House : a Satire in prose after the manner of Monsieur Le Sage*. 1747.

In the same way as the Diable Boiteux of the French author uncovers the roofs and displays to his charge

---

[6] This was a small three-cornered silk Court hat for carrying only. It could not be worn for fear of ruffling the wig. It was sometimes called the " Nivernais " hat, being supposed to be the invention of the Duc de Nivernais, who came to England in 1762 to arrange the preliminaries of the peace between England and France. He was a very thin person, which gave rise to one of Charles Townshend's witticisms, who said that the French had sent over the preliminaries of an ambassador to arrange the preliminaries of a peace. The Duc brought with him as his secretary the famous D'Éon de Beaumont, then a captain in the D'Autichamp regiment of dragoons (*vid. inf.*).

HORACE WALPOLE IN 1754
After the portrait by J. G. Eckhardt

the vanities of the sleeping town, the Demon in the English satire takes one Philonides to Ranelagh House and explains to him the characters of the various folk they meet :

" Pray inform me ", interrupted Philonides, " of the character of that conceited coxcomb whom I hear talking Italian so bad. He has the air and dress of a foreigner."

" He is indeed ashamed to own himself an Englishman ", answered the satirical Demon, " and by disuse has forgot his mother tongue. He has just returned from travel, and sets up as a great virtuoso. He imagines he has an exquisite taste in Paintings, Statuary and Medals, and is inviting his friend to come and see a genuine Otho which I assure you was coined at Rome two years ago. He is at this moment making a panegyric on the charming green rust of his favourite medal that hinders the inscription from being read. He is perpetually railing at the climate and manners of his native country : and pronouncing the word ' Gothic ' fifty times an hour. He has built a house so much in the Italian taste for shade and coolness that half his family are dying of violent colds. He imported into this country some very valuable commodities—a headless statue of Helen, a Count who fled from Florence for murder, five suits of Genoa velvet, the first edition of Pastor Fido and a cook who makes the best soup in Christendom and who has had the education of a Cardinal's kitchen."

This, of course, is a clever satirical sketch of Walpole, whose Gothic house at Strawberry Hill was one of the show-places of the latter half of the eighteenth century. Here, with old Kitty Clive, the actress of a former day, on one side of him, and the deaf Mrs. Howard, once Countess of Suffolk, mistress of George II., on the other, he passed the autumn of his life in the midst of a good deal that was beautiful and much that was trumpery, with a private printing press whence he might send forth such of his precious thoughts as he chose to put into words, and, when wearied of letters and the arts, the naughty Court tales

N

of " my good Howard ", or the spicy greenroom
reminiscences of Kitty Clive to refresh his brain withal.
He was generally known as " The Abbot of Strawberry ", and was really very much offended if not
taken at his own valuation. When the Duc de Nivernais (*see* note 6) visited him he said, " I cannot say
he flattered me much or was much struck ". He was
probably indignant when Nivernais removed his hat
on entering the Gothic room, thinking it was a
chapel !

Many of the stories retailed by him to Mann,
Selwyn, Lady Ossory [7] and others must have reached
him through one or other of his fair neighbours. He
took them all on trust, swallowed them whole, so to
speak, making no inquiries as to their truth, lest
haply a good story be lost.

My Lady Suffolk was a very old woman by this
time, for she had been lady-in-waiting to the Electress
Sophia before the Guelphs came to England, and she
was very deaf. She also may have been rather odd to
look at. She probably wore a wig, for when she
married Mr. Howard they were so poor that, having
to give a dinner to friends, she was forced to sell her
hair to furnish the entertainment. Long wigs were
then in fashion, and her hair being fine, long and fair
fetched twenty pounds. This is a story of Walpole's,
and may, or may not, be true. Mistress Clive had also
lost all her beauty, and was of such a ruddy complexion
that my Lady Townshend declared Walpole's place at

---

[7] Countess of Ossory, *née* Anne Liddell, married Duke of Grafton : was
divorced and married Earl of Ossory. On the day her bill of divorce passed
the House of Lords, or on the day before, she signed a letter to a friend,
" Anne Grafton ", added a little to it the next day when the bill was passed,
and signed it " Anne Liddell ", and then got remarried and added a final
bit, signing it " Anne Ossory ".

Twickenham would be very pleasant if Mrs. Clive's face did not rise on it and make it so hot. Female beauty had, however, no attractions for Horace. His lady friends might be old and deaf and purple as to their complexion, so long as they duly fed him with "good stories" and tit-bits of scandal.

Very few men have been so indiscriminately praised and blamed as Horace Walpole. Macaulay could see no good in him, and describes him in his usual pontifical manner as follows:

The most eccentric, the most artificial and the most capricious of mortals, his mind a bundle of inconsistent whims and affectations—his features covered with mask within mask, which when the outer disguise of obvious affectation was removed, you were still as far as ever from seeing the real man.

Old Miss Berry, on the other hand, as is perhaps only natural, in the advertisement of the edition of the *Letters* which appeared in 1840, takes up the cudgels on his behalf, defending him from all "the Reviewer" (Macaulay) had had to say against him, urging as proofs of his non-artificiality and unaffected good nature, his long attachment to his cousin Harry Conway from the time they were at Eton together to the end of his life—and his devoted friendship for the blind old Marquise du Deffand.

Conway was a handsome and distinguished soldier of a strikingly manly type (what my Lady Townshend would have called "a very pretty fellow"), the very sort of man for whom such a person as Walpole would have an extravagant liking, to whom he would attach himself as a faithful dog to its master. Effeminate men like Walpole always admire a man of the Conway type, though it may be in his particular case there was something more than mere admiration for good looks and thews and sinews, for he clung to him and loved him to the end of his life.

Marie de Vichy Chambond, Marquise Du Deffand (1697–1780), who had a famous salon in Paris in the latter years of the eighteenth century, was one of the aristocrats lucky enough to escape the guillotine. When very young she had been married to a notoriously unfaithful husband, and the young couple had been among the most dissipated of the Court of the Regent of Louis XV. Being, however, an intellectual woman, she decided to give up the dissipations of the Court and settle down to a quiet life, which she proceeded to do by entering into a liaison with a clever lawyer called Renault ! The liaison lasted a short time as such : he was not faithful to her and she was doubtless not faithful to him, so the intercourse by degrees became more respectable and settled down into a firm friendship. When her husband left her a very rich widow, but also well advanced in years, she gave up the Court altogether, and occupied a suite of rooms in the Convent of St. Joseph, Rue de Dominque, thus gathering about herself the aura of respectability which such an abode would give her, without having to observe any of the tiresome restrictive rules that a regular inmate of a convent would have had imposed upon her.

*Rangée*, and comfortably settled for her old age, a great calamity overtook her. She became completely blind. It was necessary that she should have some one with her in her misfortune, and so she invited a young girl, Julie de L'Espinasse, a lonely neglected creature, to live with her as a sort of secretary and general help in her blindness.

The result was not a success. Julie de L'Espinasse

was young and attractive, Madame Du Deffand was old and blind. A brilliant circle gathered round this odd couple in the Convent St. Joseph; for, besides Horace Walpole, who was often there, the visitors included Turgot, D'Alembert, Marmontel and others. D'Alembert fell in love with Julie; Marmontel and Turgot followed suit, and the blind old lady found herself absolutely put on one side for the young girl whom she had rescued from a dull country life and given everything that could make her life a pleasant one.

The climax came when the old lady found that Julie held receptions of her own before she herself was " up and about ". Banishment followed promptly enough; but Julie, with a true feminine instinct for what would be most disagreeable to her benefactress, took a suite of apartments immediately opposite the Convent, and D'Alembert installed himself in the same house.

Retribution followed closely on this act of spite. Julie fell really in love with a wealthy young Spaniard, who wished to marry her but died before the arrangements could be completed. Then she fell in love again, this time with a Comte de Guibert, who did not care for her but made her his mistress first, and then deserted her to get married in earnest. Under this final blow the miserable young woman died. Old Madame Du Deffand, who must have known of the whole series of comedies and tragedies from the convent opposite, had the satisfaction of hearing the body of her ungrateful protégée taken to its last resting-place. I have lingered over this episode, perhaps, too long, but it is so characteristic of the times as to be worthy of notice.

Madame Du Deffand long outlived Mlle. de L'Espinasse and continued her receptions, at which Walpole was a daily visitor whenever in Paris. She repaid his friendship by a devotion which has been well described as " une tendresse exaltée, dont le vrai nom échappe, tant celui d'amitié serait faible, et celui d'amour dérisoire ". This devotion, like that of the two Miss Berrys, must have tickled his vanity hugely. His regard for her may have possibly been sincere, but it was certainly tempered by a fear that it might make him ridiculous in the eyes of his friends. He told Conway that Madame Du Deffand was " an old blind debauchee of wit ".   In a letter to Gray in 1765 he described her as follows :

She was for a short time the mistress of the Regent. Is now very old and stone blind. She goes to operas, plays, suppers and Versailles. Gives suppers twice a week : has everything new read to her : makes new songs and epigrams admirably : corresponds with Voltaire and dictates charming letters to him or anybody : and laughs both at the clergy and the philosophers.

She certainly had wit, and it may have been in answer to a question as to what she thought of the infamous Jeanne Dubarry that she replied, " Une nymphe tirée des plus fameux monastères de Cythère et de Paphos "—a very elegant and typically eighteenth-century way of describing the profession to which La Dubarry belonged. The truth was that Horace Walpole never minded in the least what ridicule he cast upon others, but could not bear to be laughed at himself.

While endeavouring to judge him fairly and dispassionately, crediting him to the utmost with his love for Conway, his friendship for Selwyn, and his kindness to Madame Du Deffand in her blind old age ;

while attributing his effeminacy to the effeminate
society in which he moved and his mania for everything Italian ; and while extenuating such irritating
qualities as may have been due to a weakly constitution, we reach, all the same, the inevitable conclusion
that Macaulay's criticism (for once) was very near the
truth.

Besides being one of the most effeminate, he was
surely one of the most selfish of men. If he cared to
do a thing he did it, regardless of its effect upon other
people. If it caused him too much trouble and brought
him no personal gratification, he left it undone. He
was continually satisfying his own petty desires—if,
indeed, he experienced anything in his life worthy of
being called a " desire " !

Above all, was he the delighted purveyor of every
little bit of scandal about all his most intimate friends
and acquaintances in addition to those whom he did
not know at all. Nor did it matter in the least to him
how much pain he caused, or what mischief he made,
as long as the scandal was amusing enough to include
in his letters or retail to his cronies by word of mouth.
Yet he had the effrontery to complain of Richard
Cambridge that " he would tell anybody the most
disagreeable news, rather than not be the first to
trumpet it ". This was humorous enough for one who
was always particularly anxious that his own correspondents should have the first-fruits of the scandals
of the town.

He was more jealous than the most jealous woman
—as witness his conduct in doing what he could to
prevent a marriage between Harry Conway and Lady
Caroline Fitzroy (in which he succeeded), lest Conway
should cease to care for him after marriage.

He was also more spiteful than the most spiteful woman. He never forgave a personal slight, real or imagined. He put on record for the diversion of scandal-mongers of a future generation (for he intended his letters to be given to the world, and more than once said they should be regarded in their proper light as newspapers) personal details of the private lives of men and women whose hospitality he had accepted and whom he had pretended to number among his closest friends. A *mauvaise langue* in a woman is bad enough ; but it seems to fit many of the sex, to go well with false hair, painted face and padded figure. In a man it is far worse. Male scandal-mongers are, or should be, " taboo " to all decent folk.

My Lady Townshend, as was to be expected in a lady of quality of those days, loved a dish of scandal ; many must have been the racy gossipings she had with the "Abbot" of Strawberry Hill. But hers was a more open nature than Walpole's, and though often bitterly sarcastic, she was far less malicious in her talk.

In his extreme old age, after he had succeeded to the Earldom of Orford, this contemner of women and selfish old intrigant proposed marriage to the two Miss Berrys, one after the other. They were young and attractive women, and Walpole was very kind to them in many ways ; but it is impossible even to hazard a guess at the reason which impelled him to invite them successively to be his countess. I have often wondered what the thoughts were of the first sister to whom he proposed when he made a similar offer to the other one !

Students of the social life of the eighteenth century owe much to Horace Walpole. Many of his historical works are valuable as written by a contemporary of the persons of whom they treat. His art catalogues and works on painting are excellent for reference, but his criticisms on art must be considered worthless, when one remembers that in writing on Sir Joshua Reynolds he said: "Mr. Reynolds seldom succeeds with women". Such an astonishing opinion delivered, as all his opinions were, in an *ex cathedra* manner, makes one recall that he was essentially a dilettante and collector of rubbish, with all the ignorance of such folk.

His novels (*Castle of Otranto* and *The Distressed Mother*), in the style of Mrs. Radcliffe—but a long way behind her in merit—are never read now; but his *Letters* are unique, a key which unlocks many a mystery of the Age of Wig and Hoop. A library is appreciably duller without them; they are read and re-read with many an inward chuckle, but frequently, so to speak, leave a nasty taste in the mouth, and one cannot help wondering how it was that he escaped the kicking which, according to our modern ideas, he must have so often and so richly deserved.

George Selwyn, one of the most devoted of all my Lady Townshend's set, was a very different sort of man from Horace Walpole. They were, however, firm friends all their lives, from school days at Eton in 1732 to that January day in 1791 when Walpole wrote to Miss Berry—

I am on the point of losing, or have lost, my oldest acquaintance and friend, George Selwyn, who was yesterday at the extremity . . . him I really loved, not only for his intimate wit, but for a thousand good qualities.

These words were perhaps as sincere as Walpole ever wrote. Though he had not as extravagant an admiration and deep affection for Selwyn as he had for Conway, he was really his friend, and so much should be placed to his credit.

Selwyn was at Eton with Walpole, Gray (the poet), Glynn (the celebrated physician), Conway and many others who made names for themselves in the social world of the day. He was a very extravagant youth, his father having to pay his debts over and over again. After Eton he entered at Hertford College, Oxford, becoming associate of such men as Richard Rigby and Sir Charles Hanbury Williams, the writer of lampoons. He left the university under a cloud. He was in fact expelled. He attempted to avoid the disgrace of an expulsion by taking his name off the books of the College, but his conduct was considered bad enough to deserve whatever disgrace could follow on the severe punishment of a formal expulsion carried out as publicly as possible, his name being, as usual, posted up everywhere within the jurisdiction of the university.

The cause of all this was really bad enough. It appears that at a wine-party in 1745 he produced a church chalice, and, filling it with wine, imitated the institution of the Eucharist, using Christ's words of consecration.

Some biographers of Selwyn seem to look upon this as a sort of young man's frolic, and try to make excuses for him; but it was too much for the university to swallow, and he was never allowed to return. Yet, it does not appear to have affected his career in after life, and certainly lost him no friends in the polite world. London society in those days had a most capacious maw and rejected no one who was well born, well dressed and amusing.

The Hell-Fire Club or " Society of Medmenham

Monks" is a case in point. This was an association which numbered among its members many who were gladly received in the best circles of society, but who were some of the worst debauchees of the day. They were twelve altogether, including Charles Churchill, the poet; John Wilkes, the demagogue (one of the most vicious and immoral men of all ages); Robert Lloyd, son of a master at Westminster School, a minor poet, who died in the Fleet Prison for debt; Sir Francis Dashwood, afterwards Lord Despencer, of the suite of Frederic Prince of Wales, who had had to flee Rome for horse-whipping the penitents taking part in the services on Good Friday in the Sistine Chapel; Bubb Doddington, afterwards Lord Melcombe; Lord Orford; Paul Whitehead, another minor poet (secretary of the society); Dr. Bates, M.D., of Aylesbury; John Hall Stevenson of Crazy Castle, Yorkshire; Thomas Potter, son of the Archbishop of Canterbury, a friend of Pitt; John Montague, fourth Earl of Sandwich, nicknamed " Jemmy Twitcher " (after a character in the *Beggars' Opera*), who gave his name to the article of food so called; Sir William Stanhope, second son of the Earl of Chesterfield; and Sir John Dashwood King, half-brother of Lord Despencer. Sterne, author of *Tristam Shandy*, belonged to the same set, but does not appear to have been one of the monks. These rakes, living only for pleasure and the gratification of their passions, rented a large house on the banks of the Thames, which had been at one time a convent of Cistercian monks. Over the entrance was the motto of Rabelais from the Abbey of Thelma—" Fay ce que voudras ". At one end of the chapter-room was a statue of Harpocrates, the Egyptian god of silence; at the other a figure of Angerona, a

Roman divinity with finger on lips. At the end of the passage as you entered was the motto : " Aude hospes, contemnere opes ". The old Abbey Church was restored and painted with licentious emblems. The ancient cellars were filled with the choicest wines. Meetings were held twice a year, lasting about a week. In the grounds of the abbey there was a small temple dedicated to the goddess Cloacina (divinity of drains !), inscribed " This Chapel of Ease was founded in the year 1760 ". Within this little temple, and facing the entrance, was the inscription :

> Aeque pauperibus prodest : locupletibus aeque :
> Aeque neglectus pueris senibus nocebit.

which may perhaps be freely translated thus :

> Alike it benefits the poor, alike the rich.
> Alike, when slighted, it will harm youths and old men.

In this blasphemous caricature of a conventual establishment the most scandalous orgies were said to be carried on, assisted by the mistresses of the members and loose women from the town, though actual proof of the fact is wanting. Generally, there was a mock celebration of the rites of the Catholic Church, but always there was a deliberate parody of sacred things carried out with the fixed idea of bringing religion into contempt. One of the " properties " of the place, which I have heard is still in existence, was a large portrait of Sir Francis Dashwood, dressed in the habit of a Franciscan monk, kneeling before a nude Venus with a chalice in his hand.

John Wilkes was a leading spirit of the association, and from his notoriously immoral life one cannot be surprised at the fact; but it is more curious to note in such a *galère* the name of Bubb Doddington, who is generally set down as nothing worse than a conceited fool. He also belonged to my Lady Townshend's set.

Those interested in such matters may be referred to *Chrysal : or the Adventures of a Guinea*, a novel of the period, by one Charles Johnston, now practically forgotten, and perhaps too outspoken for modern readers, even in these days of prurient sex novels. It should, however, be added that Johnston's account of the Medmenham monks is much discredited; and as he was not a member of the society his facts are probably founded a good deal on hearsay alone. A weaker imitation of the Medmenham monks existed during the Regency, to which the Prince Regent and some of his choice associates belonged. It was known as the " Harry the Fifth " Club, or sometimes as " The Gang ". The principal feature of The Gang appears to have been an extreme licence in all kinds of sensual enjoyment.

Selwyn succeeded to his father's estates, his elder brother having predeceased him. He obtained afterwards the post of Surveyor-General, and also got for himself a sinecure in connection with the island of Barbados.

He was connected with the Townshends by marriage, his sister Mary having married the well-known " Tommy Townshend ", half-brother to the husband of Ethelreda Townshend. His friendship for my Lady was a lasting one. This is proved over and over again in the *Walpole Letters* and in his own correspondence with the Carlisle family. It was a much finer friendship than that of Walpole. Horace very seldom cared for any one except in so far as they could in some way contribute to his own pleasure or advantage. On the other hand, it is not too much to say that George Selwyn was her constant visitor and devoted admirer to the day of her death. He was eleven years her junior, but survived her only three years, dying in 1791 at the age of seventy-two.

In a letter to Lady Carlisle in 1786, when he was sixty-seven and my Lady Townshend was seventy-eight years of age, he says :

The Parliament, I find, does not meet for business till after the Christmas holidays, and that makes me afraid that, till then, I shall have no parties but with my immortal friend Lady Townshend.

Five years previously he had told Lord Carlisle that he was going with Mie-Mie to the opera in Lady Townshend's box to see the famous dance of " Medea and Jason ", and that my Lady Townshend herself had " made the party ". This astonishing old lady was seventy-three years of age when she made that party, and we may be sure enjoyed it every bit as much as Mie-Mie did. Mie-Mie was the pet name given by Selwyn to Maria Fagnani, the reputed daughter of the Marchese and Marchesa Fagnani. Selwyn, however, believed himself to be her father. He adopted her and had her educated at a very fashionable school at Campden House, Kensington, an old Jacobean mansion built in 1612, the residence of the Princess Anne before she was Queen, afterwards allotted to the young Duke of Gloucester, her only son who survived infancy. It was the scene of many smart amateur theatricals in Victorian days, and was destroyed by fire in 1862.

Old Q., the Duke of Queensbury, also believed himself to be the favoured lover of the Marchesa Fagnani, and therefore the father of Mie-Mie, who eventually inherited £33,000 from Selwyn and £150,000 from the Duke.

In 1798 she married the Earl of Yarmouth, famil-iarly known as " Red Herring ", from the colour of his hair and the chief industry of the town from which he took his title. He succeeded his father as Marquis of Hertford, and has been immortalised by Disraeli in *Coningsby* and by Thackeray as Becky Sharpe's Marquis of Steyne.

Mie-Mie Fagnani's life was a very miserable one in spite of her great wealth, and she left Lord Hertford to wander Europe with a Frenchman, Marshal An-droche, and bear children, one of whom has been supposed to be Sir Richard Wallace, whose widow left such a magnificent art collection to the Nation. There is a portrait of her by Romney, showing her to have been a very beautiful woman.

Selwyn was the recognised cavalier of my Lady Townshend on many occasions. When that curious personality, " Mlle." the Chevalier D'Éon, was in London, Selwyn wrote to Lord Carlisle :

Mlle. D'Éon goes to France in a few days, she is now in her *habit de femme* : in black silk and the diamonds which she received from the Empress of Russia when she was in the army and at her Court as Minister. A German of her acquaintance has promised Lady Townshend to contrive that she and I shall have a sight of her before she goes.

This D'Éon, or, to give him his full name, Chevalier Charles Geneviève, Louis Auguste André Timothée D'Éon de Beaumont, deserves a few lines to himself. He was really a man, living as a man for the first forty years of his life—captain of dragoons, doctor of civil and common law, barrister, ambassador extra-ordinary and minister plenipotentiary. Suddenly he assumed female garb and called himself " La Chevalière D'Éon ", and became engaged to the witty Caron de

Beaumarchais, author of the *Marriage de Figaro*. His portrait as a woman was painted by Angelica Kauff- mann, his miniature as a woman by Cosway, his portrait as a man in uniform by Hugener. At the time he was seen by Lady Townshend in London he was probably living in his own house in Brewer Street, Golden Square, for we hear of a dinner given by him there in 1777, among the guests being Bach, Cramer and the two Angelos. The younger Angelo, then a boy, describes him in his *Reminiscences* as " a lusty dame, dressed in black silk, with a head-dress in rose toupet, and laced cap, a diamond necklace, long stays and an old-fashioned stomacher ".

A week after that dinner party he left London *as a man*, arrayed in his red and green dragoon uniform, with the cross of St. Louis glistening on his breast. Several years later—three years after the death of my Lady Townshend; that is, in 1791—he is again in London as a woman, as seen by a note he wrote to the first Marquis Townshend :

Mlle. D'Éon est bien fâchée de ne s'être point trouvée chez elle quand Milord Marquis de Townshend lui a fait l'honneur de passer. Depuis ce tems, elle a été incommodée. Sans cela, elle aurait été lui présenter ses respectes et à Milady. Si Milord a la bonté de lui faire dire le jour et l'heure qu'elle peut le voir, elle se rendra avec empressement ; l'homme qui garda la porte de Milord dit à toutes le (*sic*) personnes qu'il ne connoît pas que Milord n'y est pas.

Many wagers were made as to the sex of this individual. Large deposits were made in banks for these bets ; but no bet could be decided, as D'Éon always refused to be examined in the presence of witnesses.

He eventually died in London in the dress of a

LE CHEVALIER D'ÉON
(in female attire)
From a miniature of the period

woman, only to be discovered by doctors after his death that he was really a man !

Hannah More met D'Éon once and said of her (or him) : " She is sure to be a phenomenon in history : and, as such, a great curiosity. But one D'Éon is enough, and one slice of *her* quite sufficient ! "

Both George III. and Queen Charlotte received D'Éon very graciously as a man ; but the story that was afterwards spread about concerning his intrigue with that very proper person, Queen Charlotte, and which rested entirely on the assertion of a biographer, Gaillardet, has been conclusively proved to have no foundation.*

To return to George Selwyn and my Lady. It is a rather pleasant picture which these two friends make in their old age. She is not happy till she gets all his news ; she wishes to see him, does see him, almost daily. She expects him to keep a friendly eye on her favourite grandson, Jack Townshend, who is to inherit all her property. He dines constantly in the Privy Garden, and is the most intimate of all the intimates who meet there in the evening. The *bon viveur*, the acknowledged wit of the day, welcome in every house and in every club, gives up all other feasts and refuses all other invitations so that she shall not be disappointed.

From Almack's, in 1774, he writes : " There was a turtle to-day, but I dined upon a haunch of venison at Lady Townshend's with her two grandsons ".

A year or two before her death he says : " I dine

* See an interesting memoir by Mr. Ernest Vizetelly called, *The True Story of the Chevalier D'Éon, his experiences and his metamorphoses in France, Russia, Germany and England, told with the aid of State and Secret Papers.* The book is rarely met with, but may be consulted at the British Museum, and is full of curious interest.

to-day at Lady Townshend's with Williams, Lord Dudley, General Vernon and Jack. It is a kind of *anniversaire*. Williams furnishes half a doe ".

Whenever my Lady received a present of venison she sent for Selwyn to come and help to eat it; or so it would appear from the references which abound. The Williams referred to above was probably Gilly Williams (George James Williams), fourth son of W. P. Williams, law reporter, M.P. for a Shropshire borough, and uncle of Lord North, through whom he obtained a post in the Excise worth £500 a year. He was a celebrated wit of the day, and formed one of the famous *partie carrée*, consisting of himself, George Selwyn, Duke Edgcumbe and Horace Walpole, who met at Strawberry Hill at stated periods of the year, and constituted what Walpole called his " out-of-town " party. He married Lady Diana Coventry and died in 1805 at the age of eighty-six.

Who but Selwyn would have dared to chaff my Lady about her admirers, her religion, her Jacobitism, and her politics ? Not spitefully, like Walpole, who reported every bit of spicy scandal he could get hold of, adding his own malicious comment; but banteringly, or with that quiet demureness, as we should say, " without moving a muscle of his countenance ", which imparted an extra keenness to the edge of his wit.

A marked idiosyncrasy of Selwyn's was his morbid delight in all the details connected with death, funerals and corpses. This has been denied by some of his biographers, but is too well established on incontrovertible evidence to be disbelieved. He loved to see a hanging, to note how the victim behaved on the scaffold, and to view the corpse after death. When

Damiens was sentenced in 1757 to be broken on the
wheel for his attempt to assassinate Louis XV., Selwyn
went over to Paris on purpose to see the sentence
carried into effect. Wraxall says he was the first among
the crowd to be repulsed by the executioners for
approaching too near the scaffold; but having informed
the person who opposed him that he had made the
journey from London solely with a view to be present
at the punishment and death of Damiens, the man
immediately caused the people to make way, exclaim-
ing : " Faites place pour Monsieur c'est un Anglais
et un amateur ".

When the first Lord Holland was on his death-bed
he was told that George Selwyn had called. " The
next time that Mr. Selwyn calls ", said the dying man,
" show him up. If I'm alive, I shall be glad to see him,
and if I'm dead, he'll be glad to see me " ! Walpole
was wont to declare that George never thought at all
but *à la tête tranchée*, and that when he went to have a
tooth drawn he told the man he would drop his
handkerchief for a signal.

Selwyn's wit was celebrated in his day, and his bons
mots were repeated on all sides. His biographer, Jesse,
has made a sort of collection of them, digging them
out of contemporary memoirs and letters. But they
do not bear the process at all well. When removed
from the context of time and place there is a decided
air of unreality about the person uttering them, and
considerable banality in the utterances themselves.

What are we to think of the man himself? Like
his friend, Lady Townshend, we cannot judge him
by the standards of the twentieth century. His great
love for all children is one point in his favour. He
was devotedly attached to many small persons of his

time, not only to Mie-Mie, whom he looked upon as his own child, but equally to the children of the Carlisle and Coventry families. In their way, his friendships were sincere. He was certainly fond of Walpole, and a very faithful friend of my Lady Townshend. For the rest, though not so selfish as Walpole, he was also a type of a supremely selfish age, living to amuse himself, to dress showily, to drink deeply, to gamble heavily—a lounger of the eighteenth century.

He was rather a heavy-looking and by no means handsome man, if his appearance may be judged from the pastel by Hamilton in the collection of Lord Carlisle.

# CHAPTER VIII

## SOME OF MY LADY TOWNSHEND'S WOMEN FRIENDS

The Countess of Harrington (*née* Fitzroy) : her passion for hand-some Harry Conway : ladies of Mrs. Warren's profession : Lady Vane ; her love for soldiers : Lady Orford ; her marriage to Mr. Shirley : Keith's Chapel in Mayfair : Fleet marriages and Fleet parsons : Kitty Edwin : the " preachings " at the Countess of Huntingdon's.

ONE OF HER LADYSHIP'S most intimate women friends was that fascinating and typical lady of quality, Lady Caroline Fitzroy, eldest daughter of the second Duke of Grafton, and great-granddaughter of Charles II., who in 1746 married Viscount Petersham, eldest son of the first Earl of Harrington. In later years, as Countess of Harrington, she disputed the leadership of " the Coterie " and the premiership of the lively dowagers with my Lady Townshend herself.

These two brilliantly handsome and audaciously witty women were cousins in a somewhat remote degree. Lady Townshend's grandmother had been Audrey Villiers, daughter of Viscount Grandison in the peerage of Ireland, and Lady Harrington's great-grandmother had been Audrey Villiers's cousin, Barbara Villiers, who became the mistress of Charles II. as the notorious Duchess of Cleveland. The ad-mixture of Irish blood in my Lady Townshend's veins would, in the opinion of many, account for much of

her wit and for a good deal of her unconventionality.
Lady Harrington was witty too, and twice as un-
conventional. When it is realised that, prior to her
marriage with Lord Harrington's son, these two were
constant companions in the rush and excitement of
the life of a person of quality, it can be well imagined
that startling adventures were sometimes the result.

They are said to have quarrelled every year, but
always made it up on the spot. Though Lady Harrington was indeed a notorious woman in more ways than
one, due allowance, as in my Lady Townshend's case,
must be made for the tainted sources of much of the
scandalous tales that have come down to us.

Walpole pulls her to pieces in his letters over and
over again; but no woman's character was safe at his
hands, at any rate not before the latter years of his
life, when old age seems to have somewhat blunted the
point of his spiteful pen.

In early life she conceived a violent passion for
handsome Harry Conway, who was Horace Walpole's
first cousin, their mothers having been both daughters
of old Alderman Shorter. Conway, it is believed,
returned her affection, and they were actually engaged;
but he had only his pay as a young officer, and so they
agreed to part.

In a letter, apparently sincere, written in 1744,
Walpole also dissuaded him from the match, when his
advice was asked; while pretending to remain neutral,
he practically counselled the breaking off of the engage-
ment. One passage of this letter may be quoted as
showing an honest attachment on her side :

You never had fortune enough to make such a step at all
prudent : she loved you enough to be content with that : I can't
believe this change will alter her sentiments, for I must do her

the justice to say that it is plain she preferred you, with nothing, to all the world. I could talk upon this head, but I will only leave you to consider without advising you on either side, these two things : whether you think it honest to break off with her after such engagements as yours (how strong I don't know), after her refusing very good matches for you, and show her that she must think of making her fortune : or whether you will wait for her till some amendment in your fortune can put it in your power to marry her.

Two years after the despatch of this letter Lady Caroline married the fop, Lord Petersham ; and eight years later, in 1754, there is another letter to Conway from Walpole about the same lady, having a good deal to say in her disfavour, and enlarging on it as follows :

I fear there is too much truth in what you have heard of your old mistress. When husband, wife, lover and friend tell everything, can there be but a perpetual fracas ? My dear Harry, how lucky you was [1] in what you escaped, and in what you have got.[2] People do sometimes avoid, not always, what is most improper for them, but they do not afterwards always meet with what they most deserve.

He lost no opportunity of congratulating Harry Conway at having escaped marriage with Lady Caroline. In 1761 he cautioned him against allowing Lady Ailesbury to go to Brunswick, adding that he might

[1] " Was " is often found for " were " in the eighteenth century and before. It has the sanction of Vanbrugh, Addison and Pope, to say nothing of Walpole and Mrs. Delany. Count Bassett, in *The Provok'd Husband*, asks " Was you at White's this morning sir ? " Examples could be multiplied indefinitely. But towards the middle of the century " were " became the correct form. Miss Polly Wilkes, daughter of the notorious demagogue John Wilkes, wrote " you was " in a letter to her father, and that old libertine who, with all his vices, loved his daughter, corrected her very prettily in his reply, saying, Not " you was ", if you please, but " you were ". The phrase is not " you is " but " you are . . . a charming girl ! "

[2] Conway got for wife the widow of the third Earl of Ailesbury. She was a daughter of General Campbell (afterwards fourth Duke of Argyll) and the lovely Mary Bellenden. Her father was one of the most intimate friends of my Lady Townshend, though he did lead the attack against Prince Charlie in the '45. *See* Chapter XI. for a letter of his to my Lady.

have had a wife who would not have thought it so terrible to fall into the hands (or arms) of hussars. And all this time he was rattling about town in the company of my Lady Caroline and pretending to be the best of friends.

She was a young woman, particularly bright and charming. Walpole thought her " gloriously handsome ", and speaks of her, Lady Euston and Lady Conway as the three beauty Fitzroys.

In 1755 she appeared at a masquerade, " powdered with diamonds and still handsome ". Six years later she was at the coronation of George III., " covered with all the diamonds she could borrow, hire or seize " (Walpole says she borrowed them of actresses), " and with the air of a Roxana,[3] the finest figure at a distance ". She appears to have been extravagantly fond of diamonds and blazed in them in and out of season.

As Countess of Harrington she lived in Stable Yard near the Royal Palace of St. James's, and was a great hostess and leader among persons of quality. Her Sunday parties were celebrated, and she may be said to have been the originator of Sunday suppers, discountenanced afterwards by the decorum of the Victorian social code, but flourishing now more than ever in a less hypocritical age.

She was an inveterate gambler, and her Sunday card-parties were exceptional because, although there was a law against gambling on Sundays, she was exempt as living within the precincts of a royal palace.

Very gay these parties must have been, an added attraction being the presence of her four beautiful daughters, who married respectively the Earl of Sea-

---

[3] Roxana, rival of Statira, wife of Alexander the Great, in a popular play by Lee, called *Alexander the Great ; or the Rival Queens*.

forth, Earl of Sefton, Earl of Barrymore and Lord Foley.

Every one in society went there, as it was one of the few places on Sunday night where the law allowed you to enjoy yourself. In the *Sunday Rambler* there is an account of a visit paid to all the tea gardens of the town, and a note is made of a string of fashionable equipages in the Mall which were "evidently on their way to Lady Harrington's rout".

Casanova was at one of these parties in 1763. He writes in his *Memoirs* :

J'avais une lettre de recommandation pour Lady Harrington qui recevait le Dimanche. Je savais le jeu autorisé chez elle ce jour-là, parce qu'elle habitait St. James Park qui se trouve placé sous la jurisdiction royale. Dans tout autre endroit il est rigoreusement défendu de jouer le Dimanche et même de faire de la musique. Cependant les tavernes et les mauvais lieux sont ouverts ce jour-là comme dans la semaine, et les bons Anglais peuvent s'amuser partout à leur aise excepté dans l'intérieur de la famille. Milady Harrington était une femme de quarante ans au moins, qui s'en donnait trente-quatre : on la citait pour ses aventures galantes : elle n'était plus belle mais elle avait quelques restes. Elle me présenta son époux, et ses quatre filles, toutes quatres nubiles et assez jolies.

At her house at Petersham, near Richmond, she also entertained lavishly, giving great card-parties and very late dinners, which Selwyn said were as late as her compassion. That same candid friend of her ladyship told Lord Carlisle that her peculiarity of character was more displayed at Petersham than in London, but that people thought it was only like a woman of quality, and would imitate her if they could; that they desired to cultivate her because she was a woman of quality, and at the same time were shocked to death with her *propos libres et brouillés avec la pudeur*.

My Lady Harrington had parties in town as well as suppers at home. She once assembled a brilliant little company "at an alehouse on the Ranelagh Road", near the Pimlico end of the present Ebury Street, which was called, like so many other similar places, "The Spring Garden", and there they supped off what Selwyn pronounced to be a " very good turtle ". He gives also a list of the company. " Lord and Lady Harrington, two of her daughters, Mrs. Boothby, Richard from his quarters at Hampton Court, Craggs, Barker, Langlois and myself." Her ladyship would have been about sixty years old at that time.

In 1768, when the King of Denmark was on a visit to England, my Lady Harrington made a dead set at him. He had the reputation of being very generous and fond of giving presents. Ladies of fashion had their private debts to pay then as now, and were often not too particular, then as now, as to where the money came from. Lady Harrington's attentions to the Danish King did not, we may be sure, pass unnoticed in those censorious days. Lady Mary Coke noted in her journal : " Lady Harrington, it is remarked, pays him particular attention. She met him upon the road, and followed him from Ranelagh to Lady Hertford's."

From a worldly point of view she was quite a good mother to her daughters, sometimes even assuming a most matronly and proper air as their chaperon.

A certain Mrs. St. John, wife of General St. John, and generally known as Mrs. St. Jack, once wanted to take one of them to a ball without her mother; but my Lady Harrington, even when an old woman, always refused to be left out of any gaiety, and would not let her go. Mrs. St. John argued that if the girl went to the opera without her mother she might surely go to a private dancing; but Lady Harrington, instead of storming at her in her usual manner, replied in the softest voice: " Mrs. St. John, if you *could* have a child, I am sure you would think as I do " ! Walpole remarks on this to Mann: " Imagine this addressed to a porpoise covered with flowers and feathers ". She dreaded death exceedingly, but in the end died very suddenly from a fall on the staircase, in 1784, four years before her cousin, Lady Townshend.

The circle of her lovers was a very wide one; she once fell very much in love with James McLean (or Maclaine), a notorious highwayman, and when he was arrested and lodged in Newgate she paid him a visit in his prison cell. This McLean was the son of an Irish Dean, and his brother was a Calvinist minister in a good position at The Hague. He had been a grocer in Welbeck Street, but on the death of his wife, of whom he was very fond, he took to the road with a friend who was an apothecary. He was captured in 1750 through selling a rich laced waistcoat to a pawnbroker, who afterwards offered it to the actual owner for sale. McLean was a tall, very handsome man, with all the airs of a fine gentleman. He had a lodging in St. James's Street when in town, and was well known as a frequenter of Button's Coffee-House in Russell Street. He was certainly a bold and successful highwayman, frequently waylaying and robbing persons of the highest quality — Horace Walpole *inter alios*. He seems to have eluded the runners for a long time, but came to the usual end of such gentry, and quitted the world " by the steps and the string " at last. Like most highwaymen he was a popular hero, and after his death broadsides and Catnach ballads

celebrated his exploits, one of which has two verses
as follows :

Ye Smarts and ye Jemmies, ye Ramillie Beaux
With golden-cocked hats, and with silver-laced clothes,
Who by wit and invention your pockets maintain,
Come pity the fate of poor Jemmy Maclaine,
> Derry down derry, etc.

He robb'd folks genteelly, he robb'd with an air,
He robb'd them so well that he always took care
My lord was not hurt and my Lady not frighted,
And instead of being hanged, he deserved to be knighted !
> Derry down derry, etc.

My Lady Harrington was as bold and outspoken
in her loves and hates as was my Lady Townshend,
but one scruple is recorded of her which certainly
reads rather oddly in these days. She piqued herself
upon observing strictly one point of honour, viz.,
never to be false to her lord's bed when she was
breeding by him. This choice example of prudishness
comes of course from Walpole, who inserted it in one
of his books in a marginal note.

Lady Harrington's passion for the good-looking
Harry Conway had evidently been the talk of the
town and not confined to the *beau monde* either. A
certain Mrs. Comyn, described as an elderly gentlewoman, but who really was of Mrs. Warren's profession, had her house in Air Street nearly pulled
about her ears one night. She said it was the doing
of my Lady Caroline Fitzroy, who had given the mob
ten guineas to demolish her house " because her
ladyship fancies I get women for Colonel Conway ".
How they were all mixed up in those days of the
Georges ! Ladies of fashion and ladies of pleasure—
ladies of high-sounding names and titles and ladies

with no titles to any name at all. "Mother Needham", who lived in Park Place, St. James's Street, in the midst of clubland and surrounded by residences of "the nobility and gentry", was another of the same breed as Mrs. Comyn. She was more than once convicted of keeping a disorderly house, and had to stand in the pillory, from the effects of which she died. Pope gives her a line or two in the *Dunciad*, and there is a note which reads delightfully:

She was a matron of great fame, and very religious in her way: whose constant prayer it was that she might get enough by her profession to leave it off in time to make her peace with God. This, however, was not granted to her, as she died from the effects of her exposure in the pillory.

But they all lived in the same quarters of the town, and seemed to be in the same set and to know each other quite well personally. In this we seem to have improved in the twentieth century; or is it that we manage things better, are more reticent, more discreet? In those days, in the world of fashion, there was little discretion and no reticence; and Walpole begs Montagu when he comes to town to visit "the elderly gentlewoman", as he assures her "she has infinite humour".

In Georgian days the taverns were dirty untidy places, the best of them not to be compared for a moment with the gorgeous palace restaurants of to-day. But it was the custom for ladies to have supper-parties of their own at these places and invite their friends, men and women, just as is done in the big hotels and restaurants of to-day.

To such taverns did my Lady Vane, another contemporary of my Lady Townshend, invite her soldier friends. This lady must not be confounded with her namesake, Miss Vane, a lady of very similar tastes and character, daughter of Lord Bernard and maid of honour of Caroline of Anspach, wife of George II. Frederick Prince of Wales fell in love with this young lady. Warburton tells us in his quaint way that the world first became acquainted with the affair by the birth of a son at St. James's Palace, who was publicly christened in 1732 with the name of Fitz-Frederick Vane! She was satirised in innumerable pamphlets and ballads under the soubriquets of Vanessa, Vanella, etc. The royal seducer tired of her after he had taken up with Lady Archie Hamilton, and the boy never grew to manhood.

But Lady Vane was not connected officially with the Court. She was a nymph who cared only for soldiers as lovers, and was much more of a free-lance in her doings with them than any of her sisters of the same set. She had no blushes for her own misdeeds, and actually gave Smollett materials for an interlude in his novel of *Peregrine Pickle*, which, under the title of " Memoirs of a Lady of Quality ", is neither more nor less than the story of her own life.

She was the daughter of a South Sea director named Hawes, and married, first Lord William Hamilton, son of the fourth Duke of Hamilton, and secondly, Viscount Vane (caricatured as " The Nosegay Maca-roni "), an officer in the Guards, madly and foolishly in love with his own wife and always ready to condone her worst misdeeds and begin the honeymoon all over again. But she constantly left him to live openly with other men (generally soldiers), with whom she would disappear for more or less protracted periods.

On such occasions her lord would sometimes go so far as to advertise for her in the public prints.

He was ready to do anything for her. She was a very extravagant woman and always in need of large sums of ready money. When not able to get as much as she required from her husband she left him and took up with some one else for the time being. Walpole told Mann that the Duke of Newcastle gave Vane £60,000 to cut off the entail of the Newcastle estates (Lord Vane's mother was sister and co-heir of the Duke), and adds, " The fool immediately wrote to his wife to beg she would return to him from Lord Berkeley, that he had got so much money and that *now* they might live comfortably : she is at Lord Berkeley's house whither go divers after her ".

This was the fourth Earl of Berkeley, a very handsome soldier of the type that my Lady Vane never could resist, and a great friend also of my Lady Townshend's. She certainly fascinated all kinds of men, though, as we have shown, confined her favours to soldiers usually. She was nicknamed a " Living academy of love-lore ". People sometimes pitied her for being tied to the " Nosegay Macaroni ", though the tie might be of the slightest. Yet he was, if weak as regards his wife, an honourable man and a fine soldier, especially mentioned for gallant conduct at Fontenoy. He died in 1789, one year after his wife, and the title died with him. An obituary notice in the *Gentleman's Magazine* states that nothing could induce him to withdraw his protection from his wife, and though obliged at one period of his life to submit, on her account, to much financial embarrassment, being compelled at one time to live within the precincts of the King's Bench, he supported her with a noble liberality. Such devotion to a woman is beyond the understanding of a man like Walpole. Hence he calls him fool.

My Lady Vane in her passion for soldiers or men of a military type was in no way different from gay ladies of all ages. Colonel Russell, writing to his wife from Ghent in 1742, says :

The greatest beauty we have here has followed us from England, which is Lady Vane, who arrived here last Monday night, and in reality has followed the Brigade of Guards, which as soon as she is tired of, intends to proceed to Brussels. She has no woman with her and walks about each evening with an officer each side of her.

The soldiers of that age, both officer and private, were generally a very dissolute lot. General Wolfe complained of those under his command, that the officers were loose and profligate and the soldiers very devils. But women of the time, like the women of all times, loved the soldier man, and my Lady Vane was as proud as any modern nursemaid when walking down the street with one on each side of her, " in all the glory of their scarlet shag ".

One of her lovers was certainly, however, a civilian. This was the notorious John Wilkes, that ugly, squint-eyed, dissolute patriot whose boast it was that it never took him very long to make a woman forget his face ! He was in exile in Paris, hiding from the English officers of justice, when my Lady Vane was also there.

Lady Mary Wortley Montagu of course had her say about my Lady Vane. She wrote to that arch-gossip, Lady Pomfret, in 1738, saying :

Lady Vane is returned hither in company with Lord Berkeley, and went with him in public to Crauford, where they remain as happy as love and youth can make them. I am told that, though she does not pique herself upon fidelity to any man (which is but a narrow way of thinking), she boasts that she has always been true to her nation, and, notwithstanding foreign attacks, has always reserved her charms for the use of her own countrymen.

She was of course in my Lady Townshend's set, her husband being a cousin of the Townshends. She died in the same year (1788), but my Lady Townshend was a leader of fashion even in her old age, and the other had sunk into obscurity years before. The latter part of her life must have been very sad. She lost the use of her legs long before she was confined to the bed in which she lay many years more before she died.

In a copy of the fifth edition of *The Abbey of Kilhampton* there are some annotations in the handwriting of a contemporary. The following is one of these marginal notes, and refers to my Lady Vane :

She died a great penitent, and tried to reconcile herself to Popery, that she might have received Extreme Unction. She endeavoured to make her acquaintance believe that she possessed an excellent heart, but it was a false and rotten one : and if her heart had been good, her other conduct might have been in some measure overlooked. I was present when she came home to her lord big with child by another man. . . . Lord Berkeley settled £800 a year upon her, which she returned when she left him : yet she lived to be denied the loan of twenty guineas from the noble lord when she wanted bread, and was obliged to be content with my purse which contained only four or five, but I always despised her after she gave Peregrine Pickle to Lord Vane to read. . . . He died mad, but after her, and she had lived forty years praying for his death.

There was another of my Lady's friends, who was, as one might say, " no better than she should be ". This was my Lady Orford, *née* Margaret Rolle, the wife of Baron Walpole, afterwards created Earl of Orford. Thus she was a sister-in-law of Horace Walpole, who was not at all fond of her, and compared her to the notorious Lady Vane, and even to Moll Flanders of Defoe's novel. She quarrelled with her husband and separated from him, travelling in Italy with Lady Pomfret, a typical gossip of the day but a far more respectable dame than she was herself. They found themselves in Florence at the same time as Horace Walpole and the poet Gray. My Lady Mary Wortley Montagu was also on the Arno then—"An old foul, tawdry, painted, plastered personage", Walpole calls her, "with greasy black locks that hang loose, never combed or curled, and old mazarine blue wrapper that gapes open and discovers a canvas petticoat". She must have been rather a trial to Lady Orford, who, although she had youth and cleanliness on her side, was sadly handicapped by the brilliance of Lady Mary's conversation, being but a dull woman herself. Add to this that they were both in love with the same man at one time and used to quarrel over him as a partner at the assemblies.

In after years my Lady Mary, with an assumption of virtuous propriety which would be very amusing were it not so absurdly out of place, wrote to her husband on the subject of Lady Orford's marriage to young Mr. Shirley:

I am not surprised at Lady Orford's folly having known her at Florence; she made great court to me. She has parts and a very engaging manner. Her company would have amused me very much, but I durst not indulge myself in it, her character being in universal horror. I do not mean from her gallantries, which nobody troubles their heads with, but she had a collection of free thinkers that met weekly at her house to the scandal of all good Christians. She invited me to come to one of these assemblies, which I civilly refused not desiring to be thought of her opinions, not thinking it right to make a jest of ordinances that are (at least) so far sacred as they are absolutely necessary in all civilised governments : and it is being in every sense an enemy to mankind to endeavour to overthrow them.

My Lady Mary was certainly a typical woman of her day. She did not mind the " gallantries "—a euphemism for infidelities, intrigues and general loose-ness—for she liked to indulge in all that kind of thing herself; but her feelings as a Christian woman in a Christian age must on no account be outraged by mixing with freethinkers and immoral folk of that sort. The truth was she was not a little jealous of women younger and more attractive than herself, for the beauty and charm which had made of my Lady Mary Pierpoint a reigning toast were no longer apparent in the more elderly Lady Mary Montagu. So the marriage of my Lady Orford to young Mr. Shirley very much vexed her feminine soul, and she also wrote querulously and spitefully about it to her daughter, Lady Bute.

Though her love affairs were so notorious, my Lady Orford endeavoured to pose as a serious-minded woman, something of a bluestocking in short. She once expressed great concern that her son did not like Latin or Greek. If Coventry in his *Pompey the Little* has satirised my Lady Townshend in the char-acter of Lady Tempest, he most certainly had my Lady Orford in his mind when he drew the portrait of the learned Lady Sophister.

She was a terror to her relations, who were always heartily glad when she chose to remain in Italy, dread-ing her reappearance in England. She was equally a terror to Sir Horace Mann, British Minister at Florence; for she lived there more or less openly as the mistress of a Comte de Richecourt, who had much power at the Court of the Grand Duke. She was also somewhat of a terror to Horace Walpole himself, and his letters to Mann at one time were full of condolences on her account, and apologies for the extra trouble occasioned to his friend by the presence of his sister-in-law in the gossiping Italian city and for her open intrigue with de Richecourt.

When she became Countess of Orford, she intrigued incessantly to return to England and take up the proper position pertaining to her new rank. Walpole, in a flutter, writes to Mann :

> She is not arrived yet, but is certainly coming ; she has despatched several letters to notify her intention ; a short one to her mother saying—" Dear Madam, as you have often desired me to return to England, I am determined to set out, and hope you will give me reason to subscribe myself your most affectionate daughter ". The poor Signora Madre is in a terrible fright, and will not come to town till her daughter is gone again which all advices agree will be soon. Another letter is to my Lady Townshend telling her that as she knows her Ladyship's way of thinking, she does not fear continuance of her friendship. . . . My brother [4] is entirely obliged to you for all your notices about her, though he is very indifferent about her motions. If she happens to choose law (though on what foot no mortal can guess) he is prepared, having, from the first hint of her journey, feed every one of the considerable lawyers.[5] In short, this jaunt is as simple as all the rest of her actions have been hardy. Nobody wonders at her bringing no English servants with her ; they know, and consequently might tell, too much.

In a later letter he tells Mann she has arrived, and calls her mother a poor weak woman for offering her the use of her house.

On her way home she stopped at Hanover, where the King (George II.) then was. A newspaper of the day chronicled her arrival in its issue of July 11, 1745: " Lady Orford, who has spent several years in Italy, arrived here (*i.e.* Hanover), the 3rd, on her return to

---

[4] George, third Earl of Orford, Lord of the Bedchamber, and Ranger of Hyde and St. James's Parks. He died unmarried in 1791.

[5] A remarkable instance of how lawsuits could be satisfactorily settled in those days if only one's purse were long enough ; that is, if the statement were true. But one can never be quite sure that Horace is not setting down inventions of his own brain to amuse his correspondent. He had no scruples.

England and was graciously received by His Majesty."
Perhaps this was a *communiqué* of my Lady herself;
for the King afterwards declared publicly to his
ministers that he had been told of the great civilities
which he had been said to have shown her at Hanover;
that not only had he showed her no more than the
common civilities due to any English lady, but he
had never intended to take any particular notice of
her and had forbidden my Lady Yarmouth to do so.
As a fact, when she did get back to England, Lady
Yarmouth peremptorily refused to take her to the
Court, and she had to go with that accommodating
person, Lady Pomfret. This sounds odd to modern
ears; it is difficult for us to imagine an English
peeress presented on her marriage by so notorious a
royal mistress as was my Lady Yarmouth.

Walpole kept Mann *au courant* with the doings of
the lady whom they both detested so cordially. He
reported that she made little progress in popularity,
and that neither the protection of my Lady Pomfret's
prudery nor my Lady Townshend's libertinism did
her any service. He said that women stared at her
and thought her ugly and disagreeable, and what was
worse, men thought so too. He met her twice at my
Lady Townshend's, and noticed that she " dressed
English " and played whist.

In 1751 she married, *en secondes noces*, the Hon. S.
Shirley, son of the first Lord Ferrers, and later established a claim in her own right to the Barony of
Clinton and Say. But she soon separated from Mr.
Shirley, as she had from her other husband, and finally
adopted as " the companion of her peregrinations "
an Italian, Cavaliere Mozzi, to whom, at her death in
1781, she left the greater part of her fortune.

Her marriage to Mr. Shirley took place at that Mayfair Chapel presided over by the Rev. Alexander Keith, an accommodating divine of the period, famous, or infamous, for the number of marriages he celebrated between parties who had their own reasons for privacy.

In his chapel the young quakeress Hannah Lightfoot is said to have been married to Isaac Axford (as arranged by that great go-between, Miss Chudleigh, for the convenience of the young Prince George), only to be parted from him at the chapel door. Another of these marriages was the youngest of the beautiful Gunning sisters to the Duke of Hamilton.

On the other hand, he refused to get out of bed one early dawn when " Handsome Tracey " was decoyed into marrying the butterwoman's daughter, but sent the couple " over the way " to his brother instead. The bridegroom in that case was the notorious beau, Robert Tracey, great-grandson of the second Viscount Tracey. He is said to have destroyed himself by his vices before he had reached his thirtieth year.[6]

Keith advertised his profession in the most open manner possible. In the *Daily Advertiser* in 1753 appeared the following notice :

Mr. Keith's chapel in Mayfair, Park Corner, where the marriages are performed by virtue of a license on a crown stamp, and certified for a guinea, is opposite to the great chapel and within ten yards of it. The way is through Piccadilly, by the end of St. James's Street, down Clarges Street and turn on the left hand.

Keith was imprisoned in the Fleet for debt, and continued his marriages while there, and also, with the help of curates, at his Mayfair chapel. He was

---

[6] See *Notes and Queries* for 1908–9 for some particulars concerning this same Tracey, contributed by Mr. Horace Bleackley, who knows his eighteenth century so well.

perhaps the most notorious of all the " Chaplains of the Fleet ", marrying, it is said, as many as 170 couples in one day. Other well-known parsons of the same kind were Dr. Guynham (or Gainham), usually known as " The Bishop of Hell ", the Rev. J. Evans, the Rev. J. J. Flint, Edward Ashwell, Walter Wyatt, Peter Symson, D. Wigmore (who was convicted of selling liquor without a licence), and Starkey (who ran away to Scotland to escape a prosecution for bigamy). Burn in his *History of Fleet Marriages*, enumerates eighty-nine of these Fleet parsons by name, all of whom had neither cash, character, nor liberty to lose, and were always ready to pander to the demands of extravagance or vice. The notices in which these persons appealed for patronage were couched in much the same terms. A reference to one will suffice for all. Here is the notice of the Rev. Peter Symson:

G.R. At the true chapel, at the old Red Hand and Mitre, three doors up Fleet Lane, and next door to the White Swan, marriages are performed by authority by the Rev. Mr. Symson, educated at the University of Cambridge and late chaplain to the Earl of Rothes. *N.B.* Without imposition.

These marriages were sometimes solemnised at the chaplain's own lodgings, but mostly at the taverns, whose landlords styled themselves also " Keepers of Marriage Houses ". In this latter case the parson and the landlord divided the fee between them, the landlord generally acting as clerk.

Many well-born people, for one reason or another, took advantage of this lax state of affairs to be married in the Fleet.[7] Among them were Lord Abergavenny,

---

[7] It should perhaps be explained that the " Rules " or " Liberties " of the Fleet, within which these marriages were celebrated, were certain limits within which prisoners for debt could reside without fear of arrest. They were apparently also made use of by others, not prisoners, who were in danger

Hon. John Bourke (afterwards Lord Mayo), Lord Montagu (afterwards Duke of Manchester), Viscount Sligo, the Marquis of Annandale, and perhaps most notable of all, Henry Fox (afterwards the first Lord Holland). Horace Walpole, with that usual want of delicacy and taste which characterises his correspondence with Mann, wrote to him about this private marriage :

> Mr. Fox fell in love with Lady Caroline Lenox (eldest daughter of the Duke of Richmond), asked her and was refused, and stole her. His grandfather was a footman, her great-grandfather a king :—hinc illae lachrymae! All the blood royal have been up in arms. . . .

The allusion to " footman " is explained by the fact that Stephen Fox, the grandfather of Henry, had been a servant and very faithful follower of Charles I. up to the date of his murder, had followed Charles II. into exile, and had been rewarded by a baronetcy and a coat of arms. The lady was certainly the great-granddaughter of a king, as she was descended from the son of Charles II. and Louise de la Querouaille, the Duchess of Portsmouth. The petty soul of Walpole (what Mr. Austin Dobson has so aptly called his " Court-usher soul ") could not miss the opportunity of a thoroughly cattish remark written with a snigger, and received with delight by the other " Court-usher Horace " in Florence. When Lord Chancellor Hardwicke introduced his bill in 1753 for the suppression of these monstrous marriages, Henry Fox was among the most violent of his opponents ; but the bill passed by a large majority.

---

of arrest. These limits were well defined within the boundaries of certain streets, and as long as an arrested debtor, or one in danger of arrest, kept to the boundaries, he could not be proceeded against further.

The same sort of marriage was solemnised in the Mint and at the Savoy Chapel. The latter place did not come into use till after the passing of the Act in 1753. The proprietor of the Savoy was one Wilkinson (father of Tate Wilkinson so well known in the theatrical world), who fancied the law could not apply to him as the Savoy was extra-parochial. After marrying more than two thousand couples he thought it prudent to hand over the conduct of the ceremony to his curate Grierson. But Grierson was arrested and sentenced to fourteen years' transportation. Wilkinson surrendered himself later, in the hope of getting off altogether; but he got the same sentence, dying, however, before the convict ship left England.

Notebooks are still extant containing entries made by these old scoundrels. One such entry by Evans runs as follows :

Paid one shilling only. The bridegroom a boy of about 18 years of age, and the bride about sixty-five. They were brought in a coach, and attended by four θυμπινγ όρες (*sic*) as guests.

Another one reads :

Paid three shillings and sixpence, certificate one and sixpence ; it being pretty late, they lay here, and paid me one shilling for bed. (A kind girl.)

But the history of Fleet marriages with its mingled tragedy and comedy, is not to be lightly dismissed in a few words. Besant has made the iniquitous system the basis of one of his best novels—*The Chaplain of the Fleet*, and Burn's book is very full and complete from the purely historical point.

To return to my Lady Orford. She was in England with Mozzi in 1770, and both of them paid a visit to Lady Holland on a day that Walpole happened also

to be there. It is described in Horace's inimitable way
to Mann :

"I must write to you this very minute. I have just seen Lady
Orford and Cavalier Mozzi. I came to town this morning on
some business, and after dinner went to Holland House where
I was sitting with Lord and Lady Holland when the Countess
and her knight-errant were announced. Lady Holland was
distressed and offered to go down to them : I said, ' by no means,
it was quite a matter of indifference to me ; nay, I would rather
see her than not '. Up they came; we bowed and curtsied,
grew perfectly free immediately, and like two persons that are
well-bred, easy, and not much acquainted. She stayed a full hour,
we pronounced each other's names without any difficulty, and
when she took leave, for she sets out on Tuesday, she asked if
I had any orders for Paris. I find her grown much older, bent,
her cheeks fallen in, and half her teeth fallen out ; but much
improved in her manner and dress. The latter is that of other
old women, her face not flustered and heated as it used to be,
her impetuosity and eager eyes reduced within proper channels,
and none of her screams and exclamations left, though a good
deal of kissing remains at her entry and exit."

Lady Orford died in Pisa, an old woman, in 1781,
seven years before my Lady Townshend. Her son
erected a magnificent monument to her memory, with
the usual laudatory epithaph, in which she was said
to have been " universally lamented ". This provoked
an exclamation from Walpole, who wished that it had
been in Greek or some language that English sailors
would not be likely to understand ! Cunningham sums
her up as being as dissolute as Lady Mary Wortley
Montagu, without one particle of her wit.

In the early days of her married life my Lady
Townshend went about a good deal with a Miss or
Mrs.[8] Kitty Edwin. This was the lady with whom

---

[8] Unmarried ladies were often addressed as " Mrs." (or " Mistress ") in the
eighteenth century. Hannah More, who died in 1833, was probably the last
spinster to be thus addressed.

she had a famous quarrel at the Wells, of which some account has been already given. The quarrel must have created some little stir at the time among persons of quality, for both my Lady Mary Wortley Montagu and my Lady Hertford send a full description of the affair to the Countess of Pomfret, who appears to have been a chartered receiver of scandal. Some years later Mistress Kitty Edwin was reported to have turned Methodist. Perhaps she simply became one of the penitents encouraged by the Countess of Huntingdon, but in any case she seems to have dropped out of the circle of my Lady Townshend and her immediate intimates.

Of quite a different type was another of my Lady Townshend's dearest friends. This was the famous methodist Countess of Huntingdon, to whom some reference has already been made in the chapter dealing with the country spas. She was Lady Selina Shirley, a daughter of Earl Ferrers, and married the Earl of Huntingdon.

In her earlier years she moved much in Court circles and made many friendships which endured long after she had renounced the giddy pleasures of society and adopted a religious life. Sarah, Duchess of Marlborough, had been one of those friends of early days, and the old virago once wrote to her after many years to express regret that she had not heard a certain sermon of Mr. Whitfield's at St. Sepulchre's, which was said to have greatly pleased the Duchess of Ancaster, Lady Townshend and Lady Cobham. For my Lady Townshend was also a great crony of Countess Selina; and whatever may be said about her " eccentricities and her gallantries ", she was ever faithful to those who had once been her friends.

In her younger days Lady Huntingdon had been as fond of dress and display as any of her flightier friends, but in later life she became strictly religious in the puritanical sense, devoted to prayers and sermons —a dour old fanatic. After the renunciation of the world's delights she was known as the " Queen of the Methodists ", or, as Walpole has called her, the " Saint Teresa of the Methodists ", and she had certainly a most extraordinary vogue. At the date of her death, in 1791, the number of chapels belonging to " Lady Huntingdon's Connection " was said to have been as many as sixty-four.

This " Connection ", known by her name, was really a branch of the sect of Calvinistic Methodists, founded by George Whitfield after he had broken with Wesley on the subject of Predestination.

In spite of her dour ways and strict notions there must have been something fascinating about her. Elizabeth Montagu called her " a well-meaning fanatic ". Sarah Marlborough and my Lady Townshend both loved her.

In common with all fanatics, one of her great delights was to make converts to her own way of thinking—to " save souls ", as she would have put it ; and some very odd fish she appears to have landed in her net at times ! In a letter to Lady Hertford, included in the Russell-Astley collection, she says :

"I have seen Lady Archibald, Lady Pomfret, Lady Bath : these are the enquirers after truth, but I might hope their progress quicker than it is."

She might indeed sigh for quicker progress with the good ladies mentioned. If, as is probable, the Lady Archibald referred to is Lady Archibald Hamilton, daughter of the sixth Earl of Abercorn, who

SELINA, COUNTESS OF HUNTINGDON
From an engraving of the original picture by T. Russel

married a son of the third Duke of Hamilton, she was a royal mistress! My Lady Pomfret, though a great scandal-monger, was outwardly a more prudent dame; but my Lady Bath, *née* Miss Anna Gumley, and better known as Mistress Pulteney, was a woman of the loosest morals and lived more or less openly with the Earl of Cadogan.

The " Queen of the Methodists " was an aunt of that Earl Ferrers hanged at Tyburn in a silken shirt and with a silken rope for the murder of his servant. She visited him constantly while in prison awaiting execution, boring him sadly it is to be feared. She took on herself to beg the governor of the prison not to allow him to see his mistress, one Mrs. Clifford, of whom he was very fond, for she said that would be for him to " die in adultery ! "

# CHAPTER IX

## INTERMEZZO—DRESS OF LADIES OF QUALITY IN THE EIGHTEENTH CENTURY

Mysteries of fashion among ladies of quality : hoops and farthingales : stays and jumpers : petticoats, gowns and sacques : dress regulations at " the Bath " : a dress of Selina, Countess of Huntingdon and of Mrs. Delany : shopping in the eighteenth century : stuffs of the period : singular male shop assistants : toilette " levee " of a lady of quality : artificial aids for improving the figure : " négligées ", " trollopées " and aprons : hoods, cloaks and travelling dresses : shoes : the fantastic head-dresses of the time : *Poufs aux Sentiments* : a dust-yard and a farm-yard on a lady's head : the " opening " of a pouf after several weeks : rules for " conserving a head " : fashionable hairdressers of the day : introduction of feathers instead of poufs by Georgiana, Duchess of Devonshire : outcry against the " immorality " of using feathers : hats of the century : the calash : signalling to a lover by the colour of the hood : patches : muffs : a dressy nun : umbrellas : masks and vizards : fans : invariable variability of ladies' fashions : the fate of old wigs.

A WELL-INFORMED LADY of my acquaintance once said to me, not without a note of regret in her voice, that the best milliners and dressmakers, like the best cooks, were always to be found among the male sex. She did not attempt to account for this, but said it was an undoubted fact, instancing the names of Woerth, Doucet and others in Paris, and Redfern in London, to which she might have added Paul Poiret and Reville. The case of cooks is still less in·doubt. One has only to mention Carême, Vatel, Ude, Soyer, Francatelli (to take a few names at random), to realise that women have not taken the highest rank in a profession which one might have thought should have been pre-eminently theirs.

I am aware that nowadays there is a race of males who know all about the frills and furbelows of woman-kind, and can discourse fluently on crêpe de chine, marocain, georgette, diamanté, etc., all of which are veiled mysteries to me, but I have always regarded them as rather a race apart and not as the " common or garden " man.

I approach this " intermezzo ", therefore, with a certain amount of fear and trembling, as of one profaning the mysteries of Bona Dea, for it deals with ladies' toilettes, and all I know about them has been gathered from books on the subject. I do not pretend to expert knowledge, and must shelter myself behind works of reference and magazine articles, and such illustrations of fashions of the period as are to be found on the shelves of the British Museum and elsewhere.

The mere donning of a complete lady's toilette has been ever one of the great mysteries of all times and all countries. At the time when all female characters in plays were taken by young boys or men, the business of getting a youngster dressed for his part was a very serious one :

" It is five hours since I set a dozen maids to attire a boy like a nice gentlewoman : but there is such doings with their looking-glasses, such pinning, unpinning, setting, unsetting, forming and conforming, painting of blue veins and rosy cheeks : such a stir with combs, cascanets, purls, falls, squares, busks, bodices, scarfs, necklaces, carkonels, rabatoes, borders, tires, fans, palisadoes, puffs, ruffs, cuffs, muffs, pustles, fusles, partlets, frislets, bandlets, fillets, corslets, pendulets, amulets, annulets, bracelets, and so many ' lets ' that the poor lady of the toilet is scarce dressed to the girdle ; and now there is such calling for fardingales, kirtles, busk-points, shoe-ties and the like, that seven pedlars' shops, nay, all Stourbridge Fair, will scarcely furnish. A ship is sooner rigged than a nice gentlewoman made ready."

I may say that, to the mere man who ponders over the arcana of a lady's toilette, whether of the present or the past, two problems at once present themselves as insoluble :

1. Why do ladies of " ton " and fashion dress as Paris pleases ? I mean why do they await the models of the Parisian modistes before deciding on their new season's clothes, or even their style of attire—models which, I am credibly informed, are first " tried out " on the ladies of the half-world ?

2. Why do all ladies, once a fashion has come in, adopt it whether it suits them or not ? What is attractive on a young person cannot be suitable for an old one. The dress which sits well on a short, stout figure cannot become a lady who is tall and thin. Yet they must wear all the same, and are miserable if they cannot !

But enough of riddles. Let us get back to the eighteenth century and see what kind of clothes the sex did put on. They were changeable then—as it was in the beginning, is now, and ever shall be ! " Souvent femme varie—fol qui s'y fie ". But one item of dress seems to have lasted in one form or another all through the century. This was some kind of hoop, lineally descended from the farthingale of the Virgin Queen.

It had already appeared in the reign of good Queen Anne. Sir Roger de Coverley speaks of it as the new-fashioned petticoat, and he says that his great-great-grandmother, who may be supposed to have flourished somewhere about the spacious days of Elizabeth, appeared as if she stood in a large drum, " whereas the ladies now walk as if they were in a go-cart ".

These hoops were large frameworks, stuffed out

with cordage and stiffened with whalebone, and though they may have ceased to form part of everyday attire at the end of George II.'s reign, they were retained in full Court dress for many years later, to be again revived as a general part of every woman's dress (though in a somewhat changed form) as the crinoline of the Victorian era.

The hoop of 1760 was also made of whalebone with canvas over it, but took the shape of an elongated oval, very flat at front and back, drawn round the waist by a string and with a pocket-hole at the side. Cane was afterwards substituted for whalebone. The hoop shown lying on the floor in Hogarth's *Marriage à la Mode* (the night scene) was a collapsible arrangement just like the crinoline of the 'sixties, which the owner could hang up on a hook flat against a cupboard wall. There was also another kind, made in two halves, and put on one on each side, fastened together in the middle by a string.

A very stiff sort of stays, colloquially called "jumpers", were worn to keep these huge structures in their place, and jumpers of a kind were in use until the Empire style allowed women to appear without stays of any kind at all, their figures barely confined by a fillet or band. But that was long afterwards. In the eighteenth century ladies of fashion laced very tightly. I am unaware if there be any truth in the tradition that these tightly laced stays were invented by the mistress of Marshal Saxe.

Becky Sharp approved of stays, and rather tightly laced ones too. When she was at Queen's Crawley in the capacity of governess after her release from the thraldom of the Semiramis of Hammersmith, she wrote to Amelia all about the house and its contents, de-

Q

scribing the portraits in the gallery there, and contrasting the various fashions.

"Some dressed in long straight stays, and gowns that look as stiff as towers, and some with long ringlets, and, oh my dear! scarcely any stays at all!"

Hoops were often the subject of the keenest satire. In 1773 appeared a rhyming description of the dress of the period, which referred to the very voluminous skirts as follows :

"Make your petticoats short that a hoop eight yards wide
May decently show how your garters are tied."

Over the hoop was generally worn a very elaborate petticoat with a vast deal of embroidery and ornament, and over this a gown, open in front to show the petticoat, gathered up into a train behind and having sleeves with abundant lace at the elbow. An addition to the gown about the middle of the century was the "sacque", an extra piece hanging down from the shoulders, and gathered up into folds over the hoop as before ; this added greatly to the general effect.

The regulations drawn up by the autocratic Beau Nash for the dress of visitors attending the Rooms at Bath when there was a ball on, give us some idea of the full dress of ladies at that time.

"Ladies who intend to dance Minuets are to be dressed in a suit of clothes, a full-trimmed sacque, or full-trimmed Italian Night-gown,[1] with Lappets and dressed Hoops such as are usually worn at St. James's. *N.B.* Hoops of the smallest size, commonly called Pocket-Hoops, are by no means proper to be worn with Lappets : it is therefore expected that every Lady who chooses to dance a Minuet, will wear a Hoop suitable to the Fashion, and proper for the Occasion. It is also expected that no Lady will appear in an Apron of any kind at the Monday's Ball."

[1] That is, evening gown.

And then follow more regulations for the dress of gentlemen on similar occasions.

There is extant a description of a Court dress worn by Selina, Countess of Huntingdon, in her younger and perhaps more flighty days, ere she had succumbed to the fascination of Wesley and Whitfield. It gives a good example of what ladies wore at the Georgian Courts, though Mrs. Delany, through whom it has come down to us, does not seem to have altogether approved of it.

" Her petticoat was of black velvet embroidered with chenille,[2] the pattern a large stone vase filled with ramping flowers that spread almost over a breadth of the petticoat from the bottom to the top : between each vase of flowers was a pattern of gold shells and foliage embossed and most heavily rich. The gown was white satin embroidered also with chenille mixed with gold, no vase on the sleeve, but two or three on the tail; it was a most laborious piece of finery, the pattern much properer for a stucco staircase than the apparel of a lady."

The same chatty diarist describes her own dress at the wedding of the Princess Anne in 1734.

"I have got my wedding garment ready. 'Tis a brocaded lutestring white ground, with great ramping flowers in shades of purples, reds and greens : I gave thirteen shillings a yard : which looks better than it describes, and it will make a show. I shall wear it with dark purple and gold ribbon, and a black hood for decency's sake."

But of course all dresses were not of the heavy pattern of my Lady Huntingdon's, and materials, even in those days, were very varied, from which a choice could be made.

Where did persons of quality go to choose their

[2] Chenille : Edging of silk corded thread, so called from its resemblance to a hairy caterpillar.

material ? There were no West-End *magasins de mode* in those days. Towards the middle of the century, Tavistock Street, near the Piazza, Covent Garden, seems to have become the fashionable shopping quarter; the long line of equipages waiting there for ladies of quality was considered one of the sights of the Town; but in the reigns of Anne and the early Georges, it was to the City—to Cheapside and St. Paul's Churchyard—that my Lady went to choose the stuff for her gowns.

These City shops were managed very differently from the modern enormous drapery stores, where young ladies or fashionably got-up young men await the orders of the customers with a more or less supercilious air of " I'm as good as you anyhow ! " Personal solicitation was still the most common form of advertisement for traders and shopkeepers in the eighteenth century. There were, of course, paragraphs in the news-sheets and journals, and perhaps a few bills on hoardings here and there. One of the modern methods of calling the attention of the public to goods or shows appears to have been quite unknown. I allude to the sandwich-board men. These were invented by one Doudney, who was also the first cheap tailor, and advertised his trousers at 18s. the pair, and other cheap articles of men's clothing, by means of peripatetic men dressed in boards. It is curious to note that by means of his successful advertising he amassed a fortune and died a clergyman of the Church of England. But in the eighteenth century a buyer was at once attacked on entering the shop, or even importuned as she passed by the door. The personnel of these fashionable establishments were all men. The *Tatler* described them as " the sweetest, fairest, nicest, dished-out creatures, and by their elegant address and soft speeches you would take them to be Italian ".[3]

As the customers come in, they press on them their goods. Italian silks, brocades, tissues, cloth of gold and silver, " very fine Mantua silks ", lutestring (or lust-ring), buckram, " any right Genoa velvet ", English velvet, velvet embossed, ruffs, muffs, puffs, shoes of all kinds, peels, pantofles, buskins, garters, shoulder-knots, head-dresses, modesties, tuckers, corkins, minni-kins, fans and patches, slammakins, round-robbins ; and for the lower classes, thread satins, striped and plain, satinettes, Persianets, Norwich crapes, anterines, hair camlets or sagathies, shallons, durances, etc.

Many of these articles of ladies' shopping have dropped out altogether, or changed their names. Lutestring (previously known as " armazine ") was a very fine corded silk ; buckram was a cloth of silk stiffened with gum (Fr. *bougran*) ; peels seem to have been a kind of shoe ; modesties (or modesty-bits) were narrow laces to pull together the top of a corset—a delightful example of an appropriate name ; corkins were large pins to fasten head-dresses or skirts ; minnikins, the smallest kind of pin ; a slammakin [4] was a loose morning-gown with lace cuffs and ruffles—perhaps, a sort of tea-gown ; and a round-robbin was a smaller kind of ruff. Camlet was a mixture of wool and silk first made in England near the river Camlet, in Montgomeryshire ; shallons was a light woollen stuff, imported, as the name implies, from Châlons ;

[3] Anything effeminate, as applied to men was said to be " Italian ". Venice, Florence and North of Italy generally were certainly the headquarters of decadent vice and intrigue. Yet all these places had a singular fascination for such a man as Horace Walpole, intellectual though he was.

[4] Compare "Mrs. Slammakin", one of Macheath's ladies in the *Beggars' Opera*. She may be said to have been more than " loose ".

sagathy was a coarse cloth for the apparel of serving-men and maids; durance was a still more lasting material made of tanned leather; what anterines were I do not know.

In one particular the old mercers' shops were the same as to-day. There was a person known as the " gentleman usher of the shop "—in our days, shop-walker—though now, I suppose, he has become "deputy manager " or " department superintendent ". His sole business was to stand, properly dressed, near the entrance, bow to passing customers, hand ladies out of their coaches or chairs, and direct them to attendants and a seat.

The dandy shop assistants were more free in their manners than their dignified successors of to-day, and in private life were said to be as great fops as any in the kingdom—having their chocolate in the morning, and their " green tea " two hours afterwards, and especially addicted to perfumes and fine linen. They were, however, energetic enough in business hours. Listen to their conversation with their fair customers:

This, madam, is wonderful charming. This, madam, is so *diverting* a silk. This, madam, my stars ! how cool it looks ! but this, madam, ye gods ! would I had ten thousand yards of it ! It suits your Ladyship's face wonderful well.

He asks fifteen shillings a yard. The lady offers ten. He is astounded.

" Fan me ye winds ! Your Ladyship rallies me ! Should I part with it at such a price, the weavers would rise upon the very shop. Was you at the Park last night, madam ? Have you seen the *Tatler* to-day ? Your Ladyship shall abate me sixpence "—and so on.

To the feminine mind, the attractions of shopping, whether the articles are really wanted or not, remains the same throughout the centuries ; at the times of the sales it is ever true what was sung in the *Pall-Mall Gazette* years ago :

> Packed are the halls of Maple and of Shoolbred,
> Fierce is the fray where flies the flag of Whiteley,
> Scarce shall a Sandow penetrate the throng at
> Marshall and Snelgrove's.

> Now is the hour of genuine reductions.
> Now you may buy for seven and elevenpence,
> Goods that we know are usually sold at
> Eight and a penny.

The mercers are there, but they have moved further westward. The goods are there under different names. The bargains and " genuine reductions " (abatement of sixpence) are still dangled to tempt the buyer. Only the people of the shop are changed. Nowadays, you may be served across the counter by a young gentleman who the same evening will take you in to dinner at the house of a peer !

A curious custom of the century was the reception of visitors by my Lady while she was still at her toilette. This was probably adopted from continental use, for it is well known that Le Grand Monarque did both his undressing at night and his dressing in the morning in public. These receptions were known respectively as the *coucher* and *lever* of the monarch, and the latter expression still survives in England (in the modified form levee), applied to the reception of gentlemen by the king. In like manner the anti-chamber of my Lady was always crowded with all sorts of people, parasites generally, dancing attendance while their patroness was completing the very elaborate toilette of the day. *Faire antichambre* became a regular expression for dancing attendance or awaiting a patron's pleasure. In the first act of Strauss's *Rosenkavalier* we witness Her Highness having her hair dressed by a barber whose own toupee is in the very height of the mode. A crowd is assembled in her anti-chamber. There are the orphans whom she has befriended, come to pay their respects ; there is the musician with an aria composed in her honour, which he sings to her, and is then admitted to the privilege of kissing her hand ; there is a poet to ask subscriptions for his new poem ; there is a dog-dealer with a couple of puppies for her inspection ; there are dressmakers and milliners with new caps and silks for gowns ; and there is a host of gallants and admirers, sipping chocolate, and awaiting the opportunity of addressing their compliments.

Perhaps it was not quite so public in England, and I do not think my Lady Townshend, for one, would have been bothered with more people than those she really wanted to see. The note of the period was ceremony on all occasions, and the stiffened hoop and elaborate head-dress lent themselves to ceremonious behaviour, stilted movements and artificial life at all times. Perhaps my Lady Townshend was less artificial than the general run of women in society, and when she had the handsome youth Frederick Campbell and other Westminster schoolboys to sleep in her dressing-room, it was *faisant antichambre* very literally indeed !

The *tout ensemble* of a woman of fashion of those days would make an ungainly sight according to our notions, but it was not so ill-adapted to an age when most women walked slowly and with dignity ; it was certainly suited to a Pavane or a Minuet de la Cour. Moreover, a great deal of the stiff appearance of a woman's dress was taken away by the sacque which, as we have seen, was a kind of loose over-robe hanging from the shoulders.

COSTUMES OF THE LATE EIGHTEENTH CENTURY

From coloured prints in the British Museum

Artificial aids to the figure were, of course, not wanting then, as always. There was, for instance, an article called a " buffont ", a projected covering of gauze or linen for a lady's breast to make her look like a pouter pigeon, which was the fashion about 1750, and there were things called " bearers " to put under the skirts of ladies' gowns for raising the skirt at that point to any height desired. A more obvious make-up was the " plumper ", a very thin, round and light ball inserted in the cheeks to make them look plump— " much used by old Court countesses ", says a writer at the beginning of the century. Swift mentions these " plumpers " in his coarse description of a " nymph " going to bed. The curious reader may be referred to the same rather disgusting piece for an enumeration of other articles of make-up.

Flowers were used as extra ornaments both for the head-dress and the stomacher. A little glass or tin vessel was sometimes hidden in the hair or in the lady's belt to contain water for keeping the flowers fresh. Another sort of trimming was a " furbelow ", a term which still survives. These were flounces, chiefly on the petticoat. A writer speaks of " furbelow'd gowns, furbelow'd petticoats, furbelow's aprons, and, as I have heard, furbelow's *smocks* also ". Not to intrude too far into the secrets of a lady's clothing, I may just say that a smock was the name for a chemise. These were sometimes highly embroidered and ornamented in various ways, according to Strutt, as early as the thirteenth century. Cambric smocks and perfumed smocks came later. City madams gave sometimes as much as three pounds for a smock. The modern tea-gown had its prototype in the eighteenth century in the " negligée " occasionally called a " trolloppée ", a name which, like "slammakin", would seem to imply a certain looseness ! Aprons were originally only worn by the working classes or by ladies for preserving the front of their dress from stains while performing their household duties ; but in the reign of William III. they seem to have been adopted as part of a lady's toilette in almost all circumstances, and were often richly decorated with lace, spangles or needlework or with little pictures painted or printed on satin, inserted in panels. In 1744 aprons reached to the hem of the petticoat : they then became shorter, more like the apron of a modern housemaid, but afterwards were worn long again. The Duchess of Queensbury's apron, which was torn off her by Beau Nash with such anger, saying it was " only fit for an abigail ", was perhaps a plain white one, though, as it was said to be of great value, it was probably ornamented with the finest lace.

For outdoor wear, ladies had several kinds of cloaks. "Capuchins ", at first called "cardinals ", were hooded cloaks like those worn by friars, and a " Brunswick " was a stiffer arrangement with lappels and a man's collar. It was probably a sort of " capuchin ", under cover of which Lord Nithisdale escaped from the Tower in the aftermath of the '45, for it was certainly hooded; but, whatever it was, the name " Nithisdale " stuck to the hood of this kind of garment for many years, and the word is to be found in the *Century Dictionary* (a dictionary of the American language) with a drawing of the hood itself.

Ladies of quality made a brave show on their travels when they could afford it. Lady Mary Coke's travelling dress of pea-green and silver attracted much attention on the continent — which was perhaps exactly what was intended. She was what Herrick had once called a "tempestuous petticoat". Pea-green must have been a very popular colour, for Mistress Winifred Jenkins, waiting-woman to the Brambles, wore "a plain pea-green tabby sack" when on her travels.

What is so elegantly called "footwear" by the Americanised public of to-day [5] was a very important item in the expenses of a person of quality in the eighteenth century. They were often highly ornamented with lace, rich embroidery and needlework, or set off by jewelled buckles. The heels were worn high for the greater part of the century, coloured heels being very fashionable. A writer in the *Lady's Magazine* in 1776 says that flat heels were introduced about that time (perhaps it was only for a time) simultaneously with a rage for plain dresses, simple caps and a forced simplicity, when ladies would go so far as to attire themselves as milkmaids or shepherdesses, crook and all; yet it does not seem that they ever forgot the diamonds and gold-headed canes such as could not have been possessed by Phyllis or Chloe.

Shoes were, however, looked upon as a snare and as being a proof of extreme worldliness, if nothing more, when very highly decorated. The great Isaac Bickerstaffe, early in the century, issued the following amusing proclamation :

The Censor having observed that there are wrought ladies' shoes and slippers put out to view at a great shoemaker's shop towards St. James's end of Pall-Mall, which create irregular thoughts and desires in the youth of this realm : the said shop-

[5] The English language is fast being spoilt by the affectations of America. "Footwear" and "shirt-waist" are bad enough as substitutes for boots and shoes and blouses, and there are other blots which will occur to every lover of English undefiled. We may be thankful that up to now we have been spared "casket" and "cuspidor" for "coffin" and "spittoon".

keeper is required to take in those eyesores or show cause the
next Court day why he continues to expose the same : and he is
required to be prepared particularly to answer for the slippers
with green lace and blue heels.

The youth who could be seized with improper desire
at the sight of a slipper with green lace and blue heels,
must have been more susceptible than the youth of the
present day. An advertisement of a shoemaker, *temp.*
George I., shows the kind of " footwear " worn in the
early decades of the century. He boldly states that he
" makes and sells all sorts of boots, shoes, slippers,
spatterdashes (*i.e.* gaiters), double and single chan-
nelled pumps, rich quilted shoes, clogs and turned
pumps of the neatest work and genteelest fashion ".

But it was in the decoration of the head that the
lady of that time differed so much from all who have
preceded or followed her. There were hoops before,
and crinolines after the time of the Georges ; high-
heeled shoes have been known before and since ; cloaks
and hoods have not varied very much. But it may be
safely asserted that anything like the head-gear of the
eighteenth century had never been seen before, and
will never be seen again.

In the days of William and Mary the tall head-dress
was called a " commode ", and has been defined as
" a frame of wire two or three stories high, fitted for
the head, and covered with tiffany or other thin silks ".
Some authorities say it was also called a " Fontange ",
from Mlle. de Fontange, the mistress of Louis XIV.,
who is said to have invented it ; but, according to the
*Dictionnaire de l'académie*, a Fontange was the knot of
ribbons on the coiffure itself. The structure did not
differ very much (except in the actual form, for it was
always shaped like a tower) from that curious head-gear

"THE FINISHING TOUCH"
From an old print

of the Middle Ages seen sometimes in the shape of horns and at other times like an enormous extinguisher. The commode fell into disuse about the time of Queen Anne, though readers of *Esmond* will remember the Dowager Viscountess Castlewood, who retained the fashion from a tender remembrance of her old sweetheart James II. and his days. After the decline of the commode, ladies began to wear smallish caps more elegant than the towers, but which must have appeared out of all proportion to the size of the hoops. Then, somewhere about the middle of the century, it was noted that ladies were going (as usual) from one extreme to the other, especially with regard to the size of their heads.

It is not so very long since this part of their sweet bodies used to be bound so tight and trim, so amazingly snug, that they appeared like a pin's head on the top of a knitting needle. But they have now so far exceeded the golden mean in the contrary extreme that our fine ladies remind me of an apple stuck on the point of a small skewer.—(*London Magazine*.)

As the hoop declined in size the coiffure grew in height. Addison said that there was no such variable thing in nature as a lady's head-dress, which rose and fell in his own memory more than thirty degrees. In 1767 women took to wearing towers or " pompons " of hair stuffed with wool or horse hair, or even meal, covered with powder and reeking with pomatum.

These exaggerated high head-dresses were the height of fashion when Marie Antoinette married the Dauphin in 1770 ; but I think they were in use in London before that, and all the French Queen did was to give the sanction of her use of them and so set the fashion in Paris, which then, as now, still led in all question of modes in dress.

It came to be the general opinion that these high coiffures were indispensable to a woman's beauty : they were supposed to tone down the defects of a badly shaped face, rounding off square ones and making them appear more of an oval shape, while they also concealed irregularities of features that were too marked. Their height grew as time went on, till the chin of a fashionably dressed woman became the central point of her total height.

Later still, the head-dress had become more monstrous, consisting of a still larger heap of tow and padding of all sorts over which the lady's own hair (or some one else's !) was arranged and hung with ropes of pearls, ribbons, feathers, artificial flowers. On these wonderful erections were stuck ornaments of various kinds, often an indication of a wearer's tastes, such as a coach and six, or a frigate in full sail, or a bunch of flowers or vegetables, butterflies, caterpillars, etc., and other little articles, all of blown glass or some brittle substance.

One lady planned her head to represent a dustman's sorting-ground. On the top was a group of cinder-sifters, a dust cart was winding its way up the side, and a sow with a litter of little pigs lay among the bottom curls. Another had a sedan-chair, with a lady inside—chairmen and all complete, and all made in the blown-glass material. Large bows, called " top-knots ", were also placed on the summit of ladies' heads. In Durfey's *Songs and Ballads* it is said that " sable top-knots are religious and scarlet ones lewd "—perhaps calculated to have the same baleful effect on youth as slippers with green lace and blue heels !

Towards the end of the century the head-dress became larger and more fantastic still, and the stupendous erections were often known as " Poufs aux Sentiments ". The following description is of the coiffure of the Duchesse de Chartres :

At the back of the coiffure, a woman is sitting with a baby in her lap : on the right a parrot is playing with a cherry : on top, there is a curl of her husband's hair, one of her father's the Duc de Penthievre, and one of her father in law's, the Duc D'Orleans.

Another " Pouf aux Sentiments " presented a stormy lake :—ducks on its banks, a hunter with a gun, and, behind a mill, a shepherdess flirting with an abbé, while near by stood the miller with his donkey.

Sometimes these " Poufs aux Sentiments " were arranged or ornamented according to some passing event or whim of the moment. When Marie Antoinette was vaccinated, there was a " Pouf à l'Inoculation ", and the Princess Dorothea de Montbeliart once appeared at Court wearing a pouf on which there was the portrait of a woman with a large bunch of household keys. She said it was the likeness of her confidential housekeeper at the chateau, and that her desire was to show her appreciation of the good woman's fidelity and trustworthiness.

The *Marchande de modes* of Marie Antoinette was the moving spirit in Paris of all these extravagant and unwieldy fashions. She was one Rose Bertin, a clever milliner and dressmaker, who had obtained such a hold over the vain Queen that she began to give herself great airs, and would receive ladies of the highest nobility of France lying on a sofa and not attempting to rise when they entered her establishment. She ruled the extravagant fashions of that extravagant time, inventing all the new headdresses and hats and urging the Queen ever to greater

excesses. All Europe sent for her models. She despatched mannequins dressed in the latest mode to
every capital. Besides making for the Queen herself,
she supplied toilettes and designed hats for Jeanne
Dubarry, the fallen favourite of Louis XV., who,
though living in obscurity since the conversion of the
Court to virtue, would still be attired in the height of
fashion. One cannot help thinking that Rose and
Jeanne had much in common, or the fashionable
milliner would not have kept as a customer one who
had fallen so low from her former greatness.

La Bertin, in spite of the immense sums of money
she must have made, was bankrupt over and over
again. The Queen always paid her debts in full, and
the amount spent by this royal lady on clothes and
jewels must have been enormous. Bertin was clever
enough to keep well in with those about the Court,
and was hand and glove with Leonard the Queen's
coiffeur, one of those fortunate enough to escape the
guillotine. He got safely to St. Petersburg and became
coiffeur-in-chief to the Empress.

Of course such gigantic and elaborate erections
made it impossible for ladies to have their heads
dressed every day. The false locks which supplied
deficiencies in natural hair, the profusion of pomatum,
the greasy wool to bolster up the pouf, and the powder
to conceal dust had, however, to be renewed from
time to time. Once in three weeks, at the very least,
and more often if the lady could afford the time and
the expense, was the great pouf demolished and rebuilt.
It was not considered safe to leave it longer than that,
especially in the hot weather. That they would not
" keep " longer is evident from the numerous recipes
advertised as being good for the destruction of the

insects which bred in the pomatum and flour. In the *London Magazine* of 1768 appeared the following :

I went the other morning to make a visit to an elderly aunt of mine, when I found her pulling off her cap, and tendering her head to the ingenious Mr. Gilchrist, who has lately obliged the public with a most excellent essay on hair. He asked her how long it was since her head had been opened or repaired. She answered, " not above nine weeks ". To which he replied that it was as long as a head could go well in the summer, and that therefore it was proper to deliver it now : for he confessed that it began to be " un peu hazardée."

The irritation produced by the tight arrangement of the hair of these toupets, and also, it is to be feared, by the presence of other irritants inside them, necessitated the carrying of a sort of head-scratcher. These were openly taken everywhere and used in company, at the opera, at the gaming-table, or at private parties. According to the position in society and the wealth of the owner, they were made of bone, ivory, silver or gold. It seems incredible that ladies of quality could thus go into the world ready prepared to scratch their heads in public !

The art of hairdressing having reached such a height could not, as a rule, be entrusted to the hands of a mere lady's maid, however clever an abigail she might be. We find, therefore, that the hairdressers of the day were very important people, who trained a number of apprentices to follow in their footsteps. An artist in hair who could successfully build up one of those fearsome erections, surmounted perhaps by a ship in full sail, or a windmill, or the complete model of a dust-yard, would be in great request throughout the London season, and doubtless follow his fair clients to the Bath or the Wells.

The " ingenious Mr. Gilchrist " mentioned above

R

was probably a well-known hairdresser of the day.
Another one, Monsieur Toussaint, a Frenchman, was
also celebrated for the excellence of his coiffures. But
the name that has lingered longest of all these useful
gentlemen is that of Mr. Rowland, of " Macassar Oil "
fame. He was a French *émigré* who came to London
with the exiled Bourbon sovereigns on the outbreak
of the Revolution, and returned to France in 1814.
He was the most fashionable hairdresser of the day,
his charge for cutting hair alone being five shillings.
In his advertisements he speaks of " les vertues incom-
parables de l'Huile de Macassar ". Byron remembered
this hairdressing puff when he wrote in *Don Juan* :

> In virtues nothing earthly could surpass her
> Save thine incomparable oil " Macassar ".

Another important matter was that these erections
should be most carefully preserved once they were
made, if they were to last some time. In Stewart's
*Plocacosmos*, an essay on the art of hairdressing, minute
directions are given to his apprentices as to the manner
of " conserving " a lady's head at night, especially if
they had to be " conserved " for at least a month. The
curls are to be secured on rollers, and the hair straight-
ened with pomatum. The instructions continue :

> After that, take a very large net fillet, big enough to cover
> the head and the hair, and put it on, and, drawing the strings to
> a proper tightness behind, till it closes all round the face and
> neck like a purse, bring the strings round to the front and back
> again to the neck where they must be tied ; the finest lawn
> handkerchief is night covering sufficient for the head.

Fresh powder could be added to the pouf daily.
In many old houses may still be seen the old " powder
closet ", with a hole through which the head was
placed to receive the daily dose of powder.

COIFFURES OF THE EIGHTEENTH CENTURY

(British Museum)

Powdering the hair is a very old-world custom. All the Roman ladies did it under the ancient Empire. The Emperor Commodus (who in many ways was very like a lady) made his head look as if it were on fire from the quantity of essence and gold dust poured on it. Various coloured powders were used. Fox, a great dandy in early life, though neglectful of the barest decencies when he was an older man, was very partial to colours. He wore red-heeled shoes and blue powder on his hair.

When this absurd fashion was at its height, it began to be severely satirised in prints and on the stage. In July 1776 Samuel Foote appeared at the Little Theatre in the Haymarket in the character of a Mrs. Pentweazle in his own comedy of *Taste*. Probably with the sole intention of raising a laugh, he wore the most exaggerated type of female head-dress then in fashion. It was stuck full of feathers of enormous size; it was a yard in width; and finally the whole construction of tow, hair, wool, pomatum and feathers fell off his head as he left the stage. It has been asserted that this was one of the things that started the reform of the extravagant fashion; but, setting aside the fact that the same fashion lasted for a long time yet, it is hard to believe that followers of the mode among the female sex will abandon what is recognised as the fashion merely because it has been ridiculed on the stage. Else how did the hoop last so long and then reappear as the crinoline?

The Mrs. Pentweazle in Foote's comedy was an amusingly exaggerated person, a very vain type of an ignorant City madam. She boasted of being a Griskin by birth (I seem to remember a Mrs. Sparsit who was a " Powler "), that all her family on her mother's side were famous for their eyes, that her aunt was " a beauty of Windsor " (with only one eye, it is true, but that one a piercer), and that her portrait was done after Venus de Médicis, the sister of Mary de Médicis ! Smollett also had a sly hit at the outrageous style of the hair. When Winifred Jenkins went to the play at Newcastle, she was induced to go rouged " with her hair dressed in the Paris fashion ", and she was mobbed by the colliers for a " painted Issabel ".

Some ladies did have their heads done daily. Perhaps they did not wear such outlandish " poufs ". One such was Lady Austen, Cowper's friend at Olney, who was accustomed to have her hair done by William Wilson, the Olney barber. After Wilson joined the Baptists he declined to dress the ladies' hair on Sundays. Lady Austen was therefore obliged to call him in on Saturday evenings, and often had to sit up all night to avoid the disarrangement of her " head ".

After the disappearance of the big poufs, turbans seem to have gradually taken their place, and must have lasted for a considerable time, for some of us may remember an account in early Victorian days of a turban trimmed with a bird of Paradise, whose feathers were ruthlessly burned to restore a younger lady who had fainted. Was it Frank Fairleigh or his friend Colman who thus destroyed the old lady's head-gear ?

In the meantime feathers also came into vogue, as we can see from the delightful caricatures of Rowlandson and Gillray. It was the young Duchess of Devonshire (Georgiana) who introduced the habit of sticking very tall feathers in her hair. These were often over a yard in height and sometimes two or three of them together.

There was a loud outcry against them when first introduced, not because they were extravagant or unbecoming but because they were immoral! Ladies wearing them were insulted, mobbed and persecuted whenever they appeared, were abused in the papers and denounced from the pulpits. There is a delightful pamphlet which was published under the title of a *Letter to the Duchess of Devonshire*, in which the question is seriously asked what kind of wives and mothers were those ladies likely to prove who borrowed their favourite decoration from a creature so unnatural as to leave her eggs scattered in the sand like the female ostrich!

With regard to ladies' hats, they varied in the eighteenth century much the same as they do in the twentieth. Enormous hats were of course required to cover the huge heads of false hair and substructure of tow, and giant pins, called "corkins", were necessary to fasten them on. The frame of the hat was usually made of light wire and gauze, covered with silk and flowers in profusion. Sometimes they were high and sometimes low, perched on the top of the pouf, or lying flat on the head at the time when a wave of simplicity induced ladies to dress like country lasses and shepherdesses. Now they were covered with a mass of feathers, and now they were simply a small mob cap. Some were evidently imitated from the hats of men, such as we may imagine my Lady Ancaster (daughter of the Newmarket jockey) to have worn, who always loved to wear the breeches at a masquerade! Anstey in his *Bath Guide* notes straw-built hats and bonnets green, but this may have been a country mode.

Towards the end of the century hats grew at one

time very small only to be enormous again in the early years of the nineteenth. The weird Lady Mary Coke, who died in the days of the Regency, insisted on dying in a high-crowned beaver hat such as is seen in some of the pictures of Queen Caroline of Brunswick.

Occasionally instead of a hat a sort of hood was worn to protect a big pouf. This was called a "calash", from *calèche*, the hood of a carriage, which it resembled in that it was constructed in sections that folded up or opened out on pulling a string. In the garden scene of Goldsmith's *She Stoops to Conquer* old Mrs. Hardcastle always wears one of these calashes. Hoods were also worn instead of hats, and, like patches, were sometimes indicative of the politics or sentiments of the wearer, generally signified by their colour. Mr. Spectator says that a black hood signified the lady's husband was absent, and constituted a sort of signal to her lover. A white hood meant "at peace with all the world", and so on. Later in the century there were ribbons and trimmings of special significance. These mostly originated in Paris in the artificial days just before the Revolution. There were ribbons of "marked desires" and of "Venetian sighs", a gown of a "stifled sigh"—trimmings of "honest arrangements" and of "superfluous regrets" —a cap of "assured conquest" and a muff of "momentary agitation". Nor were shoes omitted in these sentimental signals. In the time of Marie Antoinette there was a long narrow shoe, set with gems, known as "Venez y voir!"

Perhaps one of the most astonishing vagaries in those days of vagaries of all sorts was the invention of new names for odd shades of colour. In our time we have "crushed strawberry", but it may not be generally known that the very proper and sedate colour of early Victorian times known as puce is really " crushed flea ", puce being, of course, the French for flea. The story goes that a fine lady of the Court of Louis XVI. once crushed one of these wandering insects on her dainty rose pink nail. She exclaimed " What a marvellous colour! Neither black nor brown: black without being too black, and brown without being too brown, but truly delicious ! " After that discovery puce colour made the round of the fashionable world as " La couleur puce qui fait oublier toutes les autres ". And with many variations : there was a tint of " a young flea " and the tint of an " old flea " and there was a somewhat mysterious colour known as " Coleur de ventre de puce en fièvre de lait ", the translation of which I will leave to my readers. Shades of colour of a " flea's leg " and of a leg of " an emotional young maiden " (" Couleur de Cuisse de Nymphe émue ") — and many other fantastically coarse expressions came into use and were adopted by Rose Bertin and her frivolous horde of customers.

Muffs, as I have observed in a previous chapter, were carried by men as well as women, though, of course, they are now purely a feminine article of attire. They were always a mark of luxury and date from long before the eighteenth century. In Naples when Sir William Hamilton was minister there, luxury was at its height, and even the nuns were " dressy " and partial to their muffs. Nelson's Emma wrote to her husband that she had paid a visit to a convent, where she made the acquaintance of one of the nuns, a certain Beatrice Acquaviva. She said :

Their dress is very becoming, and she (*i.e.* Sister Beatrice) told me she was allowed to wear rings and mufs and any little thing she liked and endead she displayed today a good deal of finery for she had four or five diamond rings on her fingers, and seemed fond of her muf.

It will be seen that Emma's spelling is of the kitchen-maid order. But she was a good correspondent, and in one of her letters to a former " protector ", Greville, she describes the magnificence of the Neapolitan nobility and the people in general, winding up her letter by remarking : " But, Greville, fleas and lice their is millions " !

Another accessory to costume, though not strictly an article of dress, is an umbrella, and this seems to have been introduced into England early in the eighteenth, if not late in the seventeenth century. At first they were only used by women, and it was considered effeminate for a man to carry one.

Early umbrellas were made of cotton or paper prepared in some way against the wet. After the publication of *Robinson Crusoe* they were often nicknamed " Robinsons ", as later they were known as " Gamps ", after the immortal Sairey. One Jonas Hanway was the man who popularised the umbrella in London. He gave his name, perhaps, to a curious little backwater of a street (leading from Oxford Street round the back of Frascati's to Tottenham Court Road), where, by the way, the great actor Fechter was born.

Hanway was a noted philanthropist, who started societies for training poor boys for the sea, helped to remodel Coram's Foundling Hospital, founded the Magdalen Hospital and also various institutions for the care of chimney-sweeps. He travelled much for those days, in Persia, Russia and other little frequented countries. He was an eccentric in more ways than one. Pugh, his biographer, says that he habitually wore dress clothes so as to be ready at a moment's notice for any kind of polite society, and carried a small "parapluie" (*sic*) to protect his face and wig from the wet. He was very susceptible to cold feet and always wore three pairs of stockings at once. He lived in Red Lion Square and is buried in Westminster Abbey.

Various other little items there were, adjuncts to the perfect toilette of a great lady, which are only to be found now in the establishments of Mr. Willy Clarkson and other purveyors of "fancy dress".

Such were patches and masks. The former were much more elaborate in the days of the Stuarts than in the following century. There exists a well-known illustration of a lady's face in the time of Charles II., showing a daintily executed coach and horses along her forehead, and sun, moon and stars all over the rest of her face. In the times of the Georges, patches were generally confined to two or three, or at the most four, small ones in the form of dots, tiny stars or crescents, made usually of plaister, but sometimes of velvet and so placed as to show off a dimple near the mouth, or call attention to the eye.

In the days of the Stuarts ladies seldom went out without a mask, and the custom was continued far into the following century. They were first worn in England in the days of Queen Elizabeth, but much earlier on the continent, and, at centres like Venice, generally as an aid to conspiracy and intrigue. Whole masks, made of velvet or lined silk, to cover all the face, were called vizards and were kept in place by a bead that the wearer held between her teeth. Ladies usually wore their masks when riding, but if not in actual use they were fastened to a cord and suspended to the belt. Whole masks were principally worn in windy weather or for the purpose of complete concealment, but there were also smaller ones called " loo-masks ", that only covered the face to the nose.

Fans have been in use from time immemorial in all countries. About 1740 the size of the fan began to increase and they grew to a great breadth, so much so that a large green fan was commonly in use at the end of the century out of doors instead of a sunshade. But in England, as abroad, the fan was more often an instrument of coquetry and intrigue than a mere appendage of the toilette.

Men used fans as well as women. Lord March, in a letter to Selwyn in December 1766, says :

> By the neglect of my servant, you did not receive the fans that I intended to have sent you by the Bunburys. They are finer than those I hope you have received by Lord Fitzwilliam but I shall have an opportunity of sending them. Did you ever get any from Lady Townshend? She sent me two when she thought I was going to Paris—but she was in great haste to get them back again ; I believe she was afraid they might be seized upon by some of the opera people if they remained in my house.

Rather an amusing advertisement appeared in one of the eighteenth-century journals calling attention to the sale by auction of the

WHOLE STOCK OF A COQUETTE LEAVING OFF TRADE.

> . . . several valuable curiosities, including a *transparent* capuchin, an elegant snuff-box with a looking-glass in it (being a very good pocket companion for a beauty), directions for painting and the use of cosmetics, and the secret of putting on a patch in an artful manner, showing the effects of its different arrangement, with instructions how to place it about the eye in such a manner as to give disdain, an amorous languish, or a cunning glance—said to be translated from the French.

The jewels worn in the eighteenth century were

numerous and elaborate. There was always a watch and an etui hanging at the waist. Necklaces were much worn (one cannot forget the famous diamond necklace with which the vain and credulous Cardinal de Rohan was to approach the Queen). Bracelets were worn over long gloves. After the accession of George III. necklaces came to be composed of several rows of gold chains, or beads, or jewels, the upper one tight round the throat and the rest disposed in festoons. This kind of ornament was known as " L'esclavage ".

I have taken a bird's eye view, so to speak, of the chief features of ladies' dress in the eighteenth century. The account does not profess to be more than a rather discursive one, without reference to exact dates (for my notes overlap the century at each end), and without the detail that can be found in Fairholt or Planché or other books on costume. But the chapter may help to indicate the scope of the ideas of ladies of quality of the time with regard to dress. As I have already remarked, these are much the same in all ages. Anything for a change, and no limit to extravagance of design or execution so long as the result is one which will force people to look at them—women as well as men. Who was it said that a woman would be sooner looked at with disdain than not looked at at all ?

With their hoops and poufs and feathers the ladies of quality in the eighteenth century must have presented a queer sight. As Lady Louisa Stuart wrote long afterwards :

If a North American Indian had seen a well-dressed lady's stiff stays, round hoop, high-heeled shoes, her hair stuffed with bushels of powder and paste, and her neck overlaid with ruff, puff, frill and tippet, he could never have suspected that an animal like his own squaw lurked within the structure !

Ladies seem to have generally worn their own hair, though padded, puffed and decorated out of all recognition; but, as is well known, all men of all classes wore a wig of some kind, their heads being shaved for the purpose. This has been a chapter on the dress of ladies, but I may be excused the addition of a few notes on the trade in male wigs, which were almost as ridiculous an institution as the ladies' "Pouf aux Sentiments ".

Names and descriptions of all kinds of wigs would fill a chapter of themselves. Each class of individual was represented by its own particular wig. A "tie-peruke" for a barrister; a "brigadier" or a "fix-ear" for a military man; a "full-bottom" for a merchant; a "bob" or a "scratch" for a tradesman; a "fly-peruke" for a country gentleman; a tightly curled one, like the head of a spaniel, for a coachman, the only one, perhaps, outside the Law Courts which survives to-day. But there were many others. A popular journal of the eighteenth century enumerates the following :

The pigeon's wing, the comet, the cauliflower, the royal bird, the staircase, the ladder, the brush, the wild boar's back, the temple, the rhinoceros, the corded wolf's paw, Count Saxe's mode, the she-dragon, the rose, the crutch, the negligent, the chancellor, the cut bob, the long bob, the half natural, the chain buckle, the corded buckle, the snail back, etc., etc.—(*London Magazine.*)

Wigs were sold very extensively in the streets. One of the old London street cries was " Fine tie or a fine bob, sir "—one or other of which wigs was in most common use. The illustration of the cry depicts a wig-seller combing it and talking to a customer at his door in Middle Row, Holborn. Wigs on blocks stand on a bracketed board outside his window.

At that time every man, old and young, wore a wig. The cost of a common one was at least a guinea : a workman had a new one every year. In all indentures it was specified that a master should find his apprentice in " one good and sufficient wig yearly, and every year for and during and unto the expiration of the full end and term of his apprenticeship ".

What became of the old wigs ? Some of the better ones doubtless found their way to " Old Clo' " men in the same way that discarded hats and boots and shoes do still. The probability is that members of the Hebrew tribes plied their trade in wigs then as they do still in old clo'. But one use for old wigs too far gone to be renovated was to provide the public shoe-blacks with something wherewith to wipe the wet dirt from their customers' shoes. Before the coming of the great Day and Martin (whose " passing " has recently been announced) nearly all persons had their shoes polished in the street, except, of course, such of the quality as could afford servants innumerable. " Japan your shoes, sir ", which later became " Black your boots, sir ", was a very common cry of the London streets. By the time the wig got into the hands of the shoeblack it must have been almost as "hazardée" as that "head" opened by Mr. Gilchrist, to which allusion has already been made.

When wigs went out of fashion and men began to wear their own hair there were great riots and disorders between wig-makers and hairdressers, both in London and Paris. But the hairdressers triumphed in the end, and the wig finally survived only in fancy dress, on the stage, in the Courts of Justice, and on the heads of coachmen of State or of those unfortunate individuals whose natural wig has prematurely failed.

# CHAPTER X

## SATIRES AND LAMPOONS

Origin of the expression "lampoon": Wills's Coffee-house the centre of distribution for satires and lampoons: the hired lampooners of the day: the scurrility and baseness of Pope's attacks: Sir Charles Hanbury Williams: satirical attacks on my Lady Townshend: unfounded connection of her name with the character of Lady Bellaston: what a "Tom Jones" really meant: Lady Braidshaigh's anonymous correspondence with Samuel Richardson: Coventry's *Pompey the Little*: delight of Lady Mary Wortley Montagu with the satires against Lady Townshend: Mr. Winnington and my Lady Townshend: the mock auction at Carlisle House: satire on the Coterie: the Gunnings at the Opera: the Chevalier D'Eon and a jury of matrons: Lady Rochford and Lady Vane: Thompson's satires: *The Female Jockey Club*: *The Abbey of Kilkhampton*: William Combe's satires: the *Diaboliad* and the *Diabo-Lady*: curious career of William Combe: the story of Miss Letitia Piper's twins: indifference of my Lady Townshend to all lampoons.

TO GIVE ANYTHING like a complete account of the satires and lampoons of the eighteenth century would be far beyond the scope of a work of this description, and require a volume or two to itself. I have therefore confined myself to some general account of satirical and abusive writings aimed at the "Lively Lady Townshend" or at those of her friends mentioned in the foregoing pages.

It is curious that both these words—satires and lampoons—seem to be originally derived from something to do with eating and drinking. A satire was a medley of all sorts of things before it became definitely associated with attacks on persons, institutions, or manners. It may have been from *satura*, a mixed dish, though this seems to be rather far-fetched. But " lampoon " is certainly derived from the French *lampons*, which means " let us drink " or " let us carouse "; or from the kindred Italian *lampone*. There was an old kind of drinking-song containing personal allusions of a satirical nature, and the chorus was " Lampone, lampone, camerada lampone ". From a drinking-song, the lampoon became anything in the form of a personal attack on an individual.

The eighteenth century was essentially an age of satire and lampoon. No person's character was at any time safe from scurrilous attack. Every man or woman at all well known in politics, society, literature or art was liable to be openly lampooned in print, either in one of the magazines of the day, in a flying leaflet, or in a longer pamphlet specially written for the occasion.

Wills's Coffee-House in Russell Street, Covent Garden, was at one time the open market for libels and lampoons. Sir Walter Scott speaks of a man called Julian, a drunken sottish fellow, who styled himself " Secretary to the Muses ", and frequented the above-named coffee-house. He undertook to write any kind of lampoon, and also to find some means of distributing those written by others, in such a manner that their authors should remain unknown. Wills's was one of the best coffee-houses of the time, where you would meet the highest society, and a pamphlet carefully distributed among its frequenters was as good as published all over the town—or rather better, for the loungers at Wills's would include most of those whom the lampooner wished to reach.

Julian was, however, only one of many such. By means of this vile trade lived a whole army of hack writers who, for the merest trifle, were prepared to produce a lampoon in prose or verse attacking the victim under an easily penetrated pseudonym, or under their own names, occasionally thinly disguised by asterisks, often not disguised at all.

In addition to these penny-a-liners, and far more powerful, of course, in their way, were writers in the foremost ranks of literature, who, moving in the best society of the day, and with all the command of the English language that genius and education could give, were not above prostituting their talent for the gratification of a personal spite, or in the hope of pleasing a patron or intimate friend.

Pope may be reckoned as the leader of all lampooners of that day, not only on account of the literary genius which he made subservient to his spiteful nature, but because of the bitter virulence of some of his verse.

His satire attacking Lord Hervey (" Lord Fanny "), in the character of Sporus, ostensibly written with the object of exposing an unworthy politician in his true colours, betrays in every line the acrid spite of a petty and crooked disposition which is so often found in combination with a small person and a crooked back. His attacks on Lady Mary Wortley Montagu, with whom he had been on the most intimate terms, are so low as to be beneath contempt. His minor satires were generally dull. His *Dunciad* cannot be understood now without a key.

Swift's pen was as bitter, but far more virile than Pope's. Some of his writings are, indeed, strong enough in personal abuse and expressed with little restraint as to language ; but the spiteful womanish note of the

Twickenham hunchback is wanting. He wrote as a man, and could not have lowered himself to that meanness which was essentially a part of Pope's nature.

Another clever versifier and lampooner of the age, now forgotten, was Sir Charles Hanbury Williams. He was connected with the Selwyns and, by marriage, indirectly with the Townshends through his mother, Albina Selwyn, daughter of John Selwyn of Matson. A highly educated man, he made the grand tour on the continent, and was afterwards elected member for the County of Monmouth, eventually becoming ambassador at St. Petersburg and other foreign capitals.

In a memoir prefixed to an edition of his works, published in 1882, it is hinted that he was of little importance politically, but that " The wit and bitter satire which flowed from his pen in a stream apparently of careless gaiety, rendered him a very important ally ; nor did he confine the exercise of these talents to the censure of public men and manners, but frequently attacked with equal severity the faults and foibles of domestic conduct . . ."; or, in other words, he was a writer of impertinent remarks on the lives of private people, by which he hoped to inspire fear in his enemies, and at the same time gain reputation as a wit. He went mad towards the end of his life and committed suicide, though this did not prevent his burial in the Abbey.

Coarse indeed, according to our notions, were the manners, language and ephemeral literature of the day. Outspoken invective and rough satire were licensed weapons, though the value of the malicious insinuations or unveiled attacks on political and social reputations is considerably discounted by the certainty that they were hardly ever supposed to be true.

S

Fortunately, perhaps for her, the " young person " did not read much beyond the sentimental novels of the day, such as those by Richardson or by scores of writers whose very names are forgotten. The booksellers of the town and of Tunbridge, Epsom, Bath and Bristol had probably but a small stock from which to choose. It had been left to the more enlightened nineteenth and twentieth centuries to let loose in the libraries for the delectation of youths and maidens a flood of nasty novels dealing with the problems of sex, and raising in the minds of young people such doubts and questionings as would never have come into existence from reading the more downright, but withal purer, novels of Fielding, Smollett and Sterne.

By those older authors vice was called vice, and condemned as such, and virtue was called virtue and commended. In the prurient rubbish of to-day the coarse talk of earlier times is taboo, but the most degrading sentiments and the filthiest vices are described with an outer wrapping of clean language, the most flagrant immoralities are excused, and the whole unsavoury *olla podrida* is made easily accessible to all comers of both sexes by means of circulating libraries and cheap editions.

It is often asserted that Fielding took my Lady Townshend as a model for his Lady Bellaston in *Tom Jones*, but no evidence of this beyond the unsupported guesses of writers of a later age can be produced. The one witness whose word would have set the matter beyond the shadow of a doubt—Horace Walpole to wit—nowhere alludes to the supposed resemblance of the lady of real life to the lady of fiction. Assuredly, neither his friendship for my Lady Townshend, nor any motive of delicacy, would have hindered him from proclaiming the likeness on the housetops, if such a likeness were known to be intended. He was a contemporary of Fielding and knew all about him. He records that Andrew Millar, the publisher, gave £600 for *Tom Jones* and an extra £100 later on because the sales were good; but I cannot trace any hint that my Lady Bellaston was meant to be a portrait of a well-known lady of quality who counted him amongst her most intimate friends.

Nor is Sir Charles Hanbury Williams more communicative on this point. He had been at Eton with Fielding, had helped him largely in his poorer days, and was also an intimate of my Lady Townshend's; but he apparently knows nothing of the matter.

It may be, indeed, strongly doubted whether the novelist meant to draw anybody more definite than a typical lady of quality of the time, and it is just as likely that Lady Bellaston was intended for Lady Harrington or for that notorious Lady Vane who had already been before the reading public in *Memoirs of a Lady of Quality*.

But there is another explanation of the rumour that arose later attributing the original to my Lady Townshend. When Fielding's great novel attained the height of its popularity, the name of Tom Jones came to be used in the world of fashion as a synonym for a lover. Lady Bradshaigh, that curious would-be blue-stocking, whose great delight was to maintain a correspondence with well-known authors under a feigned name, notices the custom in a letter to Richardson, in which she says:

As to Tom Jones, I am fatigued with the name, having fallen into the company of several young ladies who had each a " Tom Jones " in some part of the world, for so they called their favourites. Last post I received a letter from a lady who laments the loss of her " Tom Jones ", and from another who was happy in the company of her " Tom Jones ".

The writer of this letter was well acquainted with the fact that Fielding and Richardson hated each other. It seems to me more than probable that my Lady Townshend used the same expression herself and so laid the foundation for all the malicious reports that followed.

This same Lady Braidshaigh corresponded regularly with Richardson under the pseudonym of " Belfour ", without the novelist suspecting her identity, and she was one of his many correspondents who, during the appearance of *Clarissa Harlowe* in parts, begged him not to allow the heroine to come to an unhappy end.

" If you disappoint me ", she said in one of her innumerable letters, " attend to my curse : May the hatred of all the young, beautiful and virtuous for ever be your portion, and may your eyes never behold anything but age and deformity ! May you meet with applause only from envious old maids, surly bachelors and tyrranical parents ! and may you be doomed to the company of such, and after death may their ugly souls haunt you ! Now make Lovelace and Clarissa unhappy if you dare ! "

They met at last, but the correspondence continued, and the sixth volume of Mrs. Barbauld's portentously long work on Richardson contains nothing but the later letters between these two elderly philanderers.

But there are plausible grounds for suspecting that in another popular novel of the same period the principal characters are intended for actual portraits of my Lady Townshend and her quondam friend my Lady Orford.

This is a tale by one Francis Coventry, called *The*

*History of Pompey the Little : or the Life and Adventures of a Lap-dog*, and Ouida's *Puck*, a novel which at one time had a great vogue, is directly descended from *Pompey*. On its first appearance the character of Lady Tempest was at once set down as a lifelike portrait of Ethelreda, Viscountess Townshend, the following description lending some colour to the idea:

She was a free-hearted, sprightly, jovial girl, very cheerful in her conversation and open in her behaviour : ready to promote any party of pleasure, and not displeased now and then to be assistant in a little mischief. This made her company courted by men of all sorts; among whom, her affability and spirit, as well as her beauty, procured her many admirers. At length she was solicited in marriage by a young Lord, famous for nothing but his great estate, and far her inferior in understanding, but the advantageousness of the match soon prevailed with her parents to give their consent, and the thoughts of a title so dazzled her own eyes, that she had no leisure to ask herself whether she liked the man or not that wore it. His lordship married for the sake of begetting an heir to his estate : and married her in particular because he had heard her toasted as a beauty by most of his acquaintance. She, on the contrary, married because she wanted a husband, and married him because he could give her a title and a coach and six.

This novel was sent to the Lady Mary Wortley Montagu, in exile on the continent, by her daughter the Countess of Bute, who knew well what would please her mother, for she also sent her *Peregrine Pickle*, containing the celebrated *Memoirs of a Lady of Quality* in the same parcel. Lady Mary declared she was able to recognise my Lady Townshend at once. The tale diverted her so much that she could not go to bed till she had finished it. She found it a real and exact representation of life as acted in London then and in her own time, and, as she added, " I have no doubt a hundred years hence with some variations of dress and perhaps Government ". She recognised many of her own acquaintances in the book : Lady Orford (*née* Rolle) in the character of Lady Sophister, as well as my Lady Townshend; and she declared that she had often heard those ladies say the very things now repeated in print. All this may be considered good enough testimony. Though she had been out of the world for some time, my Lady Mary knew it well enough. She had known intimately both the ladies referred to, and in more than one of her letters in bygone years had chronicled the doings of one or the other with a spiteful glee all her own.

Walpole is as silent on this novel as on the supposed likeness to my Lady Townshend of Fielding's Lady Bellaston ; but it is more than probable that the description as quoted above was really meant for her. Her conduct invited satire and lampoon. She was a reckless woman in many ways : without home ties at any rate until her children grew up, and married to an exceptionally disagreeable, morose and notoriously unfaithful husband. She defied public opinion in every direction, and though never once losing her reputation as a lady of quality and leader of society, was openly held up to keen satire in her own name and mercilessly lampooned on all sides.

Such an age of personal abuse has passed away, it is to be hoped never to return. The nearest equivalent in modern days to the lampoon of the eighteenth century is the " On dit " column of the society press, for which Americans, as they might themselves elegantly express it, "take the cake"—a New York society journal, being a publication of which any nation should be thoroughly ashamed. English papers of a similar type are not far behind in their scurrilous impertinences, and only a wholesome fear of the law of libel, with a possible heavy fine as a consequence, holds the hands of the inventors or rakers up of moral nastiness.

The law of libel, for instance, would have stood in the way of the publication of that parody of Horace's ode which was written by Hanbury Williams about 1739–40. It referred to the much-talked-of friendship of my Lady Townshend for Mr. Winnington, already mentioned, which might or might not have exceeded proper bounds. Part of it only may be quoted :

*Donec gratus eram tibi* (HORACE).

*Winnington.* For that short time that I alone was blest,
Singly admitted to that lovely breast,
There was no happier fellow in the Town,
Nor Essex, Bludworth or vig'rous Brown.

*Ethelreda.* Whilst me you loved beyond each earthly thing,
Nor Ethelreda was postponed to Byng,
I shone the foremost character in life,
Nor envied Walmod [1] or Lord Archie's wife.[2]
For Teddy Byng,[3] a passion now I feel
Who both a Pichen and my heart could steal :
To save whose life, I'd stand all Hambden's fury,
Bully the witnesses and bribe the jury.

*Winnington.* I have as odd a passion for my Kitty [4]
(The Motley breed of quality and city),
Had I as many lives as twenty cats,
I'd give them all for one dear game at . . . . . !
What if to nature I again return,
And for thy beauteous form once more should burn !

[1] Madame de Walmoden, Countess of Yarmouth, mistress of the King
[2] Lady Archibald Hamilton, mistress of the Robes to the Princess of Wales. She succeeded Miss Vane in the irregular affections of Frederic Prince of Wales.
[3] Fifth son of the first Lord Torrington.
[4] A notorious courtesan, kept by the Earl of London. Casanova knew her also during his short stay in England.

Should I quit Byng, would you take back your Winny,
An love again as if the Devil was in ye ?

.        .        .        .        .

Some of the allusions are obscure, and the remainder
of the poem, with Ethelreda's reply, are too gross for
quotation here.   The curious may be referred to the
text in the British Museum ! In another set of verses
on the Duchess of Manchester, Williams writes :

Sprightly as Orford's Countess she,
And as the wanton Townshend free,
And more than both discreet.

It must have been an astonishing society which
permitted such things to be written by members of
one's own circle, and printed and published with
impunity. The publication of such a set of verses of
course never affected my Lady's conduct at all. She
was just the woman to laugh with the lampooners
against herself, and always had the wit to turn aside
the edge of any malicious shaft directed against her.

She is also supposed to have been the original of
" Lady Bonton " in Anstey's appendix to the *Patriot*,
who is described as a " Lady celebrated for her eccentricities, her gallantries, and her wit ".

The country spas—Epsom, Tunbridge, Bath and
the rest—were naturally regular forcing beds of satires
and lampoons, for visitors had little else to occupy
their time beyond the criticism of their neighbours.
In such narrow circles every witty innunendo was soon
passed from one to the other and brought home to
London tea-tables later on.

A satire on the loose manners at Tunbridge Wells,
and the degraded condition to which the public walks
at that resort had been reduced, boldly asserts that
matters may improve.

When Townshend begins
To leave off her sins,
Then shall Tunbridge no more
In her walks see a w . . . .

One of the most amusing and amazing satires of
the century was published in the *Westminster Magazine*
in 1773, about the time that there was a sale by auction
of the goods belonging to Teresa Cornelys, which
had become a notorious place of assignation for the
female rakes of the day. In this satire Cupid is represented as holding an auction of various " used "
articles, a sort of jumble sale of goods from the Court
of Love !

The buyers include many representatives of persons
of quality. One of the lots is a macaroni arrayed in
the latest fashion. The auctioneer proceeds to enumerate his good points :

*Cupid.* It is, ladies, a thing of the neuter gender, fit for every
purpose but one. 'Tis one of the sweetest Macaronis that ever
perfumes and cosmeticks made delectable to a fine lady : and to
enhance his value the higher and make him more acceptable to
your arms, he is a Captain—a Captain, ladies ! Come, dont peep
through you fan-sticks : you are not at church squinting at a
Macaroni Parson ! Come, Belles, bid away for this monkey of a
man who can break china as fast as you can buy it. Oh, he is the
wickedest, merriest, simplest thing that ever simpered at a glass,
took snuff with a smile or dawdled with a teaspoon ! Allons, donc,
mes belles beautés, cheer up your drooping hearts and buy up
this thing of pastime and delight. Come, sniff your Eau de Circe,
and bid for this parrot of mankind !

*First Lady.* One thousand guineas.

*Second Lady.* Five thousand.

*Cupid.* Rare work. These are the baubles, Mercury, to take in
the Belles ! Martin Deard may burn his toyshop. 'Tis powdered
and perfumed flesh and blood that the reps and the demi-reps
want. five thousand, ladies ?

*First Lady.* Six and my wedding jewels—and take my lord in
the bargain.

*Cupid.* Does any Wanton say more ? I mean not to impose. There is money enough bid.

*Second Lady.* Knock him down, sir, at your peril. No partialities at auctions Mr Cupid, or you will have your wings singed. I say for the pretty fellow, six thousand, my jewels, repeating watch, miniatures and sedan-chair. I must, will have the delightful creature. Oh ! his crimson sattin breeches ! his coat cut away to nothing ! his plaited hair, and his sweet face washed every day with Warren's almond paste and best cosmeticks !

*Cupid.* Madam, I will knock him down to you. And I wish he may answer such domestic purposes as you may put him to ! Going—going—gone !

*Second Lady.* I shall take him on my knees on my chair. Air shall not blow upon him, and the nicest white meats shall be his diet.                                            [*Exit.*

Bouncing Bridget is then put up and immediately knocked down to the first bid of a " Cit " for five shillings and threepence.

A duchess is put up. Five pounds is bid.

*Cupid.* And all the Running Footmen thrown in. Five broad-backed footmen ! Luscious rogues of recreation !

*A Dowager Lady.* Five hundred pounds for the fellows—apart from the Duchess.

A maid of honour is sold and then a Nimrod macaroni.

Then another lot of quite a different type is put up. This is a youth called " Hercules Vigor ". He is over six feet in height and a splendid specimen of humanity.

*Cupid.* You wainscot-faced, wrinkled, doubly-japanned Dowagers ! Here is a source of rich recreation for you ! Here is comfort, consolidated comfort ! View him from top to toe, from shoulder to hip, from the tip of his elbow to the tip of his toe. What say ye, widows ? What an athletick hero !

*First Dowager.* Five hundred guineas. He shall drive my coach.

*Second Dowager.* Five thousand. He shall drive me in my whisky (*a sort of gig*). I am not afraid of my life under his whip.

THE MOCK AUCTION AT CARLISLE HOUSE
From an old print

*Third Dowager*. Seven thousand. He shall serve my country seat. He shall plough and harrow my ground.

*Fourth Dowager*. Ten thousand. He is just the size I want. I have rummaged every Registry Office in town, and cannot get a Thing to my liking. I hate a servant that is not fit for a grenadier !

Then the voice of my Lady Harrington is heard. She is by that time getting on in years and the mother of a family of grown-up daughters.

*Lady Harrington*. Twelve thousand ; and I will have him if all the plate in the house goes ! I say I'll have him, and who is the Dowager or widow that dare oppose the Lady Harrington ?

*Dowager*. I dare ! and I do ! I—the well-known Lady Townshend !

But Hercules Vigor is finally knocked down to my Lady Harrington, who calls her coach and bears away her prize.

Coarse and libellous no doubt, even in the small portion reproduced above ; and there is much more of it quite unprintable. The morals of the society of London must have been at a fairly low ebb when such matter could issue from the press with the names of private individuals in full, even though it were intended to be a caricature of things and people as they were.

In the same magazine is to be found another example of personal lampoon. This is headed " An extraordinary Meeting of the Female Members of the Coterie—*Veneris 23 die Octobris 1772* ".

The Coterie was that association of ladies already alluded to in connection with Mrs. Cornely's assemblies at Carlisle House. As at all ladies' clubs, then and since, the absence of men was very severely felt, and at this supposititious meeting various propositions are made by our old friend the Countess of Harrington to mitigate the evil. Among others is the following:

> That a tête à tête, provided that it is composed of one lady and one gentleman, shall form a Coterie, and shall have the privilege of retiring or mixing with the company in the great room at pleasure: that a number of retiring rooms be immediately prepared for this purpose, accommodated with sophas, refreshments, etc.: that, upon any lady or gentleman retiring, all looks of astonishment, all shrugs of disapprobation shall be considered as affronts to the whole assembly.

This is a most amusing, but indelicate article, in which the names of many of the best-known ladies of quality are but thinly disguised by the omission of the central letters. In this way are pilloried the Duchess of Ancaster, Lady Fitzroy, Lady Carlisle, Lady Grosvenor, Lady Percy and the Countess of Upper Ossory.

In a number of the *Town and Country Magazine* was the account of the proceedings of a supposititious jury of matrons empanelled to determine the sex of the celebrated Chevalier D'Éon. My Lady Harrington presided, but my Lady Townshend was also in the box, together with the Ladies Grosvenor, Sarah Bunbury, Ligonier[5] and Rochford. The last named, being declared to be "the most experienced", was therefore deputed to represent the rest, and gave her verdict as "doubtful"!

This Lady Rochford was a daughter of Edward

---

[5] Wife of the celebrated soldier, Colonel Ligonier of the "Black Horse", now the 7th Dragoon Guards, and sometimes nicknamed "Ligonier's Horse". He divorced her, after fighting a duel on her account with the poet Alfieri in the Green Park in 1771. She was a daughter of the beautiful Mrs. Pitt, of Strathfieldsaye, afterwards Lady Rivers. After the divorce she married a Captain Smith and sank into obscurity. Proper Lady Mary Coke, writing from Calais, mentions her as "one of the people I would always avoid. She comes very often to Calais, sees all the French officers, but refuses to see any one from England."

Young or Durnford, Bath King-of-Arms, and married the fourth Earl of Rochford. She had been attached to the Court at one time, and rumour said that the Duke of Cumberland (" Butcher " Cumberland) had been attracted by her. She was a notorious woman of gallantry, and many stories had been told about her when at Court.

My Lady Vane had her full share of the muck thrown by the lampooners, but possibly no more than her desserts. The story of her life is the most un-blushing confession of immorality that has ever proceeded from a member of her sex, and occupy among female memoirs much the same position as those of Jacques Casanova or the Chevalier de Faublas do among those of mere men.

Another writer of lampoons in which the names of well-known people were but thinly disguised, was Edward Thompson, author of several gross compositions such as the *Court of Cupid*, *The Meretriciad*, *The Temple of Venus*, *The Courtesan*, etc., all full of allusions to " gallantry " (as the pursuit of such pleasures was always styled) and to the gay world of the higher social scale and the better-known courtesans of the day. Thompson, or some similar writer, was the author of the following epitaph " On the Death of Kitty Fisher "—a very celebrated woman of the town, whose portrait, by Sir Joshua Reynolds, hangs to-day in the library at Lansdowne House.

> Of St. Peter 'twas said in the days of the Jews
> In Judaea no fisher could stand in his shoes :
> But this I'll affirm, and I'm sure with no drift,
> That he ne'er, like St. Kitty, was put to the shift !
> Nay, I'll bet Bishop Warburton fifty to ten
> He never, like her, was the fisher of men !

Of Lady Vane he wrote :

> With feelings, who can see and not complain
> Of the lewd actions of a Lady Vane ?

and, perhaps, in allusion to the low origin of H.R.H.
the Duchess of Gloucester the following words were
addressed to the *filles de joie* of the time :

> Hold up your heads, my girls, the manner such is
> There is no knowing who will be a Duchess !

Another famous publication of the same scurrilous
kind was *The Female Jockey Club*. This did not appear
till very late in the century, after the death, indeed, of
my Lady Townshend. It was a series of pen-pictures
of noted women, high in the social scale, each of
which was described in a more or less scandalous
light. No one was spared. The series ranged from the
Princesses of the blood Royal to Mrs. Piozzi and Mrs.
Robinson (" Perdita "), and included such ladies as
Georgiana, Duchess of Devonshire, and her successor
in the ducal honours, Lady Elizabeth Foster, the
Duchess of Rutland, the Duchess of Gordon, Mar-
chioness of Salisbury, Lady Bath, Lady Wallace, Lady
Elizabeth Luttrel, etc.

In 1780 there appeared the first edition of a book
now almost entirely forgotten, but destined at the
time to make a great sensation, run through several
editions and induce many (and inferior) imitations.[6]
It is stated in the *D.N.B.* (not always a reliable
authority) that this book, which received the title of
*The Abbey of Kilkhampton*, was written by the Rev.
Sir Herbert Croft in 1780, and that in 1781 he added
a second part, continuing to augment it through eight

---

[6] To pen with garretteers obscure and shabby
Inscriptive nonsense in a fancied Abbey.
(MATHIAS, *Pursuits of Literature*.)

successive editions until 1788. There were fourteen
editions in all.

It professed to be a collection of epitaphs transcribed from the tombstones of people well known
in the political and social world, and supposed to have
been buried in an abbey raised on the site of the
church where Hervey wrote his *Meditations* in 1746.

The idea was one that gave the greatest scope to
the lampooner and satirist, and could only have been
carried out by some person or persons who knew all
about the foremost people of the day. The description
of the contents, as given on the title-page of the first
edition, runs as follows :

The Abbey of Kilkhampton : or monumental records for the
year 1780. Faithfully transcribed from the original inscriptions
which are still perfect, and appear to be drawn up in a Stile
devoid of fulsome Panegyric or unmerited Detraction : and
compiled with a view to ascertain with Precision, the Manners
which prevailed in Great Britain, during the last Fifty Years of
the Eighteenth Century.

In an address to the reader the origin of this
imaginary resting-place of all the celebrities of the age
is thus set forth :

To the Reader.

The Church of Kilkhampton was visited by Mr. Hervey
(author of the *Meditations*) anno 1746, when in its original
obscurity. About the year 1783, some exalted characters of that
century proposed the erection of an Abbey on the spot where it
had stood. The project was considered of essential utility and
speedily put into execution. It soon became distinguished by the
interment of the most honourable personages : and when this
select collection of epitaphs was transcribed, Kilkhampton Abbey
was supposed to contain a more extensive range of splendid
monuments than that of Westminster.

In the first edition there were upwards of one
hundred and twenty epitaphs. Horace Walpole, Selina

Countess of Huntingdon, Old Q., George Selwyn, Lady Greenwich (wife of Charles Townshend), the Earl of Carlisle, the Duchess of Queensbury, John Wilkes, the Duchess of Kingston, Lady Vane and two Lady Townshends—one my Lady Viscountess Townshend and the other meant probably for one of the wives of the first Marquis.

The epitaph of Ethelreda, Viscountess Townshend, appears as No. 40 of the series and is couched in the following terms. It is the only one for which there is space to quote.

Indulge the Tribute of a pitying Tear
In kind Remembrance of her who was once the fair, the blooming
Lady V . . . . . . . . . s T . . . . . . . d.
Born and educated without the Prospect of rising beyond the
Level of Mediocrity
She cultivated the sincerest Charms that could assist in finishing
A Model of the loveliest Perfection.
The Elegance of her Attractions captivated the Heart, while the
Artless Innocence of her Conversation improved the Felicity
of those who gazed on the soft Lustre of her
Beauties with Rapture and Admiration.
The Nobleman who was *induced* to espouse her, kept guard over the
Treasure he possessed, with a Warmth of Affection that did
Honour to her Virtues,
Though it robbed her of that unsuspected Freedom of Sentiment
Which Youth and Beauty part from with Reluctance.
She lived, beloved without Jealousy by the Young and Gay,
Admired without Envy by the more rigid of her Sex, and
Distinguished with Tokens of sincere Veneration
From all who knew the Refinement of her
Accomplishments.

Such a collection of clever satirical lines about people of quality, showing up their weaknesses, and not without many a touch of spicy scandal, had an enormous success in times when, if you wished to be a welcome guest, you must be ever ready to say something malicious about your friends. After many editions, an enlarged series was published in 1799, in which the epitaphs on those who had really died in the interval were, marvellous to say, omitted. Imitations also appeared. In 1788 was issued the first number of a small periodical called *The Devil's Pocket Book*, containing some continuations in imitations of the famous Kilkhampton series, among them being lines on Old Q., the Prince Regent, Mrs. Thrale and others. But it was a far less witty production and soon died a natural death.

Before leaving one of the most unpleasant aspects of the eighteenth century, allusion may be made to another collection of scurrilous lampoons in which the names of persons were as usual but thinly disguised.

Most students of the literature of this period will know something about William Combe, the creator of Dr Syntax, but few of his works are now read except the *Tour of Dr Syntax* and *Dr Syntax in Search of a Wife*. He was, however, widely known in his day, not as an author, for all his works were published anonymously, but as a brilliant man about town, a gay bachelor who kept horses and carriages, lived in expensive quarters, spent money lavishly in entertaining his friends, belonged to the exclusive " Coterie ", and gambled and speculated with the best.

At his death it was discovered that he was the author of an immense number of books, poems, essays, pamphlets and satires, among which two especially had an enormous success on their first appearance and ran through several editions. These were the *Diaboliad* and the *Diabo-Lady*, dedicated respectively to the worst man and the worst woman in His Majesty's dominions.

T

In the latter of these, the Devil is represented as looking for a wife, and all the notorious women of the day are paraded in front of him so that he may choose the worst. A rare opportunity is thus afforded for an unscrupulous lampooner to pillory in his lines any woman who was being talked about for her reckless conduct, from the smartest lady of quality to the lowest courtesan. Combe availed himself of the opportunity to the fullest. As a specimen the following may be quoted:

> The next that rose was wanton . . . . . . . .
> With front assured, and dressed en cavalier.

It was not difficult to guess that the well-known wife of Colonel Ligonier was indicated in these lines. In the same way my Lady Townshend, with the Ladies Harrington and Vane, are dragged into the satire, with scarcely any attempt at concealment.

According to the *D.N.B.*, Combe " was said to have been successively a common soldier, a waiter at Swansea, a teacher of elocution, a cook at Douai College, and a private in the French army ". This may be just a sequence of gross inexactitudes. Horace Walpole in one of his note-books in the Waller Collection, quoted in the Supplement to the Toynbee Edition of the *Letters*, says that he was the son of an attorney, who left him about seven thousand pounds, which he wasted in two years and contracted a debt of £13,000 more. He was always talking of building seats for himself in the country. He was a fairly good artist and agreeable, and for some time kept quite good company. On one occasion he was applauded for the spirit with which he took up Lord Lyttelton (as bad a man as himself) for gross rudeness to a woman. At Almacks supper-rooms Lady Archer, a peeress remarkable for her tawdry dress and the prodigious quantity of rouge she plastered on her cheeks, reproved Lord Lyttelton for too much familiarity, upon which he said : " Why do you pretend to talk, you drunken peacock ? " and threw a glass of wine in her face. Combe happened to be sitting next to her and immediately said : " My Lord, I take the insult as intended at me for you could not be brutal enough to aim it at a woman ", following up this by challenging him. Lord Lyttelton, however, went off the next morning to France.

Combe's extravagance soon reduced him so much that he actually took to pilfering, and once stole a silver spoon. He afterwards married a common woman who had been kept by Francis, Lord Beauchamp, son of the Earl of Hertford, but had been dismissed by him for boundless infidelities. He had settled three hundred a year on her, on which she and Combe managed to live for a time. Walpole adds : " This creature egged on her husband, Combe, to satirise Lord Beauchamp and all his family, which he did in various satires with unbounded malice and virulence, but with some good poetry ". Combe died in his eighty-second year, heavily in debt and within the precincts of the King's Bench.

If it be thought that I have laid too much stress on an unsavoury aspect of the eighteenth century, it should be remembered that the ideas as to what constituted morality, or even decency, differed very greatly in that age from those of the present day. It is therefore necessary to insist once more on the difference of the standard by which men and women should be judged.

With regard more especially to Ethelreda Townshend, it is but a shallow criticism which cites her as an example of the immorality of the time, when the evidence consists so largely of the spiteful gossip of rival women like Lady Mary Montagu and effeminate creatures of the Horace Walpole type. The story of Miss Letitia Piper's twins, as related by the gossips of Sheridan's *School for Scandal*, is one instance of how reputations could in those days be blasted at the will of an empty-headed macaroni or a jealous dame.

Perhaps, after all, we are not much better off in the twentieth century. The School for Scandal flourishes as it did a hundred and fifty years ago, only nowadays language is less gross, and no words are used which cannot be found in an expurgated dictionary! The result is the same.

# CHAPTER XI

## EXTRACTS FROM LETTERS ADDRESSED TO
## MY LADY TOWNSHEND

The numerous correspondents of the Lively Lady Townshend:
letter from General Campbell when out against the '45 : letters
from Lord Hervey, George Hervey and Augustus Hervey:
entertaining letter from Augustus Hervey, describing life at
Genoa : Mrs. French.

MY LADY TOWNSHEND had a large number of
intimate friends with whom she must have kept up a
regular correspondence in that delicate handwriting
which has survived in one or two short notes now in
the British Museum. It is much to be regretted that
so few of her letters can be traced, though doubtless
many are still extant hidden away in family archives
or stacked in lofts as lumber. Her correspondence with
three generations of the Hervey family, of whom the
Earl of Bristol is the head, would make most entertaining reading if it could be found. Her letters to
adherents of the Pretender might help to settle the
question of her supposed Jacobitism. Her answers to
the wordy despatches of that Duke of Argyll who
hunted the Highlandmen after the '45 would be
amusing on the other side. Her correspondents were
many and various. They included politicians, men of
fashion, and a host of women, headed by her own
erratic cousin Caroline, Countess of Harrington, but

also including the blue-stockings and the pious entourage of Selina, Countess of Huntingdon. In col-
lections of letters available to the public very few of
hers are to be found, and it is especially curious that
only one or two unimportant notes are among Horace
Walpole's letters. Such intimate friends undoubtedly
wrote to each other frequently, and Walpole was wont
to copy out his correspondence and prepare it for
future publication.

Some few letters there are, however, addressed to
her, or to members of her family, preserved among the
papers at Raynham Hall, and among them is a very
long and interesting one from General John Campbell,
husband of the lovely Mary Bellenden, whom Lady
Louisa Stuart in her Argyll *Memoir* speaks of as " the
very handsome, very stupid Colonel Jack Campbell ".

This letter, or rather the postscript, which is three
times as long as the body of the letter itself, was
written at the time when the last remnants of Prince
Charlie's followers were being hunted down in the
Highlands or driven to sue for mercy. It has a curious
historical interest, for it shows how near the young
Prince was to surrendering himself to the Royal troops,
just before Flora Macdonald aided him to escape, and
it incidentally removes some of the glamour attached
to the received account of that young lady's doings :
for we find that at first she altogether refused to help
the royal fugitive, and afterwards told General
Campbell that she would, in like manner, have
assisted him or any one else in distress.

The letter is dated from Inveraray, September 30,
1746.

MY DEAR LADY TOWNSHEND—It is high time that I should
in private life follow the example of some of His Majesty's

rebellious subjects who have come in and surrendered to the
Royal Mercy hoping forgiveness.

You know that some time after the loss of my late Mistress,
I put myself under your wing as my Queen : as to you, my
Princess, I own but one crime, that of omission, yet, to so good,
so kind a friend, even that calls aloud and demands asking
pardon and forgiveness, I ask it, I expect it, and considering
(as I think I wrote your Fatt friend and neighbour) the crime
carried with it its own punishment by being so long deprived
of a most agreeable correspondence, I hope for the best. When
I told your Ladyship that I have wrote more for these last ten
Months by post than any clerk in office, you'll tell me it is
condemning myself, I deny it, I was not pleasing myself which
would not have been the case had I been writing to you : in
short, since I left London and arrived in this Country, I cannot
say that I have had one agreeable or pleasant moment. Nothing
but hurry and anxiety of mind : excessive fatigue, together with
a great deal of bad health. And since I returned here from my
Island Expedition mostly confined to the House, and so worn
out that I begin to think of another world. I wish it was
Whitehall. But before I leave this, Christian-like, I desire once
more to be forgiven my enemys, I have 'tis true had some
revenge off them, and may say that in my Turn, I gave them
(as they did me), no small trouble, and I think did some good
to the cause I was engag'd in : but I must, will have done with
myself, but never with you : for in truth I am with the utmost
sincerity, affection and esteem, Dear Lady Townshend's most
obedient, etc., etc.                           JOHN CAMPBELL.

P.S. I rejoyce with you, pray tell me if Miss Townshend is
as handsome as ever after that dangerous but natural operation
the small-pox.[1] Is Mr Townshend as much in love with you as
when I left him ? and lastly is his father jealous of him ? I cant
say but I am. I condole with you for the loss of a friend, make
my compliments to those you choose to see in private in Whitehall, particularly Lady Sophia T., and our Missie : tell her I must
and will kiss her when we meet, but very gently. . . .

Here the writer of the lengthy postscript wanders

[1] My Lady's third son Edward died of the smallpox. Her eldest son and
her daughter Audrey were ill of it at the same time.

off into a long account of an expedition to Skye, the
Western Highlands and St. Kilda, undertaken in conjunction with some ships under Commodore Smith,
in search of the " Younger Adventurer " ; *i.e.* Prince
Charles Edward. The latter part may be quoted :

Having forgott myself, fancying I was talking to you, this
P.S. has swel'd beyond the Bounds of a letter, so that I must
have done, and leave it to another opportunity of giving you
and His Lordship some further Account of this last afore-
mentioned Expedition in which I had very near succeeded. As
a proof of which I hereto add what Captain O'Neil who was
taken prisoner by one of my Parties and sent to the Earl of
Albemarle sette forth in his Declaration or rather Examination.
I have it under his own hand and you shall hear it.

The account which follows of the negotiations with
Miss Flora Macdonald, though said by the General to
be the statement of Captain O'Neil, is perhaps from
the lips of another of the Prince's party. It throws a
light on the actions of the popular Highland heroine,
somewhat disconcerting to those who have so be-
lauded her devotion to the Stuart cause. I transcribe
the witness's own words as quoted in the General's
letter :

The Prince (Charles Edward) and O'Neil went to the hills
and stay'd there all night, after which we heard that General
Campbell was at Bernera so that wee were then surrounded by
Forces, and was at a loss what to do. Wee mett a Younge Ladye
one Miss McDonald. Captn O'Neil advised the Younge Ladye
to assist the P. in making his Escape to the Isle of Skie, which
she at first refused, but by Force of Arguments and telling her
that the Prince should be in Woman's Dress she at last consented:
she parted with us and desired we should stay at Corrodale till
we should hear from her, which we did for two Days without
hearing from our Younge Ladye : This made the P. very uneasy
thinking she could not perform her Promise so that at last he
determined to send O'Neil to General Campbell to let him know

he would surrender himself Prisoner. But while in this thought, a Message came from the Younge Ladye desiring us to come to the Point of Ruisneath,[2] where she would wait us. . . .

The General winds up his letter to my Lady Townshend thus :

The Younge Ladye, the Lady Clanronald and all concerned in the escape are sent Prisoners to London. I cannot but say I have a great deal of compassion for the Younge Ladye, she told me that she would have in like manner assisted me or any-one in Distress. Adieu, adieu, Dear Lady Townshend. My compliments to the lively Mr. Townshend. If your Ladyship has any commands for me to direct to Edinburgh. You have spoil'd Frederick.[3] He gives himself airs and won't write to me, I have some thoughts of forbidding him Whitehall as a punishment.

From the tone of this ill-spelt and badly punctuated letter it may be inferred that a more than ordinary friendship existed between the writer and my Lady Townshend. His very open way of discussing the pursuit of Prince Charlie, his intimate messages to members of her family, and the length of the letter itself, present the General in the light of one of the inner circle of the house in Privy Gardens, and afford proof, if further proof were needed, that my Lady Townshend's Jacobitism was of a very amateur description ; it is most difficult to reconcile her extravagant behaviour with regard to Lord Kilmarnock in prison and the other lords of the '45 with her intimate friendship for such a ruthless hunter of Highlanders as was this Duke of Argyll.

A family with whom she was on terms of the closest friendship was that of the Herveys, of whom

[2] The modern Roseneath.
[3] His fourth son. He was very handsome, and my Lady was very fond of him. Walpole couples his name with the " Westminster Schoolboys ", who were said to sleep in my Lady's dressing-room.

the Earl of Bristol is the head. The celebrated Lord Hervey,[4] second son of the first Earl of Bristol, never succeeded to the title. He had three sons by his beautiful wife, Molly Leppel. Each of these three sons, George,[5] Augustus [6] and Frederick [7] reigned in turn as Earl of Bristol, and my Lady Townshend corresponded on intimate terms with at least two out of the three.

The following letter was addressed to her in 1742 by the Hon. George Hervey, Lord Hervey's eldest son. It may be noted that the writer was but twenty-one at the time and that my Lady Townshend was thirteen years his senior.

ICKWORTH, *May* 22, 1742.

MADAM—I am very sorry to find by a letter from Lincoln that, after your Lordship (*sic*) had done me the honour to write me, the post had done me the favour to loose it altogether with his, what a disagreeable miscarriage, how unkind an abortion ! I shou'd have thought that these things only cou'd have happened to Mrs. B . . . . . . l.[8] Are you not surprised, Madam, how I came to learn these technical words ? I heard them but today. Your Ladyship's friend, Mrs. Eldred, has taken no notice of us since we came into this country, but we have had the honour of two or three Aldermen with their Ladys and Misses. I beg if you hear of any Camp there is to be in England, or of any new regiments that are to go abroad, you wou'd be so good as to let me know, for else these are my quarters, and you will find my calculation about my staying in the Country too true ; for

[4] The " Lord Fanny " of the letters of Sarah, Duchess of Marlborough.
[5] Minister at Turin and Ambassador at Madrid. Died unmarried.
[6] In the Navy. He married the beautiful Elizabeth Chudleigh, who afterwards, as Duchess of Kingston, was tried for bigamy. The offspring of her marriage with Augustus Hervey, born during one of Miss Chudleigh's periods of service as maid of honour, died in infancy.
[7] Bishop of Derry. He was rather an astounding person in more ways than one, and habitually travelled in great splendour and almost royal state on the Continent, usually accompanied by one or more " fair ladies ".
[8] Mrs. Bob Brudenel, daughter of Sir Cecil Bishopp, Bart. : she was afterwards bedchamber woman to Queen Charlotte.

tho' I was told when first I came down I was only to be here ten days or a fortnight, yet now that time is expired, there is no probability of my going to town. Has your Ladyship got your house in the Country? I shall grow so rich during my retreat that if the widow insists on ten additional Guineas, you may draw for it from my Banquers at Bury. May I enquire how Lord John does? it is relatively to you that I am solicitous about his health, since I remember some very gloomy days in Grosvenor St on his account. Lord Bristol often drinks your health to me, which is seconded by infinite pleasure by me, my poor flirtation is never included; you accused me, Madam, of having a violent passion, the fact I own tho' not the person to whom it was apply'd, it was they who did apply who cou'd lay the chief claim to that, and to the entire esteem of madam.—Your Ladyship's most obedient humble servant.        G. HERVEY.

It is evident that my Lady must have flirted with and fascinated this youthful member of the third generation of Herveys as well as his old grandfather, who "often drank her health". George Hervey's own father, Lord Hervey, had, of course, always been her intimate friend. The following letter from him to my Lady in 1742 seems to show that he had sent her his portrait. The allusions are not quite clear, but the letter is thoroughly characteristic of the writer, one of the most remarkable men of his day. The extremely stilted style of the wording, more stilted than usual, seems odd to us now, and still more so when it is reflected what close friends they were.

ICKWORTH PARK, *August* 19, 1742.

MADAM—The last Post (the most welcome Messenger that ever arrived at Ickworth) brought me the honour of your Ladyship's letter; and though it is impossible for any Body to be more obliged and pleased than I was with the Favour of so agreeable a Distinction, yet it was no small Alloy to that Pleasure, to feel the Severity, as well as Politeness of your Reproach, in condescending to thank me for giving what I ought to have pay'd my humblest and warmest Acknowledgments to you for your Indulgence in receiving; since I am very sensible when you allow the Copy a Place in your House, you confer an Honor upon it, equal to the Pleasure you give the original when you admit him there.

If there was a Dearth of Talk (too often taken for Conversation) in the Party you mention, I think a more proper Addition could not have been made to it than that you tell me of, since as far as the bare Evacuation of Words can contribute to make such Partys what they call *go off well*, I will stand Godfather to all their Lungs, and would as soon answer for Articulation flowing constantly through the Channels of those Mouths as I would for water in the Channel of the Thames.

I am very sorry to hear poor Winnington has in reality been downright ill, and am sure the Symptoms must have been very strong when your infidelity on that Chapter could be converted into Faith: but if I was in his place, I could never forgive your drawing any Parallel between him and the Man with whom you coupled him on this occasion,[9] since I think Nature has made as full as great a Difference in the Furniture of the Insides of their Heads, as I daresay the faces of their Wives will do in the Ornaments of Outsides. I had some thought once of sending this Letter to my Servants in London, with orders to have it smoak'd like a Westphalia Ham, in a London Chimney, before it was presented to your Ladyship, knowing how little Chance it must have to be well received when you reflect it is the uncorrected Produce of the intolerable Rusticity that must reign three score miles from London; but upon second thoughts, fearing no Quarantine would be deemed by your Ladyship sufficient to purge it of such a Plague, I laid this Project aside, resolving to lose no time in assuring you with how much Gratitude, Warmth and Truth I am—Madam, your Ladyship's most obliged and most obedient Humble servant,

HERVEY.

There is another letter in the collection addressed to my Lady Townshend by Lord Hervey, which is not quite so "elephantine" in its wit. It bears no other date than "Tuesday Morning" and evidently refers to something on which my Lady had asked for an

---

[9] Some unrecorded sally of my Lady Townshend's.

opinion. An easy familiarity is there, in amusing contrast to the formal polished periods.

*Tuesday Morning.*

Your Ladyship does my Taste great Honor to think it worth consulting in anything, and a very undeserv'd one if you let it be any Guide to your's with regard to what I now send back to you. As far as my *Plate-Skill* goes, I think them very pretty, but as uselessly pretty as the Face of a virtuous Beauty on the Head of an injudicious Wit. I call'd at your Door on Sunday Morning but had not the good Fortune to find you, and by the Equipage I saw at the Door, should have feared you were in danger of the Ill-Fortune of going somewhere into the Country farther than halfway to Knightsbridge, had I not luckily recollected that *One Flesh* may sometimes resemble the double Man Odmar talks of in the *Indian Emperor* [10] when he says " one half lay upon the ground, the other ran away " : which half I would have you resemble I dare not suggest, but firmly believe you will guess right.—I am, Madam, your Ladyship's most obedient humble Servant.                                    HERVEY.

But the most entertaining letters from a Hervey to my Lady in this collection were received by her six years or so later than the last quoted, about 1748, from Augustus Hervey,[11] second of those three grandsons of the first Earl of Bristol, who eventually all succeeded to the title. He was in the Navy and rose to be Admiral of the Blue ; but his chief claim to note in the social annals of the time rests on his clandestine marriage with the beautiful and notorious maid of honour, Elizabeth Chudleigh. He soon got very tired of her and she of him. She would have been glad to have acknowledged the marriage after a series of deaths had made her a Countess, but he refused to do so ; so that,

---

[10] *The Indian Emperor*, a well-known play by Dryden.

[11] Casanova alludes to this Hervey in his *Memoirs*: " Parmi les autres connaissances que je fis chez Lady Harrington, je dois mentionner Lord Hervey (*sic*), illustre marin, le conquérant de La Havane. Il avait épousé Miss Chodeleig (*sic*) et s'en était séparé. Miss Chodeleig est devenue célèbre depuis sous le nom de Duchesse de Kingston.

when the amorous Duke of Kingston offered himself,
she persuaded her husband to accept a large sum of
money to hold his tongue, thus enabling her to mount
one step higher, and become a Duchess. How the
bigamy was brought to light through the greed of a
servant belongs to another story. Augustus was a very
lively youth, and, like his elder brother George, very
much attracted by my Lady Townshend.

The letter is dated May 8, 1748, on board the
*Phoenix*, Vado Bay.

Tho' I have never received one line from Dr Lady Townshend, since I left England, yet I cannot help writing one now
by Capn Foulkes who has the Admll's leave for three months
and who has been abroad with me the whole time of my being
out ; he will tell you how well Jemmie [12] is, that I have taken
him into this ship with me and shall take all the care of him in
my power. The Sea has given him an opportunity to practise
his wild Spirit, and tho' a little endanger'd by the Heat of our
warm Climate, yet all is well again ; he is forgiven on promises
of future reserve ; the young Dog got ashore when I was up at
Turin, *and went astray*. Pray now let me ask you (for I know you
are sincere) what has prevented your writing to me after
promising—was it that you had promis'd, or was it that you
heard of my success, and at once imagin'd I had become worldly?
if either, permit me to say you are to blame, I'm sure Mr. Selwyn
will agree with me, and Mr. Hume will condemn you. I have
wrote three or four letters to you and am heartily sorry if you
have never had them ; I am sure you'll repent of not having
wrote to me, when I tell you that except my Mother I have
received no letter from any Relation. I have only one from my
uncle Aston [13] ever since I have been out of England. I shall
refer to Captn Foulkes all particulars concerning myself, and
be content with telling you that, if 'tis Peace, I hope not to see

[12] " Jemmie " was probably one of the many very youthful admirers of my
Lady. Perhaps one of the precocious Westminster boys !
[13] The Hon. and Rev. Henry Hervey, D.D., fifth son of the first Earl of
Bristol and a brother of " Lord Fanny ". He took the name of Aston on his
marriage with Catherine, sister and heiress of Sir Thomas Aston of Aston.

England some time, as I'm in a Ship that I flatter myself will be station'd here. You cannot expect to hear any News from me : and to tell your Ladyship the Truth, I'm at a loss for a Style at present, lest if I write in my usual one to you I should offend, because I have not had the Satisfaction since I have been out to hear your Approbation; for which reason I had better be quick in assuring you that this is only for an Opportunity of convincing you that Nothing can prevent me ever remaining—Yours Ladyship's most faithfull and obedt humble servt.

A. HERVEY.

There is another from the same young sailor, written at Portsmouth, with no date, much in the same style, bewailing that she does not write to him and vowing that he cannot keep from writing to her :

You see that I'm as incapable of refraining from this kind of proxy when absent as I am solicitous of ever being with you in person when possible.

Then he is off again to the Mediterranean, and at Genoa sits down one day to write my Lady a long letter describing the place and the people, delightful for its chatty gossip and the light it throws upon the Italy of that day. The lively Lady Townshend must have been indeed a fascinating personality. At this time Augustus Hervey was barely twenty-eight years of age, and she was forty-four ! But years made little difference with her ; and as for her admirers, they were of all ages, from grandpapa Lord Bristol and papa Lord Hervey to grandsons George and Augustus and the Westminster schoolboys ! By that time she had perhaps got over her attack of Jacobitism, for her most intimate friends appear to have been strictly on the Hanoverian side.

Augustus Hervey, with all the faults of his years and of the age in which he lived, shows up as the best of the family in many ways. He had a profession in which he greatly distinguished himself; he was so unfortunate as to be mixed up with, and married to the most notorious and unscrupulous woman of the Court, who stopped at nothing, however criminal or mean, to advance her own ends. But for this connection (she outlived him for nine years) he might have married and his title descended to a son. As it was, the earldom at his death devolved on his brother Frederick, Bishop of Derry, one of the most dissolute and unprincipled prelates that has ever adorned the Protestant Church of England.

The letter of Augustus Hervey from Genoa to my Lady was as follows:

GENOA, *November* 27, 1852.

This is the third letter I have wrote to your Ladyship since I have been abroad; and I must repeat my usual complaint of never hearing from you—tho' I must own it has been yr former kind indulgence that has only intitled me to expect it now. As to George,[14] I look upon him as a Man burried in the Matrimonial Sepulchar, and till he is wak'd out of his Tomb by the Squalling of half a dozen Bratts expect to know no more of him: but I confess (let me vent myself by chiding) I did not imagine Lady Townshend wou'd so shortly forget one of her Chimney Corner party. Your Ladyship has a thousand subjects to write of that you know are interesting to me—your own Well Fare, George's ("toute ingrate qu'il est") in short, write of Die Junke anything that recalls the many hours you have permitted me to pass away at Whitehall. For my Part, unless I could send you a Month's Sun or a Basket of Fruit I know of nothing in this Country that would give you a moment's pleasure or amusement. For unlike our Lady Caroline,[15] our Lady that, our Miss this, our Miss that, the women are all so poor that their outsides are no better adorned than the Insides of the Men:

[14] Hon. George Townshend, eldest son of my Lady, and at that time just married to Lady Charlotte Compton, Baroness Ferrers, etc., in her own right.
[15] Again my Lady Caroline Petersham (*née* Fitzroy), afterwards Countess of Harrington, who appears to have exercised much the same fascination over all men, young and old, as did my Lady Townshend.

they are as dirty and as Frippery as their Gallants are vain and ignorant, and the Commerce as little desirable for want of a right Pride as that of the other is from a wrong one. There is nothing more common in Italy than to see a great Princess who will return a Visit to no Lady of an inferior Title, strolling round the Streets for amusement and in a continued Conversation with her own Footmen who to facilitate this entertainment walk on each side of her Coach holding by the Doors. They play for Halfpence with the utmost Avidity: and he that will be cheated of three and sixpence never fails of going away with the Reputation of being the most gallant Man of the Company. I was delighted with a thing say'd the other day by one of their own Countrymen wch putt their understanding in a light equally true and ridiculous. The Italian Women (say's he) are such Fools that if three of them are gott together 'tis possible that one may say that 2 and 2 make 4, another that 2 and 2 make 5, and whilst the dispute grows warm the third shall be embarass'd which to decide for. The Men are not in a Form one Degree higher: they are too proud to seek or suffer the Company of their inferiors: too jealous to be pleased with that of their equals: and too ignorant to be able to bear their own. However, I have had the good Fortune to meet wth two or three here who both know 'tis possible to communicate one's ideas in other languages besides Italian, and have a notion of their being inhabited Countrys beyond the Alps: two Branches of Knowledge that few Gentlemen or Ladies on this Side of them arrive at. I pass a good deal of my time wth them and with more pleasure than I have done any part of it since I left Lisbon. Indeed I have been ill with a Pleurisie, and therefore bad Health, or bad Objects, I dont know wch or perhaps both, have quite cured me of flirting: 'tis so long, tell Lady Caroline,[15] since I have seen so spruce a Toylet as hers, that I have hardly the idea of one; and if I venture ever again to accost a fine Lady, I believe it will be with blushing, stuttering, twisting my Thumbs, and so much in the style of Sr Wilfull Witwood,[16] that if the Lady refused to *fetch a Walk* I should be extremely puzzled for a second Question to putt to her: and in much greater Confusion to ask her the last Favour, than any Woman in France or Italy I believe ever felt in granting it. Your Ladysp wont credit this change perhaps:

[16] A character in Congreve's *Way of the World*—a shy, obstinate man.

and I wish I did not feel it but I am absolutely another fellow. I rejoice in basking in the Sun : every Limb is a Barometre and foretells Rains, Winds, Snows, etc.—I begin to tell the Storys of what I was : pretend to despise Pleasures I am past taking : rail at Wine because I drink none (nor have not since I left England) : condemn gaming because I have no spare Money to play : and like the Dog in the Manger stare at every charitable Gentlewoman that throws her oats to those Animals who are glad to eat them ; tho' perhaps like other Reformers, my only Quarrel to the Banquet is not being bidden or not having an Appetite. Now dear Madam, after what I have acknowledged myself dwindled into, 'twill be impudence to expect yr Ladysp will allow such a Creature much of your Time ; but till I come to a Pair of Spectacles, a Newspaper and a Pipe and confining my whole Conversation to Virtue and Vice without having a View to either in my Conduct, I flatter myself now and then you'll hear me relate extraordinary things over a Cup of Mrs. Johnson's [17] good Chocolate in a Morning : and when Mrs. French or Lord Waldegrave's engaged, sometimes allow me to make a fourth in an Evening at Whist ; and whatever changes you may discover in my *Person, Parts* or *Conversation* there is one wch I venture to assure yr Ladysp you will never find, which is my being otherwise than—Madam, your most faithful oblig'd and obedt servt.                                   A. HERVEY.

Forgive my having made as many Blotts as lines, but I have not time to write it over again. I am going to a very great Ball and Feast, and the Post will be gone too early in the Morning for me. I beg a thousand kind Things to George and respectfull ones to Lady Ferrers, for *all the rest*—" speak of me " (as Othello says)—" as I am nothing extenuate."

The Mrs. French alluded to in the above letter was an Irish lady who lived to a great age (she died in 1791), near Hampton Court. Walpole, writing in 1743, spoke of her separation from her husband, adding :

She has been fashionable these two winters : her husband has commenced a suit in Doctors Commons against her Cat, and will,

[17] My Lady's personal maid, who was with her for so many years, and to whom she left an annuity at her death.

they say, recover considerable damages : but the lawyers are of opinion that the kittens must inherit Mr. French's estate, as they were born in Lawful Wedlock.  .

The Lord Waldegrave mentioned was the one who afterwards married the beautiful Maria, illegitimate daughter of Horace Walpole's brother Edward and " a little milliner ".

# CHAPTER XII

## THE SORROWS AND LAST YEARS OF
## ETHELREDA TOWNSHEND

Her two sons in Canada with General Wolfe : letters to wife of
George Townshend : unkind conduct of Charles Townshend's
wife, Lady Dalkeith : Walpole's sneers at her sorrows : Lady
Townshend's notes to Walpole : sympathy of Mrs. Montagu and
other friends : indifference of her husband : elopement of her
daughter Audrey with Robert Orme : Roger killed at the battle
of Ticonderoga : death of her second son Charles : death of Lady
Townshend in 1788 : her devotion to her children : the good
traits of her character.

THE LIFE OF MY LADY TOWNSHEND was not
without its darker moments of sorrow and trouble.
In the early years of her married life her children were
ill of smallpox, a much more serious matter in those
days than it has been since the discovery of vaccina-
tion—and one boy died. Her husband left her in
1741, after eighteen years of married life, and lived
chiefly on his country estates more or less openly
with one of her servants, though he appears to have
sometimes come to town and lodged in St. James's
Street while his beautiful wife had her own establishment in the Privy Garden. In the year 1759 her two
sons, George and Roger, were in Canada with the
British army. On July 7 of that year Roger fell at the
battle of Ticonderoga, and his mother was expecting
every moment to hear similar news of her eldest son,

who was fighting with Wolfe before Quebec. More-over, her only daughter, Audrey, had left home with a Mr. Orme, and but for her son Charles and her daughter-in-law she was practically left alone.

Some letters to Lady Ferrers,[1] wife of George Townshend, written about this time, show an aspect of her character quite unlike that of the gay woman of fashion, and one perhaps hardly suspected by even her most intimate friends. She is revealed as a tender, affectionate mother, torn by anxiety over the fate of her eldest son and overwhelmed with grief at the death of her youngest.

*September* 1759.

DEAR LADY FERRERS—I take the benefit of being a little better in my health today to thank you for your kind letter, sometimes being very incapable of writing a single line. I hope Charles's last letter to you afforded you a relief to your spirits. I trust in God we shall all be in a much happier situation, by receiving the good news we most ardently wished for. My compliments to Lady Elizabeth Compton,[2] and affectionate love to the children.

A few days later she writes again :

MY DEAR LADY FERRERS—Believe me nothing but the being incapable of writing a single line should have prevented me thanking you for your tender concern for me. I trust in God that he will preserve the most dear thing to us in life, and from that dependance am still able to support myself enough to be in hopes to exist to receive the greatest of blessings.

E. TOWNSHEND.

P.S. Charles is with me and writes to you by this post.

[1] Charlotte Compton, Baroness Ferrers of Chartley, wife of George Townshend, only surviving child and heiress of James, Fifth Earl of Northampton. She brought into the family of the Townshends the Barony of Ferrers of Chartley, inherited from her mother, and that of Compton, inherited from her father, and two hundred and fifty quarterings, including the Royal one of Plantaganet.
[2] Lady Elizabeth Compton, daughter of seventh Earl of Northampton, and therefore first cousin to Lady Ferrers.

About this time it became known that George Townshend was safe but that his brother Roger had been killed. Four days subsequent to the date of the above letter, Lady Townshend writes again :

*September* 17, 1759.

MY DEAR LADY FERRERS—No situation of my mind or health can ever prevent me from thinking and being anxious for you and your Dear Children. Charles writes by this post to you. I trust in the Almighty God that he will soon bless us with the safe return of our most dear George.—Yours ever Affect.,

E. TOWNSHEND.

These letters show that however worldly, frivolous and eccentric my Lady Townshend had been throughout her life—and she was all these to the *n*th power—she was yet capable of strong affection for her children and those who were dear to her. She was in constant correspondence with the wife of her eldest son, and her second son was with her as much as possible, but she complained bitterly that Lady Dalkeith,[3] Charles's wife, would neither allow her husband to remain with her to await his brother's arrival, nor come up herself. There was evidently not much love lost between my Lady Townshend and my Lady Dalkeith, and, remembering what a flow of language was ever at the command of the older lady, one cannot but admire the restraint with which she expresses herself in the following letter :

[3] Lady Caroline Campbell, eldest daughter of John, Duke of Argyll. She married, firstly, Francis, Earl of Dalkeith, eldest son of the second Duke of Buccleuch ; and, secondly, Charles Townshend. She was created Baroness of Greenwich in her own right, but the title died with her. By Charles Townshend she had three children, two sons, both in the army, who died unmarried (one was found shot in his tent), and one daughter, Anne, a very . beautiful girl who eloped with a Mr. Wilson, of Tyrone, and has descendants living at the present day, who have assumed the name of Townshend before that of Wilson.

*September* 29, 1759.

DEAR LADY FERRERS—I can say nothing at present in the least favourable in respect to my health therefore will avoid dwelling upon so uncomfortable a subject.

Mr. Charles Townshend set out on Thursday night for Adderbury : he entreated Lady Dalkeith to be in town herself or to consent to his staying here with me to await Mr Townshend's arrival : but she would not hear of his proposal, persisting still that she should not be in London for an hour or at Sudbrook, nor should he remain here from Adderbury even untill fryday morning, by this fatality, for I can call it by no other name, I am now deprived of Comfort and Support of his Assistance and Company who never left me till twelve o'clock at night. The North East wind continues and is directly contrary for having any News from Quebec when it changes I sometimes think of setting out for Portsmouth : here I shall not remain.

My best wishes and Compliments attend Lady Elizabeth Compton. My affectionate love to the children.

E. TOWNSHEND.

The poor Lady was in an unenviable position as mother-in-law to Lady Dalkeith, who must have been of a particularly selfish disposition to refuse her any consolation she could have experienced from the presence of her son Charles. The other daughter-in-law, Lady Ferrers, was of a different nature and was genuinely fond of her husband's mother. She asked her to visit them at Tunbridge, and my Lady Townshend writes quite gratefully in return :

LONDON, *October* 2, 1759.

DEAR LADY FERRERS—Nothing but the apprehension that the seeing me would agitate your spirits too much and consequently be prejudicial to your health could prevent me from coming to Tunbridge. Everybody agrees that the first time the wind changes from the North-East we must hear from Mr. Townshend, but as yet it is full East. The poor Norfolk Militia, by being pent up so long in the barracks at Portsmouth, are all dying of the bloody flux.

Sir Armand Woodhouse is come to town to see Lord

Barrington to endeavour to get them relieved, but Mr Pitt's being out of town makes it impossible for their having any immediate redress, by being removed from that duty.

My health is so affected for the last three days that I can with difficulty write this.                                    E. TOWNSHEND.

A little later she received news of the surrender of Quebec and of the safety of her son George, who had succeeded to the command of the British troops after the death of Wolfe on the Heights of Montcalm. She communicates the intelligence to Walpole in a rather formal note which has been preserved in the Waller Collection, and is quoted in the Supplement to Walpole's *Letters* edited by Toynbee. The wording sounds odd when one considers the terms of extreme intimacy on which Lady Townshend and Walpole had lived all their lives; but the stilted customs of the time may account for what otherwise might appear to be due to some estrangement the lady was trying to make up!

Lady Townshend's compliments to Mr. Walpole, and begs he will believe that it is from the knowledge she has of his goodness to her and of his humanity in general that she is very sure he will now share in her joy when she acquaints him that Mr Townshend is safe and well, and has most miraculously been preserved in the midst of the most desperate enterprise in the taking of Quebeck in which he has made a glorious figure.

WHITEHALL, *October* 17, 1759.

Horace Walpole, who was by way of being one of Lady Townshend's most intimate friends, but who cared for no one but himself, except so far as they could amuse him, could not resist a sneer over what he supposed to be an affectation of grief on her part when she heard of the death of her son Roger. Writing to Lord Stafford at that time, he says :

My Lady Townshend, who has not learning enough to copy a Spartan mother, has lost her youngest son. I saw her this morning—her affectation is on t'other side : she affects grief, but not so much for the son she has lost as for t'other she may lose.

A little later he writes to Harry Conway in the same strain :

I passed the whole morning most deliciously at my Lady Townshend's. Poor Roger, for whom she is not concerned, has given her a hint that her George may be mortal too : she scarce spoke, unless to improve on some bitter things that Charles said, who was admirable.

The " most deliciously " of the above extract throws a searchlight on the cold, heartless character of Walpole. Nothing that was sincere or genuine in the way of natural feeling or affection ever found in him an admirer. He sneered his way through life, giving no credit for sincerity—for he had none himself—and careful only to note the cynicism, bitterness and shady stories of shady lives that he might store them for the amusement of posterity and gain for himself a pos-thumous fame. To any one who did not appreciate his own dilettante efforts he could be as spiteful as a jealous woman. He noted that, although he had given my Lady Townshend an epitaph and a design for Roger's tomb, *neither was used*! And it is quite likely that the sarcasm on the subject of her grief was provoked by this slight to his vanity.

My Lady must have had many friends " at court ", who kept her informed on all public matters of interest. When the Hanoverian troops were defeated in 1758 she at once sent a little note to inform Walpole of the circumstances, though it is not at all clear why she should have thought it necessary to do so, as he must have been also very much in the way of hearing the news early. Perhaps she liked to let him see how well informed she was, and maybe she is exercising a little sarcastic vein in assuring him that he had fortitude !

· Lady Townshend's compliments to Mr. Walpole, and as she is very sensible that he is always master of the greatest fortitude, she ventures to inform him that at this day an express arived at Whitehall with an account of the defeat of the Hanoverians under Counts Issenbourg and Oberg, near Cassel, by the Prince of Sobizze. The Duke of Marlborough, Marq. of Blandford, Col. Wade and Capt. Tuffnel are all down with the camp fever and bloody flux.

WHITEHALL, Saturday evening, *October* 1758.

In these days of trouble her real friends were most attentive to her. Mrs. Elizabeth Montagu writes to Lord Lyttelton in October of the same year (1859), after the news had been received of the fall of Quebec and the taking over of the command by George Townshend, as follows :

I wrote a letter to Lady Townshend to congratulate her on Mr Townshend's success at Quebec, to which I had the most obliging answer imaginable. It was as affectionate as to a daughter, and as respectful as to an Empress. She said her spirits had been so worn out, she could not recover her dejection and begged to see me. I found her very low-spirited still, though pleased with the late event. Mr Charles Townshend was excessively gracious to me, and we talked of the affair of Quebec with the regards due to General Townshend.

Other old friends also rallied round her, the Duke of Newcastle among them. Among the Newcastle MSS. in the British Museum are preserved two short notes from my Lady to the Duke, one dated October 17, 1759, congratulating him on the taking of Quebec, and thanking him for the interest he had always taken in her son George; and the other, dated five years later at the time of her husband's death, expressing regret that " she had gone out to take the air, when his Grace did her the honour to call upon her ".

Such incidents, trivial in themselves, do away with the idea, put forward by some of the modern critics of my Lady, that she was regarded as a *pêche à quinze sous*.

During all the time of her anxiety for her absent sons, her husband remained in the country, or at any rate away from her, paying no regard to her sorrows, and betraying very little concern at the death of Roger Townshend or for the safety of his son and heir.

Lady Ferrers wrote him the news of her husband's safety, and he acknowledged her letter coldly in the third person.

This estimable peer died in 1764, leaving three children by a housemaid on the Raynham estate, to whom he bequeathed fifty thousand pounds. He left nothing to his brilliant son Charles, Chancellor of the Exchequer; to his widow only what he was compelled by settlement; and to his son George what was entailed on the title. Whatsoever may have been the faults of my Lady Townshend, there can be no question as to the abominable treatment meted out to her and her children by this most selfish of men.

Walpole had his usual sneer when my Lady was left a widow. In a letter to Mann he communicates the news of the Viscount's death, and brutally adds :

We conclude that the Duke of Argyll [4] will abandon Mrs Villiers [5] for the richer widow (*i.e. Lady Townshend*) who will only be inconsolable as she is too cunning, I believe, to let anyone console her.

The Lively Lady Townshend, queen of fashion,

[4] John, Duke of Argyll. (*See* his letter to my Lady, Chapter XII.)
[5] *Née* Mary Fowke, widow of Henry Villiers, nephew of first Earl of Jersey.

toast of the eighteenth century, was thus left to bear
her sorrows very much alone. Her eldest son in
Canada, her second son kept from her by a jealous
wife, her youngest dead on the field of battle. Her
only daughter had, as we have seen, made a runaway
match of which she strongly disapproved, with one
Captain Robert Orme, a handsome young officer of the
Coldstreams. There was nothing against Orme in any
way. He came of a good old Devonshire family, was
known as an honest and capable man and a fine soldier,
and made the most favourable impression wherever
he went.[6] But my Lady had destined her beautiful
daughter for Lord George Lenox. She never really
forgave her, and the Orme grandchildren got little or
nothing at her death.

In 1767 another terrible blow fell upon her.
Charles Townshend died in that year, after a short
illness and at the zenith of his political career. This
time, even Walpole is obliged to bear witness to her
grief. To Lady Mary Coke, Charles Townshend's
sister-in-law, he writes that it is feared the old mother
will never get over her loss. Lady Mary, in her diary,
has also a sympathetic note :

The Dowager Lady, who, poor woman, is so ill that those
who have seen her think she will never recover this terrible blow,
and yet amidst her own distress she had omitted no attention or
kindness to Lady Dalkeith.

Some years elapsed before she had quite recovered
this succession of severe shocks, and, though she was

[6] A full-length portrait of Captain Robert Orme, by Sir Joshua Reynolds,
at one time in the Orkney Collection, hangs in the Western vestibule of the
National Gallery. He was A.D.C. to General Braddock in the war in Canada,
and was wounded in the action before Fort du Quesne. There is a Military
Diary of his in the British Museum, containing some interesting particulars
of this war.

never paralysed (as was maliciously reported by Walpole in one of his letters) she was no longer her gay, insouciant self, and must have been very ill for some time, so little do we hear of her doings in the fashionable world. She did appear sometimes in the *beau monde*. She had been, as we have seen, at the coronation of George III. in 1761, but quite soberly, with a large party and not as a " frolic ". This was after the death of Roger and the elopement of her daughter Audrey, but some years before the death of her son Charles.

With her wonderful vitality she rallied somewhat towards the end of her long life, fussing a good deal over her grandchildren and lavishing on them her superabundant stores of affection, especially on her dear grandson Jack, the second son of her favourite George, in later life a brilliant member of the House of Commons.

A woman who was such a bundle of nerves could not be expected to have a very great amount of physical courage. Throughout her long life she had gone in for every form of pleasure and indulgence, and gratified every whim. When the hour of trial arrived she collapsed utterly and was afraid. In 1754, when only forty-six, she was reported to be dying, and Walpole says she was " woefully frightened ", but adds, with his usual sneer, that she " took prayers and recovered even of her repentance ".

Again, in the year of the Gordon Riots, when she was nearly eighty years of age, she was terrified by the doings of the incendiaries in London, and, according to Selwyn, talked the language of the Court instead of the Opposition (though she had always loved to be in opposition in all things), putting him in mind, he said,

" of removed tradesmen who hang out a board with
' burnt out from over the way ' ".

At that time there were not many of her own
people, the Harrisons of Balls, left. Richard Harrison,
her grandfather, had lived to be seventy-nine years of
age, dying in 1725, two years after her marriage. Her
father died in 1732, her mother twenty years later. Her
uncle George died in 1759, and there remained indeed
but one old woman, his widow, Mary Harrison, eldest
daughter of Edmund Feilde, of Stantsted, Herts, who
was older than herself, and not likely to have much in
common with her niece.

My Lady died in 1788, the same year as Mrs. Delany,
Lady Vane, and many another well-known personage,
including Prince Charles Edward Stuart, the " Young
Pretender ", whose cause she had for a short time so
fantastically espoused.

Wraxall, in *Posthumous Memoirs of my Own Times*,
says that her intellectual faculties had suffered little or
no decay, and that in the Empire of Mind she might
be said to have occupied the place left vacant by Lady
Mary Wortley Montagu and Lady Hervey. An obituary
notice in the *Gentleman's Magazine* (vol. lviii. p. 275)
states that—

she possessed her faculties in amazing perfection to the last.
Her acuteness of observation and brilliancy of expression were
as forcible and brilliant as at her earliest state of life, when she
was so esteemed, and her society cultivated by the first wits of
the time.

She was buried in the family vault of the Townshends
at All Saints Church, Hertford, near her own property
of Balls, which she bequeathed to her grandson "Jack"
Townshend.

The parochial record of the day of her birth is lost,

all registers of the church having been destroyed by fire; so there is no official confirmation of the date as stated on the slab in the church, viz. 1708. If born in 1701, as gratuitously supposed by various more or less inaccurate historians, she would have been as much as twenty-two years old at the time of her marriage, which is most improbable, considering how general was then the custom for girls to marry before they were eighteen, and remembering also how beautiful she was and her claims as an heiress. Any doubt as to the exact date is set at rest by the inscription on a mourning ring, disposed of at the sale of the Townshend heirlooms in 1904. This was engraved as follows— " Audrey. Dow$^r$ Visc$^s$ Townshend *ob*: 5 Mar: 1788: AE 80 ".

Four of her sons and her only daughter predeceased her. These were Charles, the statesman; Roger, the gallant soldier; Edward, who died a young boy; and Audrey, married to Captain Orme. As already stated. she left little or nothing in her will to the children of Audrey Orme nor to George, who, as heir of the entailed property, was well provided for. To each of George's children who survived her she left six thousand pounds, except the eldest, Earl of Leicester, who got but five hundred. She left several small sums to relations and also some money for charitable purposes. The bulk of her fortune—*i.e.* the estate at Balls and a large sum of ready money went to Lord John Townshend, who had always been her favourite grandson.

Of her friends and special cronies, Walpole, nearly seventeen years her junior, survived her for ten years, and George Selwyn for three. Most of the other companions of her brilliant career were already dead.

Her actions, so far as they can be judged from letters and memoirs and other contemporary evidence, more especially her conduct with regard to Lord Kilmarnock, prove her to have been either a woman with a very highly strung nervous system (such as is called a mere " bundle of nerves ") or simply an extraordinary specimen of a fearless, free-and-easy woman of the world, who cared little for what anybody said about her conversation or her "carryings on" as long as she could amuse herself in the way she liked best and always have plenty of lively men and women about her.

One may not forget that, when still a young and very beautiful woman, she separated herself from her husband with very good cause, and launched herself alone on the high seas of the society of the eighteenth century, where so many reputations suffered shipwreck; that the chief authorities for the more lurid stories of her career are Horace Walpole and Lady Mary Wortley Montagu, who, amusing though they may have been, were two of the most malicious scandal-mongers the world has ever known; and further, that she has attained to a sort of spurious notoriety by being branded as the original of Lady Bellaston in Fielding's *Tom Jones*, though no proof has ever been adduced that the novelist had her in his mind at the time.

Remembering all these things, may we not find some excuses for such of her harum-scarum doings as we know to be true, and receive *cum grano salis* the graver accusations made against her character by spiteful gossip-mongers of that day and since ?

She was a whimsical, fearless, perhaps a somewhat lawless, and essentially an unartificial woman living in an artificial world, whose sayings have been handed down to us by two or three of the worst mischief-makers of a mischief-making age, chatterers of a cat-like nature who never failed to scratch as they purred out their amusing bits of gossip.

She was a most devoted mother to her children and a still more devoted grandmother to her children's children. All men, young and old, adored her; strange to say, in spite of her wonderful beauty, her brilliant wit and her success with the other sex, many women loved to call her friend. She was not only a notable woman of fashion, but intellectual besides and educated far above the average woman of her own set.

She steered clear of the Georgian Courts and their intrigues, but held a miniature court of her own at Whitehall, entertaining all the foreign royalties and celebrities who visited England, besides the members of the reigning family at home, and giving gorgeous balls, routs, receptions and masquerades renowned throughout the country.

She held her own—a great Lady to the very last. Nothing has ever been brought forward to support the spiteful insinuations of her own sex, or to show that she should be saddled with any worse reputation than that of a typical " Lady of Quality " of the eighteenth century.

# INDEX

THE END